Law and Philosophy Library

Volume 139

The Law and Philosophy Library, which has been in existence since 1985, aims to publish cutting edge works in the philosophy of law, and has a special history of publishing books that focus on legal reasoning and argumentation, including those that may involve somewhat formal methodologies. The series has published numerous important books on law and logic, law and artificial intelligence, law and language, and law and rhetoric. While continuing to stress these areas, the series has more recently expanded to include books on the intersection between law and the Continental philosophical tradition, consistent with the traditional openness of the series to books in the Continental jurisprudential tradition. The series is proud of the geographic diversity of its authors, and many have come from Latin America, Spain, Italy, the Netherlands, Germany, and Eastern Europe, as well, more obviously for an English-language series, from the United Kingdom, the United States, Australia and Canada.

More information about this series at http://www.springer.com/series/6210

Nicoletta Bersier • Christoph Bezemek •
Frederick Schauer
Editors

Common Law – Civil Law

The Great Divide?

Springer

Editors
Nicoletta Bersier
Thémis Institute
Geneva, Switzerland

Christoph Bezemek
Institute of Public Law and Political Science
University of Graz
Graz, Austria

Frederick Schauer
School of Law
University of Virginia
Charlottesville, VA, USA

ISSN 1572-4395 ISSN 2215-0315 (electronic)
Law and Philosophy Library
ISBN 978-3-030-87717-0 ISBN 978-3-030-87718-7 (eBook)
https://doi.org/10.1007/978-3-030-87718-7

This Springer imprint is published by the registered company Springer Nature Switzerland AG.
The registered company address is: Gewerbestrasse 11, 6330 Cham, Switzerland

Preface

The idea for this volume originated in the aftermath of a panel organized by the editors at the XXIX World Congress of the International Association for the Philosophy of Law and Social Philosophy (IVR) in Lucerne in the summer of 2019. Befitting the rather broad topic of the panel "Common Law – Civil Law: The Great Divide" a variety of proposals were submitted by scholars from all over the world. Accordingly, the papers presented in Lucerne, ranging from historical questions to theoretical and comparative aspects, covered far more than the problems discussed over and over in the past.

The fresh approaches and the diverse accounts we had the privilege to discuss in Lucerne convinced us that it would be useful to pursue the topic further and to invite still more friends and colleagues from around the globe to join the conversation. We were pleased that so many of them accepted our invitation and are even more pleased to present the result of our joint efforts in this volume.

We would like to thank Springer's "Law and Philosophy Library" for including the volume in the series and Abdus Salam Mazumder of Springer International for diligently looking after the volume and the editors. Patrik Rako and Raphael Ulbing kindly assisted in revising the manuscripts. We are grateful for their support.

Finally, we would like to thank the contributors to this volume for sharing their ideas and perspectives, thus significantly enhancing our understanding of the idiosyncrasies and commonalities of common law and civil law systems. We hope that our readers will benefit from their insights just as much as we did.

Geneva, Switzerland — Nicoletta Bersier
Graz, Austria — Christoph Bezemek
Charlottesville, VA, USA — Frederick Schauer
July 2021

Contents

Editors and Contributors

About the Editors

Nicoletta Bersier is a member of Thémis Institute, Geneva. She has authored and (co-)edited numerous publications on legal theory and legal sociology.

Christoph Bezemek is a Professor of Public Law and the Dean of the Faculty of Law at the University of Graz. His research focuses on comparative constitutional law, free speech, and legal and political theory.

Frederick Schauer is the David and Mary Harrison Distinguished Professor of Law at the University of Virginia and Frank Stanton Professor (Emeritus) of the First Amendment at the Kennedy School of Government, Harvard University. He is the author of numerous publications on constitutional law, in particular, on free speech, and on legal theory. He is a Co-Editor of Springer's Law and Philosophy Library.

List of Contributors

Stefan Arnold University of Münster, Münster, Germany

Nicoletta Bersier Thémis Institute, Geneva, Switzerland

Christoph Bezemek Institute of Public Law and Political Science, University of Graz, Graz, Austria

Ana Margarida Simões Gaudêncio University of Coimbra, Institute for Legal Research (UCILeR), Coimbra, Portugal

Han Liu Tsinghua University, Beijing, China

Patricio Nazareno Universidad de San Andrés Law School, Buenos Aires, Argentina
New York University School of Law, New York, NY, USA

Michael Potacs University of Vienna, Vienna, Austria

Alessio Sardo University of Genova, Genova, Italy

Frederick Schauer University of Virgina, School of Law, Charlottesville, VA, USA

Alexander Somek University of Vienna, Vienna, Austria

Lars Vinx University of Cambridge, Cambridge, UK

Introduction

Nicoletta Bersier, Christoph Bezemek, and Frederick Schauer

Common law and civil law are typically presented as antagonistic players on a field claimed by different legal systems: the former being based on precedent set by judges in deciding cases before them, the latter being founded on a set of rules expected to govern the decisions of those serving as a mouthpiece in applying them. Perceived in this manner, common law and civil law differ as to the (main) source (s) of law, about who is to create, about who is (merely) to draw from them, about whether the law works itself pure each step of the way or whether the law's purity may only be tarnished when confronted with a contingent set of facts.

These differences have deep roots in (legal) history, roots that allow us to trace them back to distinct traditions. Still, it is questionable whether the ideal-types presented above are in any relevant sense accurate when assessing the way these systems work. After all: International and supranational legal systems indifferent to national peculiarities seem to level the playing field. A normative understanding of constitutions seems to grant ever-greater authority to apex court decisions based on thinly worded maxims in countries that adhere to the civil law tradition. The challenges contemporary regulation faces seem to ask for ever-more detailed statutes governing the decisions of judges in the common law tradition.

These and similar observations ask for a structural re-assessment of the role of judges, the power of precedent, the limits of legislation and other features often thought to be so different in common and civil law systems.

N. Bersier
Thémis Institute, Geneva, Switzerland
e-mail: nbersier@iprolink.ch

C. Bezemek (✉)
Institute of Public Law and Political Science, University of Graz, Graz, Austria
e-mail: christoph.bezemek@uni-graz.at

F. Schauer
University of Virgina, School of Law, Charlottesville, VA, USA
e-mail: fschauer@law.virginia.edu

N. Bersier et al. (eds.), *Common Law – Civil Law*, Law and Philosophy Library 139,
https://doi.org/10.1007/978-3-030-87718-7_1

The volume at hand is dedicated to this reassessment.

It is—roughly—divided into three sections. The first of which focuses on theoretical questions associated with the 'great divide' suggested in the volume's subtitle.

Here, in a first chapter, Frederick Schauer embarks on a quest for the data that supports jurisprudential theory. Focusing on the structure of common law and civil law systems, Schauer contrasts the claims underlying legal pluralism and general jurisprudence; thus exploring the question as to whether generalizations in legal theory are, in fact, possible.

Christoph Bezemek, in a second chapter, focuses on the often-quoted image of the (common) law "working itself" pure. Is the purity thus assumed, he asks, a goal to be achieved or a regulative ideal that drives and shapes the law? In addressing this question, Bezemek pays close attention to the historical context in which the image first came to use and argues that this context continues to be relevant for our understanding to this day.

A third chapter, written by Stefan Arnold, defends the thesis that Dworkin's and Brandom's theories of law's normativity are powerful not only with respect to common law, but also with respect to civil law. Arnold discusses Dworkin's view of the law as a chain novel against the backdrop of Brandom's concept of discursive practice of law, which is characterised by mutual recognition as a social and normative attitude. Both, Dworkin's chain novel and Brandom's normative fine structure, he argues, are equally fruitful for our understanding of civil law.

Nicoletta Bersier, in a fourth chapter, focuses on the differences between common law and civil law in treating the concept of authority. In doing so, her contribution pays particular attention to the work of Roscoe Pound and, based on it, a critical reflection of the similarities and differences between common law and civil law systems.

Concluding the first section, Michael Potacs, in a fifth chapter, addresses the question as to whether the hierarchical structure of legal orders may be described more appropriately using a tree diagram than the model of a pyramid of norms. Developing his views against the backdrop of the differences between civil law and common law, Potacs answers in the negative.

A second section deals with problems of interpretation and adjudication. In chapter six Alessio Sardo explores the relation between and the complementarity of originalism and positivism, which—even though dominant models in the US and in Europe respectively—have never been an object of comprehensive comparison. Sardo's contribution aspires to fill, in part, that gap. Focusing on methodological issues he suggests that, in principle, originalism and positivism overlap and, to a very considerable extent, might complement each other.

In chapter seven, Ana Margarida Simões Gaudêncio argues that the diverse structures presented by civil law and common law systems share a partially common tradition in what concerns the methodological relevance of judicial jurisprudence. Thus conferring a specific normatively constitutive meaning to the roles played by *Juristenrecht*, and, within it, *Richterrecht*, in adjudication. Establishing a dialogue between common law and civil law systems, her contribution proposes an understanding of judicial jurisprudence not only as an effective source of law, but also as a methodologically constitutive juridical criterion.

In the final chapter of the second section Patricio Nazareno argues that comparative legal scholarship about judging typically focuses on institutional disparities among legal systems while downplaying ideological differences. His contribution has the opposite emphasis. It explores some traits of the ideological conception of judging typically associated with the American culture so as to show that remarkable differences in the judicial practice between systems may actually persist regardless of the similarities on the institutional plane.

The third and final section offers a glance at different traditions of scholarship and of law itself. In chapter nine Alexander Somek's contribution focuses on the important differences between the cultures of legal scholarship and legal education in the US and in countries belonging the civil law tradition. While North American legal academia, as Somek argues, has proudly transcended the horizon of mere doctrine and embraced a variety of interdisciplinary approaches, the civil law tradition appears to be still committed to the "science of law". In the context of the latter, Somek concludes, the moment of transcendence is the preserve of the philosophy of law.

Focusing on a particular national legal system, in chapter ten, Han Liu asks the question of whether China is to be considered a member of the civil law or of the common law tradition. The answer he develops, using historical, theoretical doctrinal and comparative analysis, is, that it is neither. Chinese law, Liu argues, is still a mélange of the socialist tradition and Western elements, including both continental and Anglo-American ones, tinged with ancient factors.

The volume is concluded by Lars Vinx' contribution which takes us to the level of international law, discussing Dworkin's last publication, 'A New Philosophy for International Law.' According to Vinx Dworkin failed to vindicate the continuing relevance of the question as to the existence of international law; a question which, as Vinx argues, Kelsen's theory of international law is better placed to answer than Dworkin's interpretative conception.

While each of these contributions is important in its own right, taken as a whole the volume indeed teaches us valuable lessons as to the similarities and differences between civil law and common law systems, oftentimes with rather remarkable results that challenge our received wisdom and enhance our understanding. Then again, sporadically, the contributions collected in this volume confirm believes we have held for quite some time. In both cases, they significantly deepen our knowledge of 'the great divide', its roots, its effects and its challenges. Thus, the volume at hand adds to our understanding of civil law as well as of common law systems: historically, structurally, and doctrinally.

Civil Law, Common Law, and the Data of Jurisprudence

Frederick Schauer

Abstract Philosophical or theoretical analysis of the nature of some phenomenon requires identifying the phenomenon whose nature is at issue. Thus, if we are seeking to understand the nature of law itself, or even, as some would put it, the nature of the concept of law, we need to have some idea of something in the world that we are examining. That is, we need to start with the *data* that supports jurisprudential theory. So-called legal pluralists claim that existing legal systems are so diverse that no useful theoretical generalizations are possible. Others claim that the features of law wherever and whenever it exists are so consistent that such generalizations are indeed possible. This essay explores these questions, with a focus on whether the differences between civil and common law legal systems are, or are not, so great as to impede jurisprudential inquiry.

1 Introduction: A Methodological Foreword

What is a legal theory a theory of? Of law, obviously. But that obvious and correct answer is also circular. What we seek when we seek a theory of law is the explanation of some phenomenon. Saying that the phenomenon we seek to explain is law gets us nowhere, because that approach just takes us back to the question of what law is, which is where we started, and what it is that we seek to explain. We require, therefore, a non-circular and non-question-begging answer to the question is just what phenomenon or phenomena a theory of law is attempting to describe, explain, justify, or criticize.

We avoid the problem of circularity by pointing to something in the world whose existence we want to theorize about, and whose definition is independent of what we are seeking a theory of. A theory of art might be, for example, a theory of the kinds of

F. Schauer (✉)
University of Virginia, School of Law, Charlottesville, VA, USA
e-mail: fschauer@law.virginia.edu

N. Bersier et al. (eds.), *Common Law – Civil Law*, Law and Philosophy Library 139,
https://doi.org/10.1007/978-3-030-87718-7_2

objects that one finds in museums and that are sold at galleries of a certain type.[1] A theory of sport would start with the kinds of activities that are widely considered to be sports, and are labeled as such, for example, football, basketball, and skiing. And once we have, even if tentatively, come up with a theory of sport, we can use that theory to decide whether certain other activities—chess, dog shows, and Sunday hiking, for example—do or do not qualify. But whether it be art, or sport, or anything else, we need to start with certain exemplars. We then attempt to determine what features of those exemplars make them exemplars of something, and then we can address whether those features are necessary, and whether those features, necessary or not, are present for certain kinds of activities or objects.

All of this is to say that the task of theorizing requires data. And the data are, commonly, or perhaps necessarily, the things whose existence we wish to explain or describe. When we seek a theoretical account of law, therefore, we need initially, to locate certain exemplars of law and then proceed to see what the features of those exemplars are, and why we think those features are important. That is, why are trying to understand why these exemplars are exemplars of the phenomenon we are looking to understand, why they might not be exemplars of something else, and why other things that might be exemplars of something else are not exemplars of the phenomenon on which we are focusing. Moreover, once we have identified the features of the exemplars that make them exemplars of the thing we are theorizing about, we may discover that we need to discard some of the exemplars. The process, with a loose analogy to Ronald Dworkin's description of the relationship between fit and justification (Dworkin 1977, 1986), and with an even looser analogy to Rawlsian reflective equilibrium (Rawls 1971), aims to explain the data whose existence is the impetus for theorizing (Postema 2018).

When we seek to explain a social phenomenon, typically have in mind a group or category of acts, events, institutions, objects, or something, and not just one of them. Yes, we might seek to understand why Judge Smith on January 15, 2013, found John Jones guilty of the crime of murder for murdering Susan Brown and sentenced Jones to twenty years in prison. But however useful it may be at times to understand and explain such singular acts, more commonly we are concerned with categories of acts, etc. And law appears to be one of these non-singular acts or institutions.

It would be tempting to explain such groups as "generics," but we need to be careful here. A recent and rich philosophical literature has focused on generics, seeking to explain, to use an example from the philosopher Sarah-Jane Leslie (Leslie 2008), why it is correct to say that mosquitoes cause malaria, even though most of them do not, and why it is incorrect to say, and here the example is mine, that Yugos and Trabants are reliable, even though most of them are. But even though generic

---

[1]With respect to art, one influential theory of art is substantially institutional, or sociological, maintaining that art is, to oversimplify, what artists, critics, and other members of a certain community ("Artworld") simply do (Danto 1964, 1981; Dickie 1969, 1993). And although there are institutional theories of law (Del Mar and Bankowski 2009; MacCormick 2007; MacCormick and Weinberger 1986), most of them become less circular by including some conception of the normative and, occasionally, some conception of the coercive.

statements differ from universal statements, and even though what is or is not a proper generic statement varies with the background facts (and that is why saying that mosquitoes cause malaria is a good generic statement, and why saying that Yugos are reliable cars is not, even though the percentage of reliable Yugos is higher than the percentage of malaria-causing mosquitoes) (Schauer 2003), the idea of a generic presupposes some similarity, with generics being the words that capture the grouping that the linguistic community has already decided bears an underlying similarity. In other words, a generic reflects but does not explain a grouping, or a category. And where the category is not a natural kind such as water or gold, just what it is that makes all of some number of things members of the same artifactual category is precisely what needs explaining. It is not surprising that George Lakoff's *Women, Fire, and Dangerous Things* (Lakoff 1987) was written by a linguist, because it is language that embodies what it is that some linguistic culture deems relevantly similar. But the task—or at least one task—of legal philosophy is to explain why, for example, statutes, constitutions, lawyers, the police, and judges are members of the same category *law*, while football, linguine, etiquette, and screw-drivers are not. And for that task merely identifying the conclusion, while a good start, is not nearly enough.

2 The Challenge of Legal Pluralism

Once we understand that a theory of anything is typically, even if not necessarily, a theory of a group of things, then we can turn to the question of what group of things a theory of law purports to explain. But here things get more difficult. Plainly there can be a theory of the French law of marriage and divorce, or the American law of freedom of the press, or the Ecuadorian law of murder, but that is not what a theory of law purports to do. First, it purports to encompass multiple topics and multiple forms. And, second, it purports to be trans-jurisdictional. So, although there might be a theory of Italian law, or a trans-jurisdictional theory of the law of negotiable instruments, both of these are too narrow, the former because it is too jurisdictionally narrow and the latter because it is too topically narrow. What we seek is something more, and on both dimensions.

The traditional theory of law—the kind of theory usually riding under the banner of *general jurisprudence*—suffers from no such narrowness. At its broadest, it seeks to offer an account of the nature of law in all possible legal systems in all possible worlds (Raz 2009a, p. 214; Raz 2009b, p. 91). Joseph Raz (Raz 1975, p. 159), Scott Shapiro (Shapiro 2011, pp. 395–398), and Leslie Green (Green 2016), for example, emphasize the way in which their theories of law apply even to societies of angels—that is, hypothetical societies of good people desirous of compliance with the law and desirous of social cooperation. A fortiori, the accounts of Raz, Shapiro, and others in their tradition apply to all actual societies, and so too for the accounts of law offered from a broadly positivist standpoint by Hans Kelsen (Kelsen 1967) and from a broadly natural law one by John Finnis (Finnis 1980). And the same applies as well to Jules Coleman (Coleman 2001), Julie Dickson (Dickson 2001), Wil Waluchow (1994), and all of the other practitioners of contemporary analytic general jurisprudence.[2] For them, the phenomenon to be explained is law, period, wherever and whenever it appears.

In response to these claims about the project of general jurisprudence, or what might more accurately be labeled universal jurisprudence, one of the strong objections is the objection from legal pluralism. For legal pluralists, with William Twining (Twining 2009) and Brian Tamanaha (Tamanaha 2017, 2018) among the more prominent names in the English-language literature, the diversity of legal systems over time and across space, from antiquity to the present, and from industrialized societies to ones that are far less so (often unfortunately mis-labeled as "primitive"), is so great that there simply cannot be a general jurisprudence. Just as there cannot be a nontrivial theory of the combination of football, giraffes, and dentistry because the three are so diverse and have so little in common, so too there cannot be a theory of the systems of social control of Germany, North Korea, and the Inuit in pre--European-settlement Canada. These systems and the cultures in which they exist are just too diverse, say the pluralists, and the same holds with all of the modern institutions that might almost coincidentally happen to bear the label "law" or happen to be thought by some people as law.

The pluralist challenge is not just that different systems and different cultures have different concepts of law. That much is acknowledged by those who practice general conceptual jurisprudence, and by Joseph Raz explicitly (Raz 2005). Nevertheless, Raz insists, *our* concept of law is universal, not in the sense that every culture has the same concept of law, but that our concept of law is what enables us to identify law everywhere, and not just here. Our concept of law is thus in one sense provincial, but in another sense universal. Consequently, our culture having one universal concept of law is compatible with there being very different legal systems in different societies.

The pluralist response at this point would acknowledge that a single concept of law could recognize the very different embodiments of that concept in different cultures, but would point out that when the embodiments are so varied as to preclude illuminating generalizations, any concept of law that includes all of them is, still, destined to failure. If there is nothing interestingly similar about the forms of social organization and control across the world's cultures, now and then, the search for a useful single concept of law, even one situated within a particular culture while looking outward at all possible cultures in all possible worlds, nevertheless remains doomed.

[2] As will be explained presently, I intentionally exclude Ronald Dworkin (1977; Dworkin 1986) and H.L.A. Hart (2012) from this list.

3 Narrowing the Inquiry

Perhaps recognizing the force of the pluralist challenge, both H.L.A. Hart and Ronald Dworkin, along with Joseph Raz the most influential of twentieth-century English-language analytic legal philosophers, acknowledged that their goals, although far more than jurisdiction- or country-specific, were at least somewhat limited in scope. Hart, who in his posthumous "Postscript" to *The Concept of Law* (Hart 2012, pp. 238–276) insisted that his project was entirely descriptive, long maintained that what he was describing and analyzing was the operation of law as it existed in modern municipal legal systems, and not law wherever and whenever it might appear (Hart 2012, pp. 82–91). And so too with Ronald Dworkin, whose narrower scope, more or less contiguous with Hart (Dworkin 1986, 2006) was one that Raz described as "parochial" (Chou 2010). And even outside the modern positivist tradition, Lon Fuller's account of law, obviously an account imbued with moral considerations, was also limited to modern state law (Zipursky 2013).

Hart, Dworkin, and Fuller, among many others, can thus be understood as limiting the geographic and temporal range of their theorizing, and in that sense to have offered a partial accommodation to the pluralist challenge. But the universe of modern municipal legal systems, even though not including those of antiquity, of less industrialized societies, and of non-state regulatory systems, still encompasses a vast number of legal systems. The question, then, is whether it is possible (or desirable) to offer general theoretical accounts of the nature of law in even that somewhat narrower universe.

4 On the Diversity of Legal Families

The dialectic between the pluralists, on the one hand, and Hart, Fuller, and Dworkin, among others, on the other hand, allows us to refine the inquiry. Are Hart, Fuller, and Dworkin correct in supposing that we can engage in useful theoretical inquiry, and thus in useful theoretical generalizations, about modern municipal legal systems? Or, to focus the inquiry even more, about law and legal systems in modern industrialized secular societies with secular legal systems.

At this point, the distinction among legal families (or legal traditions) becomes central. And although some of the contemporary scholarship on the relationship between law and economic development tends to divide the world's secular legal systems into those derived from English common law, from French law, from German law, and from Scandinavian law (La Porta et al. 1998; La Porta et al. 2008), for present purposes we can simplify by just dividing the world's secular municipal industrialized legal systems into common law and civil law systems. And if we do so, the question before us is whether it is possible to generalize about law across these two large legal families or legal traditions, or whether, to the contrary, the possibility of generalizing across the common law/civil law divide is precluded by the size of the differences between the systems on either side of that divide.

The first question to be asked is whether the divide is as great as I have just intimated. And what makes this question important is the extent to which the idea of *convergence*, a major theme in contemporary comparative law (Cappelletti 1971; Schlesinger 1995; Zweigert and Kötz 1998), accurately describes the extent of the current contrast between common law and civil law legal systems.

In examining this question, it might be useful to start with the conventional caricature of the differences between common law and civil law. According to this caricature, which like most caricatures has at least some foundations in reality, the civil law is a system dominated by a code of highly detailed legal rules, those rules being sufficiently detailed and sufficiently alert to the vagaries of human behavior that the rules are designed to deal with virtually all forms of human behavior and all forms of human conflict. Only rarely would a situation arise that was not covered by the rules, and thus the judge—as adjudicator and not simply as enforcer—is a relatively insignificant figure.

If we wanted to attach a name to this model of a legal system, the name we might choose would be Napoleon, whose image of a well-functioning legal system did not depart very much from the caricature just provided (Abi-Saab 2017, p. 217). And although modern-day descendants of the Napoleonic Code depart substantially from what Napoleon originally had in mind, Napoleon's vision stands as a useful articulation of one form of what we might think of as the civil law ideal.

Even better than Napoleon as a model for the civil law ideal type would be Jeremy Bentham, albeit perhaps ironically. Ironically because Bentham not only came from a common law country, but also was the son of a lawyer in a common law country and was himself trained as a lawyer in the same common law country. But Bentham, one of history's great haters, hated the common law, believing it to be largely a conspiracy of lawyers and judges—Judge & Co.—aimed at making the law excessively complex (Rosenblum 1978; Postema, 1986; Schauer 2015, pp. 11–15). That complexity, Bentham believed, required lawyers for its interpretation and judges for its adjudication, and thus the rise and perpetuation of the Judge & Co. conspiracy was motivated by a desire of lawyers to increase their income by creating a need for their services and a desire of judges to increase their power by leaving the content of the law largely to judicial interpretation.

As a result of these beliefs, Bentham became, even more than Napoleon, and even earlier than Napoleon, a vigorous proponent of highly detailed codes of law that would regulate all of the human behavior that needed regulating (Alfange 1969), and that would anticipate and resolve all imaginable uncertainties and conflicts, thus making judges largely superfluous and lawyers essentially unnecessary. Indeed, Bentham's presumably serious proposal that it be illegal to give legal advice for money (Bentham 1838) was based on his belief that such a prohibition would remove the incentive for Parliament to make unnecessarily complex laws, laws whose complexity benefited lawyers and judges but no one else.

If Napoleon and Bentham represent the caricature at one pole of a dichotomy, then the other pole is represented by a "pure" common law model, one in which all or most law was made by judges in the process of adjudicating individual disputes, in which statute law was minimal, and in which and in which law developed by a succession of precedential accumulations. In such a system, the judge was the primary law-maker, the legislature had little role to play, and in predicting what the law would do was largely a matter of predicting what judges would do with particular disputes (Langbein et al. 2009). And although this description is no less a caricature than the caricature of the civil law just described, it does capture the judge-centered and dispute-centered idea at the core of the common law (Schauer 1989).

Although the images just presented are caricatures, they do represent what historically been genuine differences between common law and civil law systems. Judicial law-making has long been a more important part of common law legal system than in civil law systems, and perhaps the best evidence of this is the frequency with which common law judges admit to the practice while their civil law counterparts deny it. Moreover, the judicial opinion is not only a central item of law in the common law world, but an equally central—perhaps even more so—component of legal education. Professor Kingsfield of the 1973 film *The Paper Chase* (based on a 1971 novel of the same name) is a bit (but only a bit) of a caricature of how law was taught in the United States in the 1960s and earlier, but the idea of teaching law by scrutinizing appellate decisions was and remains commonplace. Relatedly, genuine precedential constraint has long been central in the common law world, while in civil law jurisdictions what some judges have said on previous occasions was never even close to being as important as the code or authoritative interpretations of it.

5 Convergence?

As noted above. Much of comparative law scholarship starting in the second half of the twentieth century has sought to illustrate the obsolescence of the descriptions and differences just described. Typically using the label of *convergence*, a common claim these days is that the differences between common law and civil law jurisdictions are decreasing, as evidenced by the increasing dominance in common law countries, the increasing reluctance in those same countries to empower judges to create entire areas of law anew, and, on the other side of the divide, the increasing importance of precedent in the civil law world, coupled with the increased willingness of judges to support their conclusions with lengthy written opinions explaining the reasons for their conclusions.

If the convergence hypothesis is sound, then there remain no theoretically interesting differences between common law and civil law jurisdictions, and thus no differences in terms of providing the data, or raw material, for philosophical inquiry. But there are reasons to doubt the soundness of the convergence hypothesis (Mattei and Pes 2008). Although it is true that common law jurisdictions rarely any more rely on judges to create entire areas of law anew, and although many contemporary statutes in common law jurisdictions are highly detailed, the practice of intentional vagueness, leaving courts to add the necessary clarification, remains far more routine in the common law world than in the civil law (Endicott 2011; McDonnell 1978; Schauer 2021). Relatedly, the role of the judge not only as law-applier and law-interpreter but also as lawmaker is widely recognized in common law jurisdictions, just as it remains widely denied, or at least relegated to secondary importance, in the world of the civil law. And although many civil law jurisdictions have in recent years begun to take the idea of precedent seriously (Summers and MacCormick 1997), more often it is by way of precedent as analogy, and rarely, or at least less often, by way of the strong precedential constraint that, at least in theory, has long been at the center of the common law (Alexander 1989; Schauer 2008, 2012).

Obviously, there is much more to be said, and especially by people more qualified to say it than I am, about the current state of convergence and divergence between common law and civil law systems. But for purposes of this paper, and of this volume, I want to rest on the admittedly tentative conclusion that divergence remains considerable, and that in terms of the importance of judges, the nature of reasoning, and the principal sources of legal authority, among other features, there remain significant differences between common law and civil law legal systems.

6 Implications for the Philosophy of Law

All of the foregoing suggests an implication for the philosophy of law of the distinction between common law and civil law legal systems. If the task of legal philosophy, or at least one task of legal philosophy, is to offer descriptive theoretical analyses of the features of law, and if those descriptive analyses are to transcend particular legal systems at particular times, then the task must begin with data—with the features of the phenomenon we seek to explain. And, thus, it must begin not with the things that happen to be called "law" in different places and at different times, but with the features that one can find in the different exemplars of the phenomenon under examination.

In this sense the legal pluralists are on to something. Perhaps the variety of systems of social control and social ordering throughout the world and across time are so varied that no interesting and illuminating generalizations are possible at all. But that is a claim that can be tested, and it is tested by seeking to identify features that do seem to recur across what appear at first sight to be substantially different systems. Presumably that is what Raz is doing in identifying the claim to authority (and not necessarily actual authority) as being one of those features, what Hart was doing in identifying internalization of an ultimate rule of recognition and the union of primary and secondary rules as another of those features, and what Kelsen was doing with the ideas of a *Grundnorm* and a hierarchy of norms.

If legal philosophy is what in the English-speaking world is called *general jurisprudence*, then the distinction between common and civil law systems is of no moment, because what the prominent practitioners of general jurisprudence have identified and analyzed exists throughout the world of social control and social ordering. In other words, the features that general jurisprudes have identified exist across this divide, and thus the data of jurisprudence need not include some of the contingent features of some but not all legal systems, and thus need not include either the features of the civil law that do not occur in the common law world, or the features of the common law world that do not occur in the civil law world.

When the features of law that span this divide are identified, however, two gaps remain. One, the one that motivates the legal pluralists, is that looking for these commonalities may ignore differences that are not only practically but also theoretically and philosophically interesting and important. If, to give just one example, common law and civil law systems remain significantly divergent in their treatment of previous decisions by judges—precedent—then an enterprise that gives up any attempt to describe, analyze, and explain that phenomenon just because it varies across systems has perhaps narrowed itself into significantly less importance. Or, to put it differently, the differences between common law and civil law systems, insofar as those differences still exist, may be a window into thinking about just what the point of legal philosophy is in the first place. And even if the legal pluralists at times go too quickly into differences and, thus, ignore theoretically and philosophically important similarities across the differences they have identified, they deserve our gratitude for focusing us on the data of legal philosophy in ways that those we might call non-pluralists have too often either neglected or simply taken for granted.

Even if we take general jurisprudence as a valuable enterprise, however, we should not forget that one of its tasks is—or at least should be—not only to explain what all of the exemplars of law have in common, but also what makes these exemplars of law and not of something else. To give just one prominent example, Hart's identification of the importance of internalization and the importance of the union of primary and secondary rules, when combined with his identification of the non-necessity of sanctions, tells us a great deal about law, but does not tell us very much about how law differs from the formalized rule systems of football associations, private corporations, and much more. And if we think that this differentiation is also in need of explanation, and if we think that philosophical analysis can assist in this explanation, then it may turn out that even the enterprise of general jurisprudence has a lot remaining to do.

If this is right, and if the differentiation of law (Schauer 2015, pp. 154–170) is a practically, sociologically, theoretically, and philosophically important enterprise, then the distinction between common law and civil law may again remain significant. Assuming some degree of non-convergence, the characteristic features of the common law—incremental development and the central role of the adjudicator, for example—may be part of the differentiating explanation, and so too might be the characteristic features of the civil law—detailed codes and adjudicators and interpreters discouraged from modifying the content of those codes, for example—will invariably be part of what differentiates law from the things that it resembles, but only resembles.

All of which is to say that the importance of the distinction between the common law and civil law is not only a function of what the task of legal philosophy is, but also a valuable gateway into thinking about just what that task should be.

References

Abi-Saab G (2017) Remarks by Georges Abi-Saab. Proc Am Soc Int Law 11:211–220
Alexander LA (1989) Constrained by precedent. South Calif Law Rev 63(1):1–64
Alfange D (1969) Jeremy Bentham and the codification of law. Cornell Law Rev 55(1):58–77
Bentham J (1838) (1808) Scotch reform. In: Bowring J (ed) The works of Jeremy Bentham. William Tait, Edinburgh, pp 1–53
Cappelletti M (1971) Judicial review in the contemporary world. Bobbs-Merrill, Indianapolis
Chou PSC (2010) Raz on the methodology of jurisprudence. Law Philos 29(2):231–243
Coleman J (2001) The practice of principle: In defence of a pragmatist approach to legal theory. Oxford University Press, Oxford
Danto AC (1964) The artworld. J Philos 61(19):571–584
Danto AC (1981) The transfiguration of the commonplace: a philosophy of art. Harvard University Press, Cambridge
Del Mar M, Bankowski Z (eds) (2009) Law as institutional normative order. Ashgate, Farnham, Surrey UK
Dickie G (1969) Defining art. Am Philos Q 6(3):253–256
Dickie G (1993) A tale of two artworlds. In: Rollins M (ed) Danto and his critics. Blackwell, Oxford, pp 73–79
Dickson J (2001) Evaluation and legal theory. Hart, Oxford
Dworkin R (1977) Taking rights seriously. Duckworth, London
Dworkin R (2006) Justice in Robes. Harvard University Press, Cambridge
Dworkin RM (1986) Law's empire. Harvard University Press, Cambridge
Endicott T (2011) The value of vagueness. In: Marmor A, Soames S (eds) Philosophical foundations of language in the law. Oxford University Press, Oxford, pp 14–30
Finnis J (1980) Natural law and natural rights. Clarendon, Oxford
Green L (2016) The forces of law: duty, coercion, and power. Ratio Juris 29(2):164–181
Hart HLA (2012) The Concept of law, 3rd edn, In: Bulloch PA, Raz J, Green L (eds) (1961)
Kelsen H (1967) The pure theory of law. University of California Press, Berkeley
La Porta R, Lopez de Silanes F, Shleifer A, Vishny R (1998) Law and finance. J Polit Econ 106 (6):1113–1155
Lakoff G (1987) Women, fire, and dangerous things: what categories reveal about the mind Chicago. The University of Chicago Press, Chicago
Langbein JH, Lerner RL, Smith BP (2009) History of the common law: the development of Anglo-American legal institutions. Aspen, New York
Leslie SJ (2008) Generics: cognition and acquisition. Philos Rev 117(1):1–47
MacCormick N (2007) Institutions of law: an essay in legal theory. Oxford University Press, Oxford
MacCormick N, Weinberger O (1986) An institutional theory of law: new approaches to legal positivism. Springer, Dordrecht
Mattei U, Pes LG (2008) Civil law and common law: toward convergence? In: Whittington KE, Kelemen RD, Caldeira GA (eds) The Oxford handbook of law and politics. Oxford University Press, Oxford, pp 267–280
McDonnell JB (1978) Purposive interpretation of the uniform commercial code: some implications for jurisprudence. Univ Penn Law Rev 126(4):795–855
Porta L, Lopez de Silanes F, Shleifer A (2008) The economic consequences of legal origins. J Econ Liter 46(2):285–332

Postema GJ (1986) Bentham and the common law tradition. Clarendon, Oxford
Postema GJ (2018) The data of jurisprudence. Wash Univ Law Rev 95(5):1083–1095
Rawls J (1971) A theory of justice. Harvard University Press, Cambridge
Raz J (1975) Practical reason and norms. Hutchinson, London
Raz J (2005) Can there be a theory of law? In: Golding MP, Edmundson WA (eds) The Blackwell guide to the philosophy of law and legal theory. Blackwell, Oxford, pp 324–342
Raz J (2009a) The authority of law: essays on law and morality, 2nd edn. Oxford University Press, Oxford
Raz J (2009b) Between authority and interpretation. Oxford University Press, Oxford
Rosenblum NL (1978) Bentham's theory of the modern state. Harvard University Press, Cambridge
Schauer F (1989) Is the common law? Calif Law Rev 77(3):455–471
Schauer F (2003) Profiles, probabilities, and stereotypes. Harvard University Press, Cambridge
Schauer F (2008) Why precedent in law (and elsewhere) is not totally (or even substantially) about analogy. Persp Psych Sci 3(5):454–460
Schauer F (2015) The force of law. Harvard University Press, Cambridge
Schauer F (2012) Precedent. In: Marmor A (ed) Routledge companion to the philosophy of law. Ro1utledge, London, pp 123–136
Schauer, F (2021) Constructing interpretation. Boston Univ Law Rev 101(1):103–132
Schlesinger RB (1995) The past and future of comparative law. Am J Comp Law 43(3):477–481
Shapiro SJ (2011) Legality. Harvard University Press, Cambridge
Summers RS, MacCormick DN (1997) Interpreting precedents: a comparative study. Ashgate, Aldershot UK
Tamanaha B (2018) Law's evolving emergent phenomena: From rules of social intercourse to rule of law society. Wash Univ Law Rev 95(5):1149–1186
Tamanaha BZ (2017) A realistic theory of law. Cambridge University Press, Cambridge
Twining W (2009) General jurisprudence: understanding law from a global perspective. Cambridge University Press, Cambridge
Waluchow W (1994) Inclusive legal positivism. Clarendon, Oxford
Zipursky BC (2013) The inner morality of private law. Am J Juris 58(1):27–44
Zweigert K, Kötz H (1998) Introduction to comparative law. Oxford University Press, Oxford

'The Law Works Itself Pure': Reflections on a Cherished Trope

Christoph Bezemek

Abstract Centuries after its introduction the image of the (common) 'law working itself pure' still proves to be powerful. Tracing the origins of the phrase, this chapter explores how this trope can help our understanding of how (common) law emerges and who shapes this process.

1 Sentiments

"Sentimental lawyers", Ronald Dworkin wrote in the final chapter of 'Law's Empire', "cherish an old trope: they say that law works itself pure." (Dworkin 1986, p. 400)

"The figure", Dworkin continues,

> imagines two forms or stages of the same system of law, the nobler form latent in the less noble, the impure, present law gradually transform[ing] itself into its own pure ambition, haltingly, to be sure, with slides as well as gains, never worked finally pure, but better in each generation than the last. (*Id.*)

Lon Fuller, evidently, was one of those "sentimental lawyers". His seminal essay, "The Law in Quest of itself "is concluded by the author marveling at the part judges and scholars have to play "in the eternal process by which the common law works itself pure and adapts itself to the needs of a new day" (Fuller 1966, p. 140).

Both, Fuller and Dworkin, of course, refer to the same "old trope", even if from different perspectives and to a different effect. Leaving aside that Dworkin refers to "law" in general, while Fuller puts particular emphasis on the eternal process being a property of the "common law", the few lines quoted before indicate as much: it is important to see that Dworkin understands the phrase in a way that changes in the law "are (or at least can be) guided by the law itself, personified, playing out an internal program or design" (Dworkin 1985, p. 173); Fuller on the other hand

C. Bezemek (✉)
Institute of Public Law and Political Science, University of Graz, Graz, Austria
e-mail: christoph.bezemek@uni-graz.at

N. Bersier et al. (eds.), *Common Law – Civil Law*, Law and Philosophy Library 139,
https://doi.org/10.1007/978-3-030-87718-7_3

celebrates the common law for its structural capability to adapt to the ever-changing requirements of our environment.

It is against the backdrop of the two perspectives thus introduced that this chapter will discuss the supposition of "the law working itself pure". In order to do this, a first step will take us back to the source from which the "old trope" emanates to see what sentiment it is, Dworkin's "sentimental lawyers" cherish.

2 *Murray v. Mansfield*

In the search for this source, the standard account would, correctly, of course, refer to the 1744 case *Omychund v. Barker*; an important case for more than one reason: *Omychund* is, on the one hand, widely regarded to be "a major turning point in the history of law and religious toleration" (M. Hart 2019, p. 93). On the other hand, the case has gained notoriety from the perspective of evidence, having resolved the question whether testimony of non-Christians was admissible in a court of law, holding that "any religious person could testify after being sworn in the fashion most binding on her conscience." (Kaufmann 2003, p. 203).

Still, the undeniable importance of *Omychund* is of lesser consequence here; of lesser consequence in any case than the answer to the question who the creator of the phrase "of the law working itself pure" was and in which context the phrase first came to use.

The standard account, again, would typically refer to Lord Mansfield, author of the famed King's Bench ruling in *Somerset's case*[1] and originator of "Lord Mansfield's Rule of Marriage",[2] as the one to have coined this often-celebrated phrase (*see* i.a. Edin 2010, p. 74).

While this is not really wrong, it is not really right either. It is not really right as *Omychund*, as indicated above, was decided in 1744. Mansfield was appointed as Lord Chief Justice only 12 years later, his baronage having been created upon his appointment (Llewellyn 2021). So, when *Omychund* was decided, there really was no *Lord Mansfield*, as William Lee, who died rather unexpectedly in 1754, was still sitting comfortably as Lord Chief Justice of King's Bench for 10 more years (Lemmings 2021).

Still, it is not really wrong, as William Murray who should in time become the Baron, and later the First Earl of Mansfield did participate in the case as Solicitor General; a position to which he had been appointed in 1742 (Llewellyn 2021). And as Solicitor General he did introduce the phrase of "the common law working itself pure". And he did so in *Omychund v. Barker*.

---

[1]Somerset v. Stewart (1772) 98 ER 499.

[2]Goodright v. Moss (1777) 2 Cowp 591, 98 ER 1257 (592): "[T]that the declarations of a father or mother, cannot be admitted to bastardize the issue born after marriage."

3 Splitting Hairs

I am well-aware, of course, that in highlighting this, I am in immediate danger to stand accused of hairsplitting of the kind unsuited for an academic endeavor such as this volume. After all: even if not elevated to the peerage at this point. It *was* the later Lord Mansfield who coined the phrase in question. And he did so in said case.

But there is an essential difference still. And the difference concerns the context in which the phrase was introduced as well as the position of the one who did so. After all: If the phrase was not introduced by the Lord Chief Justice, it cannot be considered an integral part of the judicial opinion in *Omychund*; and it, thus, cannot be considered as a self-image of the common law viewed through the eyes of those whose duty it is "to say what the law is".[3] As the Solicitor General's remark it rather is to be considered part of a line of argument favoring, and, as in the case at hand: successfully favoring, a certain outcome.

The 'common law working itself pure', thus, started out aspiring rather than administering justice (or something akin to it). And it may be worth to bear the argumentative function at the roots of the "old trope" in mind.

Just as it may be worth to bear in mind that the style and elegance of the phrase of "the common law working itself pure" were far from self-serving but themselves employed to support the argumentative function. Murray, it seems, was not among the truest of believers of the gospel he was preaching so eloquently. In Lord Campbell's work on 'The Lives of the Chief Justices of England' we are told that Mansfield had "formed a very low [...] estimate of the Common Law of England which he was to administer" when taking office (Campbell 1849, p. 402). There was, or so it seems, still much work to do for the common law on its quest towards purity.

Still, this quest towards purity is, again, not as absolute as the standard account would make us believe. In *Omychund,* Murray makes his point by contrasting statutory law and common law, praising the flexibility of the latter when compared to the rigidity of the former: "All occasions", Murray sets out to explain, "do not arise at once; now a particular species of *Indians* appears; hereafter another species of *Indians* may arise; a statute very seldom can take in all cases, therefore the common law, *that works itself pure* by rules from the fountain of justice, is for this reason superior to an act of parliament."[4]

So: there we finally have it, the original version of Dworkin's "old trope". But it doesn't look that Dworkinian at second glance. It does not concern questions of the "nobler form latent in the less noble, the impure, present law gradually transform itself into its own pure ambition" (Dworkin (1986, p. 400). Much rather, it seems, that Murray sides with Fuller's understanding, finding the common law's genius in its remarkable adaptability when it comes to duly and adequately consider the answers the common law may give to novel questions that arise against the backdrop of novel challenges. But does this render Dworkin's take unwarranted?

[3]Marbury v. Madison, 5 U.S. 137 (1803).

[4]Omychund v. Barker (1780) 1 Atk, 21.

4 The Way You Make Laws for Your Dog

In order to explore this in more depth a close look at the cardinal features of the common law is required:

"The characteristic feature of the common law", Frederick Schauer teaches us in his introduction to legal reasoning, "in its *purest* form [. . .] is the absence of a master code of laws". (Schauer 2012, p. 104—my emphasis). "Indeed", as Schauer observes elsewhere, "the absence of a single authoritative formulation is what distinguishes common law rules from legislative rules" (Schauer 1989, p. 455)

Sure enough: such a common law system in its purest form does not exist. Schauer, at one point, refers to it as "far more as a caricature than an accurate depiction of an actual legal system" (Schauer 2012, p. 104). And yet, this caricature, or maybe rather: this 'ideal-type' of the common law as opposed to an 'ideal-type of the civil law' (as a legal order based on comprehensive and consistent codes that strictly separates the law-making function of the legislator from the law-applying function of the judge) may prove to be of great use for our purposes.

Common law rules are created, as Cass Sunstein observes, "one case at a time" (Sunstein 2001). Still, "not only are common law rules created in the very process of application, but also they are applied in – and to – the very case that prompted the rulemaking" (Schauer 1989, p. 455). It is this feature of the common law that gave rise to Bentham's often-cited snide remark on the common law being "dog law" (*see* Postema 2019, pp. 269–271) in his essay 'Truth versus Ashhurst". Writing 50 years after *Omychund* was decided, Bentham was far from being convinced of the common law's virtues or its prospects in attaining the purity it strived for, if Murray was indeed to be believed.

"It is the judges [. . .] that make the common law", Bentham famously argued, continuing:

> Do you know how they make it? Just as a man makes laws for his dog. When your dog does anything, you want to break him of, you wait till he does it, and then beat him for it. This is the way you make laws for your dog: and this is the way the judges make law for you and me. They won't tell a man beforehand what it is he should not do—they won't so much as allow of his being told: they lie by till he has done something which they say he should not have done, and then they hang him for it. (Bentham 1843, p. 235).

This is a drastic depiction, both when it comes to dog training and to law making. And we may, with some relief, assert that the methods Bentham describes are no longer employed by the overwhelming majority of dog owners who would rather positively enforce desirable behavior by luring their dogs into it; typically assisted by food and praise (*see* Hiby et al. 2004) such as handing out treats or gently petting the dog on the back. Naturally, as with any kind of positive enforcement, it would not suffice to perform this sequence once. To succeed, you would have to do it over and over again, until, at one point, the command given to becomes somewhat entrenched in the dog's mind.

5 The Law Works Itself Dure

Now, I wouldn't argue that the common law lures those subjected to it to comply with its demands by handing out treats. And evidently the strokes the common law has to offer are not just gentle brushes on the back. But the same might just as well apply to the civil law.

Still, I would argue that the common law makes good use of entrenching its rules in the minds of its subjects by applying and re-applying them over time, case after case. And, of course: the more time, the more cases; the more cases, the greater the body of law—a body of law that, if consistent, wouldn't make us miss the master code all that much, with its function well-exercised based on a mechanism of gradual law-making. In establishing this body of law, we may say (and, indeed, the pun is intended) that, while we have yet to discover whether and to what extent the common law indeed works itself *pure*, the common law does indeed work itself *dure*.[5] And already in doing so, it may provide far more guidance to its subjects than Bentham would be willing to concede.[6]

Still, at this point, we may say: if we were to seek the common law's quest of purity as a quest of perfection that, in its essence, was a quest of completion, it is easy enough to see why such a quest could never be successful. Even "in its purest form" the common law cannot reach the purity thus understood. A master code built on cases necessary is an elusive concept; the process of the common law working itself pure in this perspective is, indeed "eternal" (Fuller 1966, p. 140).

And yet, the perfect master code is just as much an elusive concept in a civil law system in its 'purest form':

> [e]ven idle reflection may conclude that every legal code is capable of improvement, for it is possible to imagine what is most glorious, exalted, and beautiful as being more glorious, exalted, and beautiful still. But a large and ancient tree puts out more and more branches without thereby becoming a new tree; yet it would be foolish to refuse to plant a tree just because it might produce new branches. (Hegel 1991, p. 249)

---

[5] Or to put it in Schauer's (1991, p. 175) words: "As the stock of [. . .] opinions increases, certain justifications recur, and certain principles become ossified."

[6] This, of course, hardly qualifies as a novel insight (see i.a. Hart 1994, p. 135). Still, it seems important to point out that even the European Court of Human Rights has long since accepted, that the requirement that a criminal "offence must be clearly defined in the law", derived from the *nulla poena sine lege* principle as safeguarded in Article 7 ECHR, may readily be met by common law systems in which "the progressive development of the criminal law through judicial law-making is a well entrenched and necessary part of legal tradition. [Accordingly,] Article 7 of the Convention cannot be read as outlawing the gradual clarification of the rules of criminal liability through judicial interpretation from case to case, provided that the resultant development is consistent with the essence of the offence and could reasonably be foreseen." ECtHR, 22.11.1995, S.W. v. UK, 20166/92 § 36.

6 Memories of Times Past

The root of the tree, in any event, the body of law itself, is maintained by the force attributed to the rules thus created. For the sake of our analysis this is to say that the *durability* of these rules needs to be safeguarded in order for their character as rules endowed with the force of law to be preserved. While in a civil law system this may seem to be ensured (primarily) by way of formalized procedure (just *see* Schauer 2004, p. 770), in a common law system this, evidently, is ensured by the handling of precedent (just *see* Bagchi 2020, p. 141).

Reading Blackstone, we learn how deep the roots of the tree run, that

> even so early as the conquest, we find the '*praeteritorum memoria eventorum*' reckoned up as one of the chief qualifications of those who were held to be '*legibus patriae optime instituti*'". For it [was] an established rule to abide by former precedents, where the same points come again in litigation; as well to keep the scale of justice even and steady, and not liable to waver with every new judge's opinion; as also because the law in that case being solemnly declared and determined, what before was uncertain, and perhaps indifferent, is now [...] a permanent rule, which it is not in the breast of any subsequent judge to alter or vary from, according to his private sentiments. (Blackstone 1765, p. 69)

Whether or not it should suffice for a rule to uphold its claim to validity to have been around for quite some time, has traditionally been the subject of debate. Holmes's line of it being "revolting to have no better reason for a rule of law than that so it was laid down in the time of Henry IV" (Holmes 1897, p. 469), is to the point today, just as it was more than a hundred years ago. Still, one might argue: the same applies to the counter-objection that to uphold such a "*rule* of law" arises from the "*rule of law*" as such properly understood (*see* Waluchow 2007, p. 198) by ensuring "intertemporal consistency" (Schauer, 174) and thereby the predictability of judicial decisions (Tamanaha 2004, pp. 86–89).[7] After all, drawing on Holmes's classical depiction: not even the worst man, let alone a simple "bad man" (Holmes 1897), can engage in predicting the decision of a court of law absent any guidance rooted in the law itself, absent any *authority* to cling to.[8]

7 When in Rome...

Against this background, and adding to this functionalist perspective, it may be beneficial to pay closer attention to this *authority* that derives from the "*praeteritorum memoria eventorum*" Blackstone referred to.

As it turns out, Hannah Arendt's observations in the context of the political order of the Roman Republic prove to be most instructive for the purpose at hand. "[T]he word *auctoritas*", so she begins her analysis, "derives from the verb *augere*, [which

---

[7] For an extensive discussion of this aspect *see* Wasserstrom (1961), pp. 60–66.

[8] For a closer analysis *see* Bezemek (2016) (18–21).

means as much as to] 'augment', and [that] what authority or those in authority constantly augment [!] is the foundation." (Arendt 1961, pp. 121–122); preparing it to be built on (similarly Kessel 1959, pp. 221–222).

"Those endowed with authority", Arendt continues,

> were the elders, [. . .] who had obtained it by descent and by transmission (tradition) from those who had laid the foundations for all things to come [. . .]. The authority of the living was always derivative, depending [. . .] upon the authority of the founders, who no longer were among the living. (Arendt, 122).

Authority according to Arendt, thus, is traced back to "*eventa praeterita*" the "*memoria*" of which is safeguarded by a tradition that spans generations united in the "the experience of politics" (Hammer 2015, p. 136).

Differing from power, Arendt goes on to argue, "authority ha[s] its roots in the past". And yet, this past is "no less present in the actual life of the city than the power and strength of the living" (Arendt 1961, p. 122). Relying on authority, the "animating forces of politics that inspired action are not just recounted but relived" (Hammer 2002, p. 137). Still, in its "contradistinction to power [authority] seems to us curiously *elusive* and intangible" (Arendt 1961, p. 122): Theodor Mommsen, as Arendt points out, insightfully called it "more than advice and less than a command, an advice which one may not safely ignore" (Mommsen 1888, p. 1034); adding to every single decision the "whole weight of the past" (Arendt 123). Thus, any political action taken in accordance with authority becomes "reinforced by a living tradition that transmits the past" (Hammer 2002, p. 142).

With "[*g*]*ravitas*, the ability to bear this weight", [as central trait of those commanding authority] Arendt concludes her survey, "precedents, the deeds of the ancestors and the usage that grew out of them, were always binding. Any thing that happened was transformed into an example, and 'the *auctoritas* of the elders' became identical with authoritative models for actual behaviour, with the moral political standard as such." (Arendt 1961, p. 123). It was for authority to serve as the "crucial source of stability" (Klusmeyer 2014, p. 141) that bare power could not (and cannot) provide.

8 The Gravitational Force of Precedent

It takes little imagination to perceive the *praeteritorum memoria eventorum* Blackstone (1765, p. 69) refers to as the link between the authority rooted in the past and the power presently exercised in the "least dangerous branch"; even less so, as Hannah Arendt herself points to the "striking resemblance to Montesquieu's judiciary branch of government, whose power he called 'somehow nil' (en quelque jagon nulle)" (Arendt 1961, p. 122). The resemblance becomes more striking still, when we realize that it is the same passage that Alexander Hamilton refers to when describing the judiciary as "the weakest of the three departments of power" in the famed Federalist No. 78; a department that may "truly be said to have neither Force nor Will, but merely judgment" (Hamilton 1961, p. 523). This judgment, however, is firmly based on authority understood in the way described above, applying "the judicial experience of the past to the judicial questions of the present" (Pound 1921, p. 182), a past that thereby is "not just recounted but relived" (Hammer 2002, p. 137) as it translates the *gravitas* of authority into "the gravitational force of precedent" (Dworkin 1975, p. 1090).

Still, the force thus described is not invincible: Precedent (whether the 'authority' it exudes technically is considered 'binding' or merely 'persuasive') is "more than advice and less than a command". Acting in the limbo between these options, judges face what occasionally (and befittingly) in legal scholarship is described as a "dilemma" (δίλημμα): a "dilemma" [that] derives from the fact that they are understood to be both bound by precedent and also to be *authorised* to depart from it." (Bagchi 2020, pp. 143—my emphasis). And while, in order to preserve the authority of precedent, the latter option is thought of as "the exception, not the rule" (Barak 2002, p. 31), the *authorization* to resort to this exception ensures that the gravitational force of the past is not to put that much weight on the present that it might find itself crushed in the "dead hand of the common law".[9]

It is against this background that Blackstone was in a position to argue that the gravitational force of precedent had to find its limits

> where the former determination is most evidently contrary to reason; much more if it be contrary to the divine law. [. . .] And hence it is that our lawyers are with justice so copious in their ecomiums on the reason of the common law; that they tell us, that the law is the perfection of reason, that it always intends to conform thereto, and that what is not reason is not law. (Blackstone 1765, p. 69).

To perceive law as the "perfection of reason", as Blackstone does,[10] is by itself a reference to Coke's famed dictum of "the common law itselfe [being] nothing else but Reason; which is to be understood of an artificial Perfection of Reason" (Coke 1738, II, 6 § 138).

Coke's choice of words may puzzle us, even if only as long as we realize that the "artificial" perfection he refers to, properly understood, is the perfection owed to the craftsmanship of the "Artifex"[11] (*see* Boyer 1997, pp. 44–45). Again: Hannah Arendt's analysis is of great use in this context:"*Auctores*", she observes,

> can be used as the very opposite of the artifices, the actual builders and makers, and this precisely when the word auctor signifies the same thing as our 'author'. [. . .] The author in this case is not the builder but the one who inspired the whole enterprise and whose spirit, therefore, much more than the spirit of the actual builder, is represented in the building itself.

[9]Rosen v. United States, 245 U.S. 467 (1918) 471 (remarkably, like *Omychund*, a case on the admissibility of testimony). For a closer analysis *see* Corbin (1918).

[10]Another phrase ridiculed by Bentham (1843, p. 235): "the reason of which you are at no great loss to see," he mocked it.

[11]Cf Coke 1832, II, 6 § 138: "[R]eason is the life of the law, nay the common law itself is nothing else but reason; which is to be understood of an artificial perfection of reason, gotten by long study, observation and experience, and not of every man's natural reason; for *Nemo nascitur Artifex*."

> In distinction to the *artifex*, who only made it, he is the actual 'author' of the building, namely its founder; with it he has become an 'augmenter' of the city. (Arendt 1961, p. 122)

It is this understanding that is weaved into Blackstone's reading of Coke. The lawyer, as an artificer in the service of the common law's spirit (Pound 1921, p. 182); with the authority of the common law shining through the body of law, permanently "augmenting" the legal system as such (for a contemporary perspective on this see Breyer 2021, p. 91). And it is said understanding that is weaved into Dworkin's reading of Murray (or: Mansfield, if you will) on the common law, or in Dworkin's words: on 'the law' working itself pure. Even if the artifex was to honestly pursue the author's grand design,[12] such a struggle was doomed to produce imperfect, necessarily tentative, results. The quest for purity, thus proves to be eternal not only as perfection as completion is concerned but also when it comes to the body of law as such. Which does not render the quest itself useless: The life of the law may well have been experience rather than logic (*see* Holmes 1881, p. 1); still, as Kant cautions, "a merely empirical system, void of rational principles, is, like the wooden head in the fable of Phædrus, fine enough in appearance, but unfortunately it wants brain." (Kant 1887, p. 44).

This does not make the life of the law necessarily logic rather than experience (*see* Schauer 1991, pp. 775–776). But it allows us to embrace the image of "two forms or stages of the same system of law, the nobler form latent in the less noble, the impure" (Dworkin 1986, p. 400)—the "Law as Will" and its various representations.

9 Slides or Gains?

To which extent we subscribe to the view underlying the "rational principle" of *the law working itself pure* thus understood and, in doing so, assent to the sentiment shared by sentimental lawyers[13] depends, however, on a variety of factors; factors neither to be considered essential traits of the common nor of the civil law 'in its purest form'. First, and foremost, this concerns the sense of direction implied by the very idea of the law's quest for purity. Whether you share Dworkin's depiction of "present law gradually transform[ing] itself into its own pure ambition, haltingly, [. . .] with slides as well as gains, never worked finally pure, but better in each generation than the last" (Dworkin 1986, p. 400) depends in the end on whether you accept a dialectic directed by the invisible hand of the law (be it guided by Dworkin's concept of *integrity* or some other way of drawing from the "fountain of justice"). This, again, makes our sentimental lawyer someone who would truly consider the law as a "brooding omnipresence in the sky";[14] as something that only needs to be

[12] She needn't necessarily (see Schauer 2004, p. 777).

[13] Which, aside from Bentham, of course, many scholars enrooted in the common law tradition would not. For a particularly vivid critique see Ewart (1904), p. 125.

[14] Holmes (dissenting), *Southern Pacific Company v. Jensen* 244 U.S. 205 (1917) 222.

validated by the argumentative function of our cherished trope as employed by Murray.

One way to avoid this, is to take the argumentative function at face value and to perceive the eternal struggle of the law working itself pure not as guided by an invisible hand but rather along the lines of something as Holmes's concept of the free trade in ideas[15] that takes place between judges, lawmakers, scholars and the wider public. In following this path, the "rational principle" of the law working itself pure may usefully serve as a regulative ideal.

This is a noble aspiration. Still, to pursue it seems risky. After all: "[i]n the hands of the wrong people, the law may be as likely to work itself impure as pure" (Schauer 2004, p. 777). That, of course, is true. And it forces us to accept that the purity thus achieved may be little more than the ever-tentative result of a quest entered for its own sake. In this struggle, we may find solace in the fact that the *gravitas* of authority rooted in the past tilts our 'trade in ideas' in favor of tradition and the '*praeteritorum memoria eventorum*' this tradition embodies. Typically, then, experience will outweigh expedience without petrifying the status quo. We may, thus, be in the position to overcome the mistakes made in the past without being bound to repeat them whenever new "occasions [. . .] arise".[16] That, at last, may be quite a fair assessment of the trope William Murray devised in *Omychund v. Barker*.

References

Arendt H (1961) What is authority? In: Between past and future: eight exercises in political thought. Penguin Books, London

Barak A (2002) A judge on judging: the role of a supreme court in a democracy. Harv Law Rev 116: 19

Bagchi A (2020) On the boundaries of normativity in law. In: Bezemek C, Potacs M, Somek A (eds) Vienna lectures on legal philosophy, Normativism and anti-normativism in law, vol 2, pp 141–150

Bentham J (1843) Truth versus Ashhurst, or, law as it is, contrasted with what it is said to be. In: Bowring J (ed) The works of Jeremy Bentham, vol V. Edinburgh: William Tait, London: Marshall Simpkin

Bezemek C (2015) The epistemic neutrality of the marketplace of ideas. First Amendment Law Rev 14:159–181

Bezemek C (2016) Bad for good - perspectives on law and force. In: Bezemek C, Ladavac N (eds) The force of law reaffirmed. Springer, New York

Blackstone W (1765 (facsimile version Legal Classics Library 1983) Blackstone's commentaries. Clarendon Press, Oxford

Boyer A (1997) Understanding, authority, and will: sir Edward Coke and the Elizabethan Origins of Judicial review. Bost College Law Rev 39:43

Breyer S (2021) The Authority of the Court and the Peril of Politics

Campbell JL (1849) The lives of the Chief Justices of England, vol II. John Murray, London

[15] Which I have discussed at greater length elsewhere (*see* Bezemek 2015).

[16] Omychund v. Barker (1780) 1 Atk, 21.

Coke E (1738) The first part of the Institutes of the law of England; or, A commentary upon Littleton, 12th edn. E. and R. Nutt, and R. Gosling, London
Corbin A (1918) The dead hand of the common law. Yale Law J 27:668–673
Dworkin R (1975) Hard cases. Harv Law Rev 88:1057–1109
Dworkin R (1985) Law's ambitions for itself. Virginia Law Rev 71:173–187
Dworkin R (1986) Law's empire. Harvard University Press, Cambridge
Edin D (2010) Judges and unjust laws: common law constitutionalism and the foundations of judicial review. University of Michigan Press, Ann Arbor
Ewart J (1904) What is the common law? Columbia Law Rev 4:116–126
Fuller L (1966) The law in quest of itself
Hamilton A (1961) Federalist No. 78. In: Cooke J (ed) The Federalist, pp 521–530
Hammer D (2002) Hannah Arendt and roman political thought: the practice of theory. Polit Theory 30:124–149
Hammer D (2015) Authoring within history: the legacy of Roman politics in Hannah Arendt. Class Recept J 7:129–139
Hart HLA (1994) The concept of law, 2nd edn. Clarendon Press, Oxford
Hart M (2019) What is an infidel? Jewish Oaths and Jewish History in the making of English Trust and Tolerance. In: Caputo N, Hart MB (eds) On the word of a jew: religion, reliability, and the dynamics of trust. Indiana University Press, Bloomington
Hegel GWF (1991 8th print 2003) Elements of the philosophy of right. In: Wood AW (ed) (trans: Nisbet HB). Cambridge University Press, Cambridge
Hiby EF, Rooney NJ, Bradshaw JWS (2004) Dog training methods: their use, effectiveness and interaction with behaviour and welfare. Animal Welfare 13:63–69
Holmes OW Jr (1881) The common law
Holmes OW Jr (1897) The path of the law. Harv Law Rev 10(8):457–478
Kant I (1887) The philosophy of law: an exposition of the fundamental principles of jurisprudence as the science of right (trans: Hastie W) Clark, Edinburgh
Kaufmann P (2003) Disbelieving nonbelievers: atheism, competence, and credibility in the turn of the century American Courtroom. Yale J Law Human 15:395–433
Kessel W (1959) Auctoritas und Potestas als Ordnungsgrundlagen der Demokratie. Archiv für Rechts- und Sozialphilosophie 45:215–233
Klusmeyer D (2014) Hannah Arendt on authority and tradition. In: Hannah Arendt: Key concepts. Routledge, Abingdon pp 138–152.
Lemmings D (2021) Lee, Sir William. In: Oxford Dictionary of National Biography (online ed) Oxford University Press. https://doi.org/10.1093/ref:odnb/16315 (04.20.2021)
Llewellyn KN (2021) William Murray, 1st Earl of Mansfield. In: Encyclopedia Britannica. www.britannica.com/biography/William-Murray-1st-Earl-of-Mansfield (04.20.2021)
Mommsen T (1888) Römisches Staatsrecht. Wissenschaftliche Buchgemeinschaft, Tübingen
Postema G (2019) Bentham and the common law tradition, 2nd edn. Oxford University Press, Oxford
Pound R (1921) The spirit of the common law
Schauer F (1989) Is the common law? Book review. Calif Law Rev 77:455–471
Schauer F (1991) Playing by the rules: a philosophical examination of rule-based decision-making in law and life. Clarendon Press, Oxford
Schauer F (2004) The failure of the common law. Arizona State Law J 36:765–782
Schauer F (2012) Thinking like a lawyer: a new introduction to legal reasoning. Harvard University Press, Cambridge
Sunstein C (2001) One case at a time: judicial minimalism on the supreme court. Harvard University Press, Cambridge
Tamanaha B (2004) On the rule of law: history, politics, theory. Cambridge University Press, Cambridge
Waluchow WJ (2007) A common law theory of judicial review: the living tree. Cambridge University Press, Cambridge
Wasserstrom R (1961) The judicial decision: twoard a theory of legal justification

Case Law

Goodright v. Moss (1777) 2 Cowp 591, 98 ER 1257.
Marbury v. Madison, 5 U.S. 137 (1803)
Omychund v. Barker (1780) 1 Atk, 21; 26 ER 15.
Southern Pacific Company v. Jensen (1917), 244 U.S. 205.
Rosen v. United States, 245 U.S. 467 (1918) 471.
Somerset v. Stewart (1772) 98 ER 499.
S.W. v. UK, ECtHR, 22.11.1995, 20166/92.

The Chain Novel and Its Normative Fine Structure in Civil Law and Common Law: *Dworkin*, *Brandom* and Law's Normativity

Stefan Arnold

Abstract This essay defends the thesis that Dworkin's and Brandom's theories of law's normativity are powerful not only with respect to common law but also with respect to civil law. Dworkin explained law as a specific genre of literature—the chain novel—where several authors collaborate in writing a novel and each author builds her chapter on the previous chapters in the chain by creatively interpreting them. Brandom built on Dworkin's chain novel of law to illustrate his theory of normativity with respect to law. Law's normativity, Brandom argues, arises through the discursive practice of law which is characterised by mutual recognition as a social and normative attitude. Dworkin and Brandom both developed their theories against a common law background and illustrated them with the practice of individual judges in the common law world. That seems to suggest that their theories of normativity are pointless and unproductive for civil law systems. Yet, this essay argues, Dworkin's chain novel and Brandom's normative fine structure of it are equally fruitful for our understanding of civil law. To support this thesis, rhetorical and stylistic characteristics of common law and civil law systems are examined with a focus on the role of legislation. Dworkin's and Brandom's theories are applied against the background of legal discourse in a broader sense—including not only judges but also other players of the law (like public officials, solicitors, barristers and the persons involved in legislation). The working of the law's chain novel in practice will be illustrated with the law on the recognition of child marriages.

I would like to thank Nils Buchholz, Moritz Grothe, Marcus Schnetter, Lea Simmler and Norman Weitemeier for their helpful comments.

S. Arnold (✉)
University of Münster, Münster, Germany
e-mail: stefan.arnold@uni-muenster.de

N. Bersier et al. (eds.), *Common Law – Civil Law*, Law and Philosophy Library 139,
https://doi.org/10.1007/978-3-030-87718-7_4

1 Introduction

This essay defends the thesis that Dworkin's and Brandom's interpretive and pragmatic accounts of law's normativity are as fruitful for the understanding of civil law as they are for the understanding of common law. In the following, normativity is understood as a form of objective rationality (*see* Arnold 2021). In the context of law, rationality is based upon sensible reasons. If law is rational in that sense, it seems worthy of compliance and thus able to conduct and control the behaviour of people. If law lacks normativity, there are no sensible reasons that it is based upon and, hence, some form of legal realism giving rise to legal nihilism seems unavoidable (Brandom 2014, p. 20; Arnold 2016, p. 11). Now, Dworkin's chain novel analogy famously compared law with a specific literary practice where each chapter of a novel is added by another author whose task is to continue the novel that has so far been written by others. Dworkin's analogy which I shall explain more extensively in the next section, inspired Brandom to illustrate his theory of normativity with respect to law. Brandom wrote, in a sense, an explanatory guide to Dworkin's law as literature analogy by arguing that law gains normativity through the discursive practice of law that is shaped by the game of giving and asking for reasons.[1] Both Dworkin and Brandom focus on judgments and the doings of individual judges and there is no doubt that they developed their theories with judge-made law in mind. Thus, one might assume that their accounts lose much of their explanatory power with respect to civil law. This essay argues against that assumption. Dworkin's chain novel analogy and Brandom's normative fine structure of Dworkin's novel are, I contend, equally fruitful for our understanding of civil law.

2 Dworkin's Chain Novel Analogy and Brandom's Normative Fine Structure of Law's Chain Novel

2.1 Dworkin's Law as Literature Approach: Law as an Interpretive Enterprise

Ronald Dworkin understands law as an interpretive enterprise that combines backward and forward-looking elements (1986, p. 225). Judges are bound to interpret law on the assumption of a coherent conception of justice and fairness—that is the core of Dworkin's commitment to law as integrity. For Dworkin, law as integrity tells law's story as a coherent, overall story stemming from the past and stretching out into the future. Dworkin captures the nature of that storytelling with an analogy between law and literature.[2] He famously describes law's development as a literary

[1] Brandom borrows that phrase from Sellars (Brandom 2001, p. 195).

[2] *See* on the narrative elements of judgments also Weisberg (1992), pp. 10–22.

enterprise: a chain novel written by a group of novelists (Dworkin 1985, chapters 6–7; Dworkin 1986; Dworkin 1982). They all together create a novel in the following way: Each author builds her chapter on the previous chapter in the chain by creatively interpreting it. Dworkin has a wide notion of creative interpretation, so that to him adding a chapter is an interpretation of the novel as a whole (Dworkin 1986, p. 232; Dworkin 1985, p. 157). The chain novel as continued by the previous author is then further interpreted by the next novelist when she creates her new chapter. An example for a real example of a literary chain novel is offered by *The Floating Admiral* (Christie et al. 2017), a detective novel for which the single chapters were written by several famous authors of detective stories—amongst them *Agatha Christie*. It is indeed surprising that Dworkin does not cite this novel given the fact that he demonstrates his understanding of literature quite often with respect to novels of *Agatha Christie*.[3]

Dworkin regards the interpretive practice of judges as a form of creative interpretation (1985, p. 158). He regards judges as authors as well as critics in the sense of literary criticism; and the enterprise of the chain novel, he argues, seems to best account for that double nature of the judge's creativity. Each novelist writes her chapter so as to create a single unified novel and to make it the best novel it can be. Now, Dworkin suggests two separate but intertwined dimensions against which the interpretations of the authors must be tested (1986, pp. 230–231). The first dimension is the dimension of *fit*. Any author must strive to offer an interpretation with general explanatory power for major structural aspects of the text. The second dimension of interpretation asks each author to choose the interpretation that makes the overall novel *the best it can be*—in case that several interpretations pass the criterion of *fit*. Similarly, Dworkin argues, law is developed by a continuous interpretation of legal texts—especially of judicial decisions. For him, deciding hard cases at law is like writing yet another chapter in law's chain novel (Dworkin 1985, p. 159). He focuses on judicial decisions at common law for his argument, even though he occasionally mentions statutory interpretation (Dworkin 1985, pp. 147–148, 161). Each judge must, according to Dworkin, interpret previous decisions with a view to the collective formation of law's rules and principles through the bulk of decisions forming the common law. Thus, each judge should regard himself "as a partner in a complex chain enterprise of which these innumerable decisions, structures, conventions, and practices are the history; it is his job to continue that history into the future through what he does on the day" (Dworkin 1985, p. 159). Thereby, judges are—according to Dworkin—to choose the interpretation which makes law's chain novel the most significant or best (Dworkin 1985, pp. 159–160). The interpretation must, firstly, fit the legal tradition established so far in order to preserve law's integrity and coherence. Secondly, judges need to interpret law with a view to law's "point or value": not artistic value as in literature, but political value in the sense of law's functions to coordinate society, resolve disputes and secure justice (Dworkin 1985, p. 160). To Dworkin, judicial interpretation

[3]For details on the *Floating Admiral see* d'Amato (1989), pp. 528–530.

therefore depends on some substantial political theory so that judges may reasonably disagree on the best interpretation of law (Dworkin 1985, pp. 160–161).[4]

2.2 *Brandom's Pragmatist Approach and the Chain Novel's Normative Fine Structure*

2.2.1 Brandom's Critique and Appraisal of the Law as Literature Metaphor

Dworkin's law and literature analogy employs a fairly narrow form of literature: The chain novel is supposed to form a coherent story. Literature, however, does not always tell coherent stories. Furthermore, to describe law as literature faces the obvious difficulty that literature—unlike law—is not easily conceptualised as a system of norms regulating social behaviour. Dworkin's analogy is nevertheless helpful to understand specific elements of law: The analogy emphasises its creative and interpretive aspects. And it stresses how law is a continuous process that is shaped by individual yet correlated propositions. These aspects might explain why Robert Brandom's project is friendly to Dworkin's chain novel approach. To him, "[i]t is clear that this model is getting at something important about case law (and about common law, which is case law all the way down)" (Brandom 2014, p. 31). Brandom uses Dworkin's law and literature analogy as a starting point to illustrate his theory of normativity with respect to law and its rationality (2014, p. 31). Brandom is neither a lawyer nor a philosopher of law. He is a philosopher and elaborated—most prominently in his influential book *Making it explicit* (Brandom 1994)—a pragmatist theory of language, meaning and rationality (*see*, for instance, Fischer 2014; Rödl 2000; Rosenberg 1997). In *Making it explicit*, there are but indications as to the relevance of his thinking to law and legal philosophy and, vice versa, to the relevance of law for his thinking (Brandom 1994, p. 130). Yet in a series of papers *Brandom* (1999, 2009, 2014, 2015) explained law's normativity as an example for normativity as a general concept that relates to everything we say and do (Brandom 2015, pp. 36–37; Honneth 2008 and Klatt 2008, pp. 115–122). In Brandom's Hegel-inspired thinking, normativity depends on practices.

> Hegel's account as I understand it is aimed at discursive practice and the development of determinate conceptual contents generally. It becomes particularly pointed and significant when applied to the explicit, self-conscious, institutionalized context in which legal concepts develop. (Brandom 2014, pp. 31–32).

It is therefore the practice of the legal discourse that, for Brandom, law's normativity is rooted in. Brandom's emphasis on the discursive character of law

---

[4]That aspect of Dworkin's theory invoked critique from a formalist perspective, *see* for instance Cass (2001), pp. 77–78. *See* also Ballingrud (2020), p. 4, arguing that Dworkin's analogy allows for law to develop in directions that contradict central concepts of the constitution.

mirrors Dworkin's idea of law as an interpretive enterprise. Thus, it comes as no surprise that Brandom shares Dworkin's focus on the practice of judging and on judges as individual interpreters of law. And like Dworkin, Brandom describes this practice as constituted by individual acts of interpretation. Brandom furthermore sharply warns of the perils of legal nihilism (Brandom 2014, p. 20), a warning that Dworkin surely would have agreed with (*compare* Dworkin 1986, p. 44).

This consonance notwithstanding, Brandom launches a severe criticism of Dworkin's law as literature approach. He underlines the difficulty of drawing analogies between law and literature and criticizes Dworkin's version of the judge's interpretive practice as extremely general and lacking systematic depth (Brandom 2014, p. 31). According to Brandom, Dworkin's model can hardly be called "a theory" at all, but rather "a set of reminders of questions to ask" (Brandom 2014, p. 31).

> The model gets a grip only insofar as one can say something systematic about what determines the relative importance of the others. It is those judgments that carry whatever practical force the model brings to bear. [...] it sketches only the form of an account. Fill in the relevant respects of assessment of 'better' extensions of legal traditions and their respective weights, or more generally interactions (in the non-monotonic inferential structure being developed) and one would have an actual account. (Brandom 2014, p. 31).[5]

In a way, Brandom seems to expand on the critiques that Dworkin's chain novel analogy has attracted from a variety of perspectives[6] and, in fact, to echo Stanley Fish who famously insisted that Dworkin's chain novel analogy wrongly assumes some form of objectivity outside the process of interpretation and that Dworkin's plea for "law as integrity" is superfluous, since a thoroughly interpretive and historically embedded conception of law is without an alternative (Fish 1982, 1983, 1987a, b, 1991).[7] Brandom's project is to supplement Dworkin's theory with "the normative fine structure" (Brandom 2014, p. 31)[8] not provided by Dworkin himself. This fine structure offers a fruitful understanding of law's normativity—even though it needs to be supplemented by justice as a virtue, as I have argued elsewhere (Arnold 2017, pp. 275–278).

---

[5] In fairness to Dworkin, Brandom attacks the judge's obligation along the general dimensions of "fit" and "the best" as expounded above. Dworkin does, of course, offer examples and detailed arguments to lend more substance to these broad interpretive guidelines.

[6] *See*, for instance, from a realist perspective d'Amato (1989), pp. 528–530; Lindquist and Cross (2005), pp. 1205-1206; from a formalist perspective Ballingrud (2020), p. 4.

[7] On the *Fish-Dworkin* debate and for further references see Robertson (2014).

[8] *See* in the general context of Brandom's philosophy Brandom (2001), p. 185.

2.2.2 Mutual Recognition as the Key to Law's Normativity

Brandom employs Hegel's model of mutual recognition to explain the normativity arising within law's chain novel.[9] He understands common law as judge-made case law which consists entirely of a sequence of application of concepts to facts. According to his view, concepts like "tort" or "strict liability" are formed by a tradition of cases that each judge inherits and applies to the actual facts of the case at hand (Brandom 1999, p. 180). Brandom regards the content of those concepts as being entirely constituted by the history of the application of them (and of related concepts) (1999, p. 180). In applying them, the judge rationally reconstructs the tradition as well as the precedents belonging to it. To Brandom, judge-made law is precisely thought of as judge-made law because the legal tradition itself is entirely formed through the process of application (2014, p. 35). But why and how can this practice achieve normativity? According to Brandom, it can, because that practice is shaped by mutual recognition (1999, pp. 179–182; 2014, pp. 30–33) as a normative social structure (Brandom 1994, p. 275 and *see* also Christensen and Sokolowski 2006). Recognition is a heavily debated concept, of course (*see* Iser 2013). Brandom regards recognition as a description of how we socially behave, as a personal attitude which we have towards others and which we expect others to have towards us (1999, pp. 169–172). Yet Brandom does not stop here. For him—and in his reading of Hegel, for Hegel as well,[10] recognition has also a normative component and functions as the lever for rationality (Brandom 1999, pp. 169–173). This normative conception of mutual recognition is promising for our understanding of the legal discourse and might help to escape legal nihilism (Arnold 2016, p. 11; 2017, p. 272).

Brandom explains mutual recognition as a personal attitude of the common law judge: Every judge recognises the other judges as recognising judges and is equally recognised herself in the same way. This echoes Hegel's famous formula in his *Phänomenologie des Geistes*: "Sie *anerkennen* sich als *gegenseitig sich anerkennend*." (Hegel 1996, p. 147). According to Brandom, recognition comprises two distinguished but interlaced elements: authority and responsibility (1999, pp. 169–172; 2014, p. 28). Both components become apparent in the historical development of law. Brandom is not concerned with the authority and the responsibility of judges towards plaintiffs or defendants but with the authority and responsibility of judges towards each other and towards the law as it is instantiated in every single judgment (2014, p. 32). For Brandom, the judge is responsible *to* the law and responsible *for* the law at the same time (2014, p. 32). When common law judges—as they often and extensively do—explicitly engage with previous judgments and with the reasons given in them, they recognise the authority of those judgments—and of the judges responsible for them (Brandom 1999, pp. 180–183; 2014, p. 32).

---

[9]The following part is partially based upon Arnold (2016), pp. 10–18 and Arnold (2017), pp. 272–275.

[10]*See* for a critique of Brandom's reading of Hegel Honneth (2008).

> Th[e] judge [...] exercises authority over future judges, who are constrained by that judge's decisions, insofar as they are precedential. But the currently deciding judge is also responsible to (and held responsible by) future judges, who can (by their practical attitudes) either take the current decision (and rationale) to be correct and precedential, or not. (Brandom 2014, p. 33).

To Brandom every single judgment is embedded in a historical process stemming from the past and reaching out into the future (1999, pp. 179–180; 2014, pp. 30–32). The judgment is rooted in the past which becomes apparent when a judgment refers to reasons which have already been given in the discursive development of the common law. Here we can see how Brandom's explanation of judge-made common law builds on the chain novel metaphor: To Brandom, each judge inherits the common law's chapters that have already been written by other judges. And they continue the common law's story on the reasoning contained in those previous chapters. At the same time, each judge writes her chapter with a view to the future[11] so that it will be recognised by future judges and therefore become relevant for the further development of law. Recognition as mutual responsibility and authority structures the historical development of judge-made law (Brandom 2014, p. 33). Each judge knows that previous judges recognised her own responsibility and authority and she is equally aware of the analogous claim of future judges. Thus, any judge claims recognition while at the same time recognising other (future and past) judges as recognising judges (Brandom 2014, p. 33). This process also shapes the content of precedents: Each interpretation of a precedent in the light of the now relevant facts affects the meaning of that precedent; it can amplify or narrow its scope of application and change its content. It is therefore the reconsideration, reconstruction and application of precedents that shape their content.

> By applying concepts to novel particulars one is 'determining' the conceptual contents in the sense of *making it* the case that some applications are correct, by *taking it* to be the case that they are. One is drawing new, more definite boundaries, where many possibilities existed before. (Brandom 2014, p. 36).

Brandom further argues that mutual recognition ensures law's determinacy, albeit only in a restricted sense:

> What we should say is that concepts have contents that are both determinate and further determinable, in the sense provided by the dynamic, temporally perspectival framework of *Vernunft*. Do we *make* our concepts, or do we *find* them? Are we authoritative over them, or responsible to them? Hegel's answer is: 'both.' (Brandom 2014, p. 37).

The practice of judges thus determines the content of law as an ongoing historical process (Brandom 2014, p. 36). The legal discourse substantiates legal content within ever changing contextual backgrounds. Every single judgment is orientated towards the past and the future at the same time. It contains previous judgments, but at the same time, it shapes them anew. The content of legal concepts can only be

[11] In fact those authors who wrote the first chapters of *The Floating Admiral* had to sketch out a theoretical solution to the criminal case (Wilson 2011).

determined *ex post* and they are permanently reconstructed with reference to specific contexts and backgrounds.[12]

2.2.3 The Game of Giving and Asking for Reasons

For mutual recognition to succeed in the practice of law, judges must advance sufficiently plausible reasons. In Brandom's thinking, recognition depends on the *game of giving and asking for reasons* (1994, pp. 141–161),[13] a game that is played in the discursive practice of law. Brandom refers to the development of the common law by precedent to illustrate the game: Each judge justifies her normative ascription with reasons which are not ultimate, formal or logical reasons but rationally plausible.[14]

This line of thinking is convincing: Whether or not a judgment will be recognised, depends on the force of the judgment's reasoning. Judges give not irrefutable, but sufficiently plausible reasons for their decisions and they do so, because the recognition of their judgments might otherwise fail: Poorly argued judgments hardly amount to influential precedents and they will hardly be followed but rather neglected, distinguished or overruled. The more plausible and convincing the reasons are, the greater is the chance that the judgment will be recognised. Reasons can be delivered in a wide variety of forms, including reference to authority or established traditions, institutions or rights, economic efficiency, justice and so forth.[15] While I cannot expand on the details of judicial reasoning here, I would like to emphasise one central aspect of the relation between normativity and reasoning: Law's normativity is deeply rooted in rhetoric if rhetoric is not conceptualised as deceitful art but rather as the art of creating agreement and of delivering persuasive arguments (Perelman and Olbrechts-Tyteca 1969, pp. 1–10). Rhetoric facilitates judges to play the game of giving and asking for reasons successfully and participate in successful instances of recognition. Since successful recognition is indispensable for law's normativity, the normativity of law is founded in rhetoric.

[12]This aspect of Brandom's theory seems incommensurable with Dworkin's famous *one right answer thesis* (*see* Dworkin 1985, pp. 119–129; 1978; 1986, p. III and throughout).

[13]Brandom borrows the concept of the *game of giving and asking for reasons* from Sellars (see Brandom 1988, p. 257; Klatt 2008, pp. 127–133).

[14]Brandom (1999), pp. 179–180.

[15]*See* on the nature of judicial argumentation Eisenberg (1991), pp. 44–46 and in a comparative perspective Hohmann (1990); with a view to the Harmonization of European Law Curran (2001).

3 The Chain Novel of Civil Law

3.1 Law's Chain Novel: A Common Law Theory Only?

Dworkin and Brandom illustrate their theories mainly with the common law judge and refer to *prima facie* common law characteristics—in particular to the common law's emphasis on judge-made case law. Both were raised and educated in the common law world (*Brandom*: Wanderer 2006, p. 1 and *Dworkin*: Guest 2012, p. 12). Is the explanatory force of their theories therefore limited to law in common law systems? That answer is suggested by Garloff (2004, pp. 70–73). He regards Dworkin's chain novel analogy as a prototype of the law as literature movement and asks why that movement figures prominently in the US while hardly being noticed in continental Europe. Garloff sees an important reason in the differences between common law—which he characterises as judge-made precedential law—and civil law—which he takes to be dominated by codification and statutory law. To Garloff it seems obvious for US-American legal scholars, to describe the social practice of law as a literary activity. He regards judicial law finding in the US as naturally close to the practices of literary critics, literary scholars and literary authors (Garloff 2004, p. 71): According to Garloff, judges have, due to the lack of codifications, leeway in their argumentation just like literary critics. They stick to the facts of the case as literary scholars to the facts of the literary text. And their reasoning is creative and deliberative as the reasoning of literary authors. Precedents, Garloff argues, gain their normative character through comparative judgments that work like metaphors according to a logic of similarity and difference (2004, p. 72). Civil law judgments, by contrast, are very different according to Garloff: He regards them as led by statutory norms under which the facts of the case are subsumed and which—since statutory law strives for coherence and completeness—deliver the programme for any judgment (Garloff 2004, p. 71). To Garloff, the Dworkinian judge is therefore based on the particularities of Anglo-American case law. If Garloff was right, Dworkin's chain novel analogy and Brandom's normative fine structure of that novel would constitute an instance for a "great divide" between common law and civil law. Neither law as integrity nor law as a normative social practice could capture the civil law's normativity.

Now, it seems plausible to assume that any theory of law is to a certain extent shaped by the structure of the legal system against the background of which it is developed and tested. That structure consists of specific legal institutions, normative commitments, modes of adjudication and so forth. A legal system's structure depends, to name but a few important factors, on a society's history, its economic, social and cultural tradition and on the dominating ideas of morals and policy. It also comprises legal methods, modes of interpretation and rhetorical traditions. Garloff is therefore right to emphasise that legal dogmatics and argumentation as well as the criteria for rationality are not universally valid—neither as logical nor as rhetorical principles (Garloff 2004, p. 69). That contingency is to a certain extent shared by any theory of law. Yet it does not follow that the explanatory power of legal theories is limited to the law of the legal system that inspired them. Dworkin himself clearly did not limit his theory of law as integrity to judge-made common law. To be sure, Dworkin regards the similarity between law and literature as "most evident when judges consider and decide common law cases; that is, when no statute figures centrally in the legal issue, and the argument turns on which rules or principles of law 'underlie' the related decisions of other judges in the past" (Dworkin 1985, p. 159 and *see* also Dworkin 1986, pp. 227–228). But this implies that the similarity does in fact hold equally true where statutes are of paramount importance—the similarity might just be less evident. Dworkin's focus on precedents and judge-made law in his illustrations of law's chain novel can be explained by the fact that precedents offer obvious and often vivid illustrations of the interpretive development of law. Case-to-case-to-case analyses figure prominently here. Moreover, common law judges engage openly in interpreting past decisions in the light of yet again previous decisions and often reformulate the rationes decidendi of those decisions with respect to the facts of the case to be decided. In a very similar manner, Brandom illustrates his theory with the practice of the judiciary. Yet Brandom, too, suggests that his theoretical endeavour is equally valid for statutory law. Brandom is motivated by the danger of legal nihilism—a danger that, according to him, can only be avoided by an account that explains law's normativity. To Brandom, the practice of law—the application of norms and the discursive practices involved in that application—is the only route to law's normativity. He does not claim that judge-made law constitutes its own specific category of law and that his (Brandom's) account of normativity should be limited to that specific category. It would be very surprising if he did, of course, given that Brandom merely uses law as an example to illustrate his much further-reaching pragmatist theory of normativity that, according to Brandom, is not limited to law, but applies to *any* proposition of language. Brandom's focus on the common law should rather be understood as a strategy of simplification: common law as "case law all the way down" is for Brandom simply "a particularly useful test-bench" (2014, p. 22).

3.2 *Common Law Versus Civil Law: Case Law, Statutory Law and the Matter of Style*

As we have seen, neither Dworkin nor Brandom limit their theories to common law systems. Nevertheless, the explanatory force of their thinking depends on the condition that civil law and common law systems share the relevant structural elements—the elements that build the foundation of Dworkin's and Brandom's theories. In the following, I will argue that this is the case and that accordingly, the law as literature metaphor and Brandom's pragmatist account of law's normativity are fruitful for the understanding of the civil law as well.

3.2.1 Case Law Versus Statutory Law

Dworkin and Brandom found their theories on interpretive practices that are related to the past and the future at the same time. Such practices seem natural in common law that "decides the case first, and determines the principle afterwards" as Oliver Wendell Holmes famously stated (Holmes 1931).[16] One might assume that such practices are less relevant in civil law that seems to decide the principle first: Civil law systems are shaped by legislation, statutory law and—in particular as regards private law—codification (*see*, for instance, Rheinstein 1952; on the role of codification for the common law *see* Weiss 2000). But firstly, even though in a historical perspective there are good reasons why common law is thought of as case law, statutory law has always played a vital and crucial part in the common law world as well (Lundmark 2012, pp. 304–305; Kischel 2019, p. 234). Dworkin himself illustrates the working of law's chain novel with reference to cases where judges interpreted and applied statutory norms (1986, pp. 313–317). And secondly, in the same vein, the relevance of statutory law in civil law systems should not be overestimated. It is true, the famous civil law codifications like the French, Austrian or German civil codes figure prominently in civil law systems. Nevertheless, case law is crucial for civil law systems as well. The codifications are filled with "open textured" norms and principles (like the principle of "good faith" in sec. 242 of the German BGB) that are case law through and through (see Merryman 1981, p. 385). Furthermore, even though civil law systems generally do not adhere to a formal doctrine of precedent, judgments of higher courts (in particular judgments of supreme courts) are generally followed in legal practice (*see*, for example, Pistor and Xu 2003, p. 947; Rheinstein 1952, pp. 96–98). Interpretive engagements with previous chapters of law are therefore indispensable in civil law systems as well.[17]

3.2.2 Law's Normativity in the Context of Statutory Law

Now, interpretive practices might still be less relevant in civil law systems because of methodological differences. Legal dogmatics in civil law systems invokes technical forms of argumentation that resemble logical conclusions (Kübbeler 2018, pp. 19–22, 111–113). Creative and interpretive aspects of the legal process are not accentuated. Legal methodology rather nourishes the impression that judges simply transfer the explicit meaning of statutory rules and principles to the factual scenarios at hand. The dominant story of the application of statutory law in civil law systems does not encourage theories where novel-creating authors or mutual recognition as a judge's attitude center as the source of law's normativity. It rather suggests the idea

[16] Frederick Schauer argues that this might be more of a demerit than a merit—not only with respect to "bad cases" but to cases simpliciter (*see* Schauer 2006, p. 918).

[17] *See* also Lundmark and Waller (2016), observing that the legal practice in civil law and common law systems are to a large exent identical.

that law gains determinacy and rationality through the determinacy and coherence of statutes—without the need to resort to the practice of their application.[18] It would indeed not be necessary to explain the normativity of civil law as arising out of law's interpretive or discursive practice if codifications or statutes could account for its rationality on their own—without resort to the practice of their application. That would, of course, equally hold true for statutory law in the common law world. But life and, thus, possible legal questions are too manifold and complex as to allow for an all-encompassing legislation.[19] Thus, even if statutory norms could account for their normativity, discursive or interpretive theories of normativity would still be needed outside the realm of statutory law. But even within the realm of statutory law, our hope for normativity without regard to interpretive practices is futile. Statutory norms generally have a rather abstract form so that they can be applied to a variety of factual situations. They cannot offer formally or logically valid solutions (Brandom 2014, p. 22; Arnold 2017, p. 272). Semantic indeterminacy threatens statutory law just like judge-made law: It is not possible to extract rational meaning from the semantic propositions that form statutory rules or principles without considering the practice of the application of these rules or principles. Brandom stresses convincingly that legal concepts contained in statutory norms are not intelligible without some implicit practical norms to be found only in the practice of law (2014, p. 22).

> Norms explicit in the form of rules or principles necessarily float on a supporting sea of norms implicit in practice. (Brandom 2014, p. 22).[20]

The rationality of statutory law therefore depends on their interpretation and application in the practice of law. Their content is not fixed *ex ante,* it is rather revealed in a historical process formed by the string of applications to concrete factual scenarios (Brandom 2014, p. 22). There are no clear-cut and never changing answers simply "contained" in statutes. While this might seem to be a philosophical insight connected with the late Wittgenstein (*see* Brandom 2014, p. 30), it might also seem quite obvious to any lawyer with practical experience: To her, it would seem foolish to assume that we could understand statutory norms—for instance on the sale of goods—by merely reading the relevant statutory rules and principles. The meaning of those norms depends on their interpretation and application in the actual practice of law. Thus, even though legal dogmatic in civil law systems suggests the idea of some objective rationality already contained in statutes or codifications, we

[18] Brandom considers this a futile idea (*see* Brandom 2014, pp. 21–22). Dworkin's one right answer thesis, on the other hand, suggests some form of objectivity outside of the actual application of rules and principles. This is an important background of the Dworkin-Fish debate, *compare* Robertson (2014), pp. 320–334; on the problem of objectivity and Dworkin's one right answer thesis for instance Leiter (2001).

[19] *See* on the imcompleteness of law and its implications for law enforcement from a regulatory perspective Pistor and Xu (2003).

[20] Brandom illustrates this point with reference to open textured conceptions in the Uniform Commercial Code ("unconscionable contractual obligation").

must look at the interpretive enterprises in the practice of law to account for its normativity.

3.2.3 A Matter of Style

As we have seen, interpretive practices are a prerequisite in order to account for law's normativity—even in the context of statutory law. Yet nevertheless, it is certainly no coincidence that this insight is much more obvious for scholars with a common law background than for those in the civil law world. That is not because civil law systems lack interpretive practices. Rather, they are less explicit in the judgments these systems produce. The reason for this is a striking difference in the style and rhetoric of civil law and common law judgments. The common law's tradition of individual judgments rather than composite judgments of the Court encourages a practice of judgments with personal style and creative appearance (Markesinis 1994, pp. 607–628). The recent rise of composite judgments in the common law world may mitigate that particularity to a certain extent (Munday 2002, pp. 321–322). That development has the potential to influence the style of judgments and it might eventually lead to greater convergence between common law and civil law systems. Still, common law precedents are often individual accounts of judges filled with personal style and reasoning (Markesinis 1997, pp. 126–127; Dworkin 1985, p. 165; 1986, p. 13). They invite analogies to interpretive practices in literature. And at the same time, mutual recognition as a personal attitude seems a natural concept for the explanation of precedent as it is reflected in the style of judgments. Civil law systems, on the other hand, generate judgments with a rather sober style and analytic appearance—much different from the style of judgments in the common law tradition (Markesinis 2000). They rather hide creative or political elements so that the judges' leeway seems restricted to the question of whether or not the facts of a given case can be subsumed to some supposedly objective content of the relevant statutory rule or principle. A somewhat extreme and famous illustration is offered by the judgments of the French Cour de Cassation; their reasoning is remarkably short (Kötz 1973, pp. 247–252).

3.3 Making the Civil Law's Chain Novel Explicit

The explanatory force of Dworkin's and Brandom's theories is therefore not limited to the common law. Both theories are founded upon the indispensable role of interpretive practices for law's normativity. That decisive structural element is a common feature of common law and civil law alike. Yet, as we have seen, the importance of interpretive practices is less explicit in civil law systems. Furthermore, neither Brandom nor Dworkin expounded upon the working of law's chain novel or its normative fine structure in the civil law. In what follows, I try to make some features of the civil law's chain novel explicit.

3.3.1 Players of the Law

Dworkin and Brandom illustrate their theories by analysing judgments and the interpretive acts of judges. At the heart of Brandom's account lies mutual recognition as a social and normative practice and he refers to the practices of common law judges to illustrate his point. In the same vein, Dworkin has judges write the chain novel of law. That focus is understandable, giving the style and appearance of common law judgments. But it is incomplete, since the practice of the law comprises many more persons and acts—some of them of greater prominence in civil law systems than in common law systems. But of course, the common law is by no means produced by judges alone, as well.[21] Whereas the judge is certainly the paradigm person whose acts of interpretation and whose attitudes represent the practice of law, the practice of law is not confined to them. Many other persons in different roles interpret and apply legal norms as well and therefore participate in the practice of law—though their participation might be less visible or obvious. I call these persons *players of the law*. Without being exhaustive, a list of the players of the law would certainly include public officials, solicitors and barristers, the persons involved in legislation and even law professors.

The application of statutory norms is not a practice reserved for judges: Solicitors apply norms when they explain to their clients their available courses of actions in a wide variety of situations. Public officials lend concrete content to statutes when they make administrative orders. Even law professors add to the content of statutory law by suggesting some form of interpretation and arguing for or against its application. Is the practice of those players equally shaped by Brandom's version of mutual recognition? As we have seen, Brandom understands mutual recognition as a social attitude that becomes apparent in the actions of persons and not in abstract norms. How is that attitude visible and relevant in civil law systems? Well, firstly, the practices of the players of the law are relevant for the content of law in action: In many instances the non-judicial application of norms determines which actions individual persons do or do not undertake. Secondly, all players of the law participate in the game of giving and asking for reasons—just like judges participate in that game. The game is played in a wide variety of forms, of course. For instance, when law professors argue for their preferred interpretation of a norm, they regularly engage deeply with arguments that already have been advanced in legal discourse. Public officials will sometimes play the game in an extenuated form. Think of police orders in situations of imminent danger. But even here, a police officer does participate in the game of giving and asking for reasons: Even if she does not say a word, she invokes by her doings her own authority and the authority of the state

[21] *See* Kingwell (1994), p. 329, Footnote 29, who argues from a common law perspective that Dworkin's chain novel is ambiguous with respect to the relevant authors and that lawyers, legal theorists and legislators are possible candidates for authors as well.

and of the (statutory or judge-made) norm that bestowed certain powers on her.[22] The players of the law also display mutual recognition as a social attitude in what they actually do. Law professors recognise the authority and responsibility of other persons—for instance judges or other law professors—by referring to the reasoning they had to offer. And, of course, they do so in the hope of being equally recognised by other players of the law in the future. Lawyers equally recognise the authority and responsibility of other players of the law and they themselves strive after being recognised—whether by judges, other lawyers or by their clients. The same holds true for public officials: Police officers recognise the statutory or judge-made norms that bestowed their powers and their authority on them and they, too, do so in the hope to be equally recognised by other players of the law—for instance by judges who decide on the legality of a police order at a later time in court.

3.3.2 Law as a Discursive Practice in the Context of Legislation

As we have seen, statutory law plays a crucial role in civil law systems as well as in common law systems and interpretive practices are indispensable to account for the normativity of statutory law. But do interpretive practices play an equally important role for the process of legislation—the creation of statutory law? How, if at all, can legislation be regarded as just another chapter in law's chain novel and as a discursive practice? Clearly, statutes do not fall from the sky. And the "legislator" is not a non-human entity residing in heaven (*compare* Cohen 1935, p. 845). Statutes are created in a discursive process that involves legal and political discussions, debates and compromises in and out of parliament. Often, those disputes are quite extended and complex. Thus, it is the argumentation, reasoning and writing of individual persons that create statutory norms—in Western societies most notably the members of parliament. But other persons, for instance scientific experts, stakeholders or law professors participate in the legislative process as well. The individual contributions of the persons involved vary and it is often hard to reconstruct them, but they are indispensable for the legislative process. Interpretive practices and the game of giving and asking for reasons are cardinal to understand that process, even though it is usually a difficult task to reconstruct the details of it.

It might be objected that legislation cannot be explained by the same structure as judge-made law: Judges are bound by the chain of law—the constitution, statutes and (to a certain extent) precedents—and they are therefore never free to break the chain novel of law. Legislation, on the other hand, generally has the power to "start a new chain novel"—untainted by past chapters of law. Otherwise, the power of legislation would remain shallow: Legislation must be free to react to new challenges, correct wrong developments and therefore to change law—within the

---

[22] Joseph Raz in his systematic approach to the role of reasons for law's normativity regards authority as a person's capability to utter a particularly strong kind of reason, so called "exclusionary reasons" (Raz 2002, pp. 62–65).

constitutional boundaries, of course. And there are, in fact, statutes that explicitly overrule judicial precedents—an example is offered by section 9 of the English Law of Property (Miscellaneous Provisions) Act 1989, according to which the common law rule of *Bain v. Fothergill* was explicitly abolished.[23]

Now, it is certainly true that statutes have a unique function within the discursive practice of law. That is due to the specific institutional authority of legislative acts, instanced in the rule of law and its binding force on the judiciary. And there is no doubt that legislative acts can and do influence the development of law profoundly. But it is conceptually impossible to break the chain novel of law—even for the legislator: Statutes must use words and concepts to be intelligible at all. They must strive to be intelligible, since otherwise they cannot regulate and shape social behaviour. Yet, the words and concepts used in statutes are only intelligible within the tradition in which those words and concepts have been applied and will be applied (*see* Dworkin 1986, pp. 314–316). Statutes are thus necessarily founded upon a wide variety of norms implicit in the future and past application of words and concepts. Any legislative practice is deeply embedded in legal tradition and conventions of language which are shaped by previous legislation, judgments, academic discussions and so forth (Krygier 1988, pp. 27–31). These conventions and traditions are sometimes even explicitly recognised by the legislator, for instance, whenever documents supporting legislation engage with previous court decisions or interpretations advanced by other players of the law, like law professors. But—and that is more important—those conventions and traditions are always recognised implicitly. And since the conventions and traditions themselves were formed within the discursive practice of the players of the law, mutual recognition as a social structure can explain the normativity of statutes along the same line as it explains the normativity of judge-made law.

When the players of the law apply statutory norms, the game of giving and asking for reasons may take specific forms, of course. To be sure: In applying a statutory provision, the players of the law do not simply transfer or recognise some objective meaning contained in the statutory norm itself. They rather interpret the statutory norms and in doing so, shape their content and contribute to law's normativity. They are just as responsible *for* the law as they are *to* the law that they apply. And through their application, they recognise the statute's authority and responsibility and, at the same time, the authority and responsibility of the persons responsible for the legislative act at hand. Yet the game of giving and asking for reasons will be shaped by the institutional authority of statutory law, backed by constitutional safeguards and the rule of law. Institutional authority matters, of course,—but that is true for the chain novel of judgments as well, and it is also true for the game of giving and asking for reasons played in the academic world.

---

[23] "The rule of law known as the rule in Bain v. Fothergill is abolished in relation to contracts made after this section comes into force."; *see* also Lundmark (2012), p. 305.

3.3.3 An Illustration of the Civil Law's Chain Novel

Legal developments that are changeful and controversial offer particularly vivid illustrations of the structures just expounded. An illuminating example is offered by the German law on the recognition of child marriages and the legal status of minors living within such marriages. For that reason, let us zoom into the civil law's chain novel chapter from Mai 2016, written by the OLG Bamberg (Higher Regional Court). The court held that the validity of a marriage of two Syrian spouses did not violate the German ordre public, even though the wife was aged 14 (and her husband 21) when the marriage had been entered into under Syrian law.[24] The decision explicitly relied on statutes as well as case law and academic literature on such cases. Politicians and interest groups criticized the ruling and the underlying legal framework as violating fundamental morals as well as children's and women's rights.[25] Law professors discussed the decision as well (critically Majer 2016; Weller et al. 2018, p. 1293; but *see* Heiderhoff 2017, p. 161; Antomo 2016, pp. 3561–3562)—in a fierce game of giving and asking for reasons. In April 2017 the conservative and social democrat groups in the German parliament reacted and motioned for a law to "combat child marriage".[26] The legislative proposal explicitly referred to the decision of the Higher Regional Court Bamberg.[27] That proposal was again discussed controversially among interest groups and scholars (*see*, for example, Deutsches Institut für Menschenrechte 2017, p. 5–6, with further references; Bongartz 2017, pp. 543–544; Antomo 2017, p. 81; but *see* Majer 2017, pp. 538–541). Enter the legislator: In July 2017, the German parliament passed the "Federal Law to combat child marriages". Since then, there is a fairly precise, even though somewhat complicated statute at play. Yet the normative discourse between the players of the law went on: Many scholars argued that the statute contravenes fundamental principles of International Private Law (Möller and Yassari 2017, pp. 282–285) and violates basic rights guaranteed by the German constitution (Coester 2017, p. 79; Coester-Waltjen 2017, pp. 431, 435). The judges entered the stage again in November 2018: The German Federal Court submitted a pending case—notably the case of the two Syrian spouses mentioned before—to the German Constitutional Court for a preliminary ruling on the constitutionality of the law reform.[28] The Federal Court argued that the (unexceptional) nullity of child marriages violates the German Basic Law with respect to the right to family life, the principle of the protection of the child's best interest, the principle of equal treatment

[24] OLG Bamberg, Beschluss v. 12.05.2016 – 2 UF 58/16 –, juris, paragraphs 20–30.

[25] *See* for instance Fraktionsvorstand CDU/CSU im Bundestag, Schutz der Schwächeren –Verbot von Kinderehen in Deutschland, resolution of 1 Sep 2016. Available online http://go.wwu.de/-ecoh. Accessed 30 Dec 2020; and TERRE DES FEMMES (2016).

[26] BT-Drucks. 18/12086. Available online http://go.wwu.de/6xzgt. Accessed 30 Dec 2020.

[27] BT-Drucks. 18/12086. Available online http://go.wwu.de/6xzgt. Accessed 30 Dec 2020, p. 16.

[28] BGH, Beschluss des XII. Zivilsenats vom 14.11.2018 - XII ZB 292/16. Available online http://go.wwu.de/bj2ha. Accessed 30 Dec 2020.

and the prohibition of retroactive effects.[29] In its request, the Court referred to opinions of legal scholars, to previous court decisions and to the intentions of the legislator. The court's decision makes the patterns of recognition between many different players of the law clearly visible. The judges' reasoning was again recognised by other players of the law—in particular law professors—, who acclaimed the preliminary ruling as a chance to reverse "a product of thoughtless political activism" (Löhnig 2019, p. 73). That development illustrates how legislation and statutory law is embedded in a normative discourse that is shaped by the game of giving and asking for reasons. At the same time, it shows how recognition is connected to the past and the future at the same time: Even in the context of legislation, law is constantly in motion, a never-ending stream of discursive practices that is both tied to its historical sources and forward looking to its future application at the same time. The practice of the law on child marriages continues as we speak—with the constitutional court as its next prominent player of the law.

4 Conclusion

The differences between civil law and common law do not threaten the plausibility of Dworkin's and Brandom's theories of law: Civil law is an interpretive affair and the civil law's chain novel is structured by mutual recognition with the game of giving and asking for reasons at its core. Interpretive and pragmatic accounts of law's normativity are as fruitful for the understanding of civil law as they are for the understanding of common law. The chain novel of civil law is, of course, not identical to the chain novel of common law: There are differences as regards the modes of recognition and the style that shapes the games of giving and asking for reasons. The civil law with its emphasis on codification, structure and coherence generates specific forms of rhetoric that evoke the codification's authority. The common law, on the other hand, emphasises facts and cases and its tradition of individual rather than composite judgments suggests lively forms of rhetoric with rich illustrations, in-depth analysis of facts and metaphorical forms of argumentation. Still, we can explain the normativity of both, civil law and common law, out of the interpretive enterprise that lies at the heart of the discourse of law as a normative practice.

[29] BGH, Beschluss des XII. Zivilsenats vom 14.11.2018 - XII ZB 292/16. Available online http://go.wwu.de/bj2ha. Accessed 30 Dec 2020, paragraphs 67–85.

References

Antomo J (2016) Kinderehen, ordre public und Gesetzesreform. NJW 69:3558–3563

Antomo J (2017) Verbot von Kinderehen. ZRP 50:79–82

Arnold S (2016) Bürgerliches Recht und Rechtsphilosophie – Gegenseitige Anerkennung und Gerechtigkeit als Schlüssel zur Rationalität des Rechts. In: Klippel D, Loehnig M, Walter U (eds) Grundlagen und Grundfragen des Bürgerlichen Rechts. Gieseking Verlag, Bielefeld, pp 5–22

Arnold S (2017) Legitimate expectations in the realm of law – mutual recognition, justice as a virtue and the legitimacy of expectations. Moral Philos Polit (MOPP) 4:257–271

Arnold S (2021) Geltung, Gerechtigkeit und Fairness in der Praxis des Rechts - Rechtsphilosophische Überlegungen am Beispiel des Sportrechts. In: Lorz S, Regenfus T, Röthel A, Spengler HD (eds) Festschrift für Klaus Vieweg. Duncker & Humblot, Berlin

Ballingrud G (2020) Law as integrity beyond the chain novel metaphor. Available at Research Gate: https://doi.org/10.13140/RG.2.2.32645.09449

Bongartz J (2017) Zur gebotenen rechtlichen Behandlung von Ehen unter Beteiligung Minderjähriger. NZFam 4:541–546

Brandom RB (1988) Inference, expression, and induction. Philos Stud 54:257–285

Brandom RB (1994) Making it explicit. Reasoning, representing, and discursive commitment, 1st edn. Harvard University Press, Cambridge (Mass)

Brandom RB (1999) Some pragmatist themes in Hegel's idealism: negotiation and administration in Hegel's account of the structure and content of conceptual norms. Eur J Philos 7:164–189

Brandom RB (2001) Articulating reasons: an introduction to inferentialism, 1st edn. Harvard University Press, Cambridge (Mass)

Brandom RB (2009) Reason in philosophy: animating ideas. Harvard University Press, Cambridge (Mass)

Brandom RB (2014) A Hegelian model of legal concept determination: the normative fine structure of the judge's chain novel. In: Hubbs G, Lind D (eds) Pragmatism, law, and language. Routledge, London, pp 19–39

Brandom RB (2015) Towards reconciling two heroes: Habermas and Hegel. Argumenta 1:29–42

Cass RA (2001) The rule of law in America. The John Hopkins University Press, Baltimore

Christensen R, Sokolowski M (2006) Neopragmatismus: Brandom. In: Buckel S (ed) Neue Theorien des Rechts, 1st edn. Lucius & Lucius, Stuttgart, pp 239–262

Christie A et al (2017) [1931] The floating admiral. HarperCollins, Glasgow

Coester M (2017) Kinderehen in Deutschland. FamRZ 2:77–80

Coester-Waltjen D (2017) Kinderehen – Neue Sonderanknüpfungen im EGBGB. IPRax (2017)(5), 429–436

Cohen F (1935) Transcendental nonsense and the functional approach. Columbia Law Rev 35:810–845

Curran VG (2001) Romantic common law, enlightened civil law: legal uniformity and the homogenization of the European Union. Columbia J Eur Law 7:63–126

d'Amato A (1989) Can any legal theory constrain any judicial decision? Univ Miami Law Rev 43: 513–539

Deutsches Institut für Menschenrechte (ed) (2017) Zum Entwurf eines Gesetzes zu Bekämpfung von Kinderehen, statement of 16 May 2017. http://go.wwu.de/r08y6. Accessed 30 Dec 2020

Dworkin R (1978) No right answer? N Y Univ Law Rev 53:1–32

Dworkin R (1982) Law as interpretation. Crit Inq 9:179–200

Dworkin R (1985) A matter of principle. Harvard University Press, Cambridge (Mass)

Dworkin R (1986) Law's empire. Harvard University Press, Cambridge (Mass)

Eisenberg MA (1991) The nature of the common law, 1st edn. Harvard University Press, Cambridge (Mass)

Fischer FA (2014) Law and analytic philosophy. Rescriptum 4:69–72

Fish S (1982) Working on the chain gang: interpretation in law and literary criticism. Crit Inq 9: 201–216
Fish S (1983) Wrong again. Tex Law Rev 62:299–316
Fish S (1987a) Still wrong after all these years. Law Philos 6:401–418
Fish S (1987b) Dennis Martinez and the uses of theory. Yale Law J 96:1773–1800
Fish S (1991) Almost pragmatism: the jurisprudence of Richard Posner, Richard Rorty, and Ronald Dworkin. In: Brint M, Weaver W (eds) Pragmatism in law and society. Westview Press, Boulder, pp 47–82
Garloff P (2004) Die Literaturwissenschaft "muß romantisiert werden". Law-and-Literature und die Poesie im Recht. Athenäum: Jahrbuch für Romantik 14:69–107
Guest S (2012) Ronald Dworkin, 3rd edn. Stanford University Press, Stanford
Hegel GWF (1996) [1806] Phänomenologie des Geistes. In: Moldenhauer E, Michel KM (eds) Werke, vol 3. Suhrkamp, Frankfurt am Main
Heiderhoff B (2017) Das autonome IPR in familienrechtlichen Fragen. IPRax 2:160–167
Hohmann H (1990) The nature of the common law and the comparative study of legal reasoning. Am J Comp Law 38:143–170
Holmes OW (1931) [1875] Codes, and the arrangement of law. Am Law Rev 1; reprint: Harv Law Rev 44:725–737
Honneth A (2008) Schwerpunkt: Anerkennung – Facetten eines Begriffs. DZPhil 56:875–876
Iser M (2013) Recognition. In: Zalta EN (ed) The Stanford encyclopedia of philosophy. http://plato.stanford.edu/archives/fall2013/entries/recognition/. Accessed 30 Aug 2021
Kingwell M (1994) Let's ask again: is law like literature? Yale J Law Humanit 6:317–352
Kischel U (2019) Comparative law. Oxford University Press, Oxford
Klatt M (2008) Making the lawexplicit: the normativity of legal argumentation. Hart Publishing, Oxford
Kötz H (1973) Über den Stil höchstrichterlicher Entscheidungen. RabelsZ 37:245–263
Krygier M (1988) The traditionality of statutes. Ratio Juris 1:20–39
Kübbeler C (2018) Notwendigkeit und Struktur juristischer Argumentation. Duncker & Humblot, Berlin
Leiter B (2001) Objectivity, morality, and adjudication. In: Leiter B (ed) Objectivity in law and morals. Cambridge University Press, Cambridge, pp 76–98
Lindquist SA, Cross FB (2005) Empirically testing Dworkin's chain novel theory: studying the path of precedent. N Y Univ Law Rev 80:1156–1206
Löhnig M (2019) Anmerkung zu BGH: Ist Art. 13 III Nr. 1 EGBGB verfassungswidrig? NZFam 6: 72–73
Lundmark T (2012) Charting the divide between common and civil law. Oxford University Press, Oxford
Lundmark T, Waller H (2016) Using statutes and cases in common and civil law. Transnatl Leg Theory 7:429–469
Majer CF (2016) Anerkennung einer ausländischen Minderjährigenehe. NZFam 3:1019–1022
Majer CF (2017) Das Gesetz zur Bekämpfung von Kinderehen. NZFam 4:537–541
Markesinis BS (1994) A matter of style. Law Q Rev 110:607–628
Markesinis BS (1997) Foreign law and comparative methodology. Hart Publishing, Oxford
Markesinis BS (2000) Judicial style and judicial reasoning in England and Germany. Camb Law J 59:294–309
Merryman JH (1981) On the convergence (and divergence) of the civil law and the common law. Stan J Int Law 17:357–388
Möller LM, Yassari N (2017) Wenn Jugendliche heiraten. Die Minderjährigenehe aus rechtsvergleichender und internationalprivatrechtlicher Sicht. KJ 50:269–285
Munday R (2002) "All for One and One for All": the rise to prominence of the composite judgement within the Civil Division of the Court of Appeal. Camb Law J 61:321–350
Perelman C, Olbrechts-Tyteca L (1969) The new rhetoric: a treatise on argumentation (trans: Wilkonson J, Weaver P). Notre Dame University Press, Notre Dame

Pistor K, Xu C (2003) Incomplete law. N Y Univ J Int Law Polit 35:931–1014
Raz J (2002) Practical reason and norms. Oxford Universtiy Press, Oxford
Rheinstein M (1952) Common law and civil law: an elementary comparison. Revista jurídica de la Universidad de Puerto Rico 22:90–107
Robertson M (2014) Stanley Fish on philosophy, politics and law. Cambridge University Press, Cambridge
Rödl S (2000) Normativität des Geistes versus Philosophie als Erklärung: Zu Brandoms Theorie des Geistes. DZPhil 48:762–779
Rosenberg JF (1997) Brandom's making it explicit: a first encounter. Philos Phenomenol Res 57: 179–187
Schauer F (2006) Do cases make bad law? Univ Chic Law Rev 73:883–918
TERRE DES FEMMES (ed) (2016) Bamberger Oberlandesgericht erkennt Ehe einer 14-jährigen Syrerin an - TERRE DES FEMMES fordert den Gesetzgeber dringend zum Handeln auf!, press communiqué of 16 Jun 2016. http://go.wwu.de/fkrkm. Accessed 30 Dec 2020
Wanderer J (2006) Robert Brandom. Routledge, New York
Weisberg RH (1992) Poethics and other strategies of law and literature. Columbia University Press, New York
Weiss GA (2000) The enchantment of codification in the common-law world. Yale J Int Law 25: 435–532
Weller MP et al (2018) Das Gesetz zur Bekämpfung von Kinderehen - eine kritische Würdigung. FamRZ 17:1289–1298
Wilson L (2011) The Floating Admiral – review. The Guardian 7 May 2011. https://www.theguardian.com/global/2011/may/07/floating-admiral-detection-club-christie. Accessed 27 Dec 2020

The Civil Law as the Foundation of the Common Law: Roscoe Pound Considers the Origins of the Common Law

Nicoletta Bersier

> Legum denique idcirco omnes servi sumus, ut liberi esse possimus. *(Cicero, Pro. Cluentio habito 146.)*

Abstract Although civil law and common law systems differ in their substantive law, and differ in the character of their institutions of law-making, law-interpretation, and law-application, they also differ in their methods of reasoning and in their use of authority. This chapter focuses on these differences in reasoning and treatment of authority. It does so, however, not so much as an end in itself, but as an entry into aspects of the thinking of Roscoe Pound. Pound, one of the founders of the discipline of sociology of law, was also profoundly interested in European law, comparative law, and legal classification more than any other American (and common law) legal theorist of the early and middle twentieth century. By looking at Pound's interest in legal classification, including the classification of legal systems, through the lens of Pound's own sociological interests, we can learn much about Pound and also about the similarities and differences between common law and civil law orders.

1 Two Legal Systems

Legal systems are generally classified into two principal groups: civil law systems and common law systems. Each is based on its own traditions, has deep roots and is conditioned by its history. Each has strong ideas about the nature of law, the role of law, the organization and operation of a legal system, and the way in which law

Language revision of this paper by Thomas Roberts, Edinburgh.

N. Bersier (✉)
Thémis Institute, Geneva, Switzerland
e-mail: nbersier@iprolink.ch

N. Bersier et al. (eds.), *Common Law – Civil Law*, Law and Philosophy Library 139,
https://doi.org/10.1007/978-3-030-87718-7_5

should be produced and applied. The legal tradition and the legal system reflect the culture to which they belong and which they express. However, civil law and common law are not two independent legal realities, and their current manifestations are the result their mutual influence and historical development. The common law is the legal system used by English-speaking countries, whereas civil law is the system of the Romanist legal systems of the countries of continental Europe, which are largely jurisprudential and doctrinal. Within civilian systems, statutory law replaced all other forms of law. The civil law system is globally the predominant system of law. Common law by contrast has grown mainly out of the law originally developed by the English king's courts. Later the British Empire exported the English legal system to its colonies. Common law is ultimately made up of the overall body of rules formed through case law that constitute the foundation of English law.

2 The Common Law Tradition

The common law tradition, which is historically derived from medieval English law is a system known as the system of judge-made law, also known as judicial precedent or case law. This means that the law is created by judges rather than by statutes or constitutions, is set out in written opinions, is based on precedential decisions (doctrine of precedent), and is applicable to the specific facts of each individual case. Common law stands in opposition to statutory law adopted according to the legislative process and executive regulations. It is premised on the principle of *stare decisis*, which lies at the heart of all common law systems, and affirms that cases should be decided according to those rules so that similar facts should yield similar results. *Stare decisis* is the principle that judicial precedent should have binding status; according to this principle, judge-made law is an actual source of law. Moreover, the common law is not in fact unwritten, as it exists within the written decisions of the courts.

The common law can also be defined as a general common law that arises out of the authority of courts to define what the law is, even in the absence of underlying legislation or regulations. Alternatively, it can be defined as interstitial common law that analyses court decisions, and interprets and determines law promulgated by other bodies. Interstitial common law includes judicial interpretation of the Constitution and legislation, as well as the application of the law to specific facts. Under the common law several stages of enquiry and analysis are required in order to determine what the law is. Facts must be ascertained, statutes and cases must be located, and principles and analogies must be extracted in order to determine how a court should proceed in establishing what the law is, and thus to apply that law to the facts of the case before it. Consequently interactions between common law, constitutional law, statutory law and regulatory law are interwoven and create a substantial complexity.

Both the common law and the civil law evolve in stages, adapting to new political, legal and social trends, so that the law can change substantively, although without sharp ruptures, thereby avoiding unruly effects. The evolution of the common law depends on the courts, and the reasons given for a decision can be more important in the long term than in the actual outcome of a particular case. The doctrine of precedent, developed during the twelfth and thirteenth century, was based on a collective body of judicial decisions rooted in tradition, custom and precedent. Judge-made common law constituted the primary source of law for several hundred years until Parliament acquired legislative powers to create statute law. In fact, common law is the traditional and older source of law, whereas legislative power has evolved on top of the common law foundation in order to ensure a balance between the powers of courts and those of the legislature.

The form of specific common law reasoning is known as casuistry or case-based reasoning. The common law as applied in private law cases is conceptualized as a means of compensating a person for wrongful acts (torts); later, the law developed by recognizing and regulating contracts. The procedure practised in common law courts is known as the adversarial system.

3 The Civil Law Tradition: The Codes

Common law systems are considered in opposition to civil law legal systems, also defined as "code jurisdictions", which are prevalent in continental Europe and South America. Common law systems place great importance on court rulings, considering them to have the same status as statutes (unless any statute stipulates otherwise) whereas in civil law jurisdictions the courts do not have any authority to act in the absence of legislation. Courts in civil law systems cannot place so much importance on judicial precedent. In fact, compared to a common law judge, a civil law judge has more freedom to interpret the text of a given statute, which results in reduced predictably. In civil law systems, which have traditionally been based on the important role performed by universities, codes and legal doctrine are of essential significance. In fact, the role of legal academia marks a significant cultural difference between the common law and the civil law. In civil law jurisdictions, the courts place significant weight on the writings of law professors, partly because civil law decisions are often very brief, with academia filling in the gaps. Whereas the common law has its roots in English law, the civil law is grounded in the Napoleonic Code (the most prominent example of a civil law code, comprising the law of persons, property law, and commercial law), as well as the *corpus juris civilis* of the Romans (who arguably had the most complex known legal system before the modern era). Common law roots can be found also in Germanic, canonical, feudal, and local practices, as well as in the foundations of doctrinal currents such as natural law, codification, and legal positivism. Roman law was received differently in different countries. In some of them it became positive law, whereas in others it was introduced into legal thinking by legal experts and scholars. Eventually, the work of civilian glossators and commentators led to the development of a common body of law and writings about the law, a common legal language, and a common method of teaching and scholarship, which was termed the *jus commune* (the Latin for "common law"), which consolidated canon law and Roman law, and also feudal law. Another prominent civil code is the German Civil Code, which came into force in the German Empire in 1900. This Code was highly influential and inspired the civil codes of other countries.

The codification movement started in the second half of the seventeenth century, and addressed specific requirements of systematization. The characteristic feature of codification was and still is to base the entire legal system on legislation as a single source of law. In particular, it sought to put a halt to the state of uncertainty in the law, which was characterized by judicial arbitrariness and abusive interpretations by lawyers. A characteristic feature of the civil law systems is that the courts apply the law, issuing judgments that become binding between the parties once they have become final. The civil law is based on legal codes made up of succinct and binding provisions of interrelated articles, which are arranged by subject matter. Codes explain the principles of law, rights and entitlements, as well as how basic legal mechanisms work. They proceed from abstractions, formulate general principles, and distinguish between substantive rules and procedural rules. The civil law thus represents a model of general and abstract law, which is pre-constituted before any disputes arise, and where the courts simply apply the law. The purpose of codification is to provide citizens with a written collection of the laws that apply to them and which the courts must follow. This model stands in opposition to the common law, where the law is created by the courts themselves in relation to disputes that have already arisen and that have been submitted to them for decision. Under common law systems therefore, judgments actually create law, as the rule laid down by the courts in any given case must then apply to all subsequent disputes concerning the same facts, even if the parties are different. Therefore, judge-made rules have the same status as general and abstract norms for other courts before which similar cases are subsequently brought. Within common law systems, judge-made law is the main source of law, whereas statutory law, with its pre-constituted and abstract norms, performs an exceptional function. Civil law systems thus differ from common law systems mainly by virtue of the different ways in which general and abstract norms are created: through legislation laying down scenarios in abstract terms under the civil law, or by judgments of the courts based on specific cases under the common law.

4 Foundational Principles and Differences Between Common Law and Civil Law

Since the two forms of legal reasoning are quite different due to the different foundational principles underpinning the two systems. Nevertheless, there has been considerable reciprocal influence between the systems in terms of ideas. Although the Roman law was not received in common law countries, common law courts were familiar with Roman law. Today the main sub-divisions of the law into property, contracts, and torts are present in both the civil law as well as the common law. Nowadays, common law decisions result both from precedent and from policy decisions based on economics, social sciences, business, and the decisions of other courts: thus, the courts derive their rulings from experience taken from other fields, as well as from other jurisdictions.

An important difference between common law and civil law is the role of written decisions and precedent. Under the common law, a disagreement concerning a case is resolved in a written opinion. The legal reasons provided in support of the decision not only determine the judgement of the court, but will be considered as a precedent for resolving future disputes, and thus constitute binding common law. Under the civil law, which only recognizes advisory and explanatory opinions, individual decisions do not have any binding effect and case law only becomes significant where a long series of cases use consistent reasoning, with the result that civil law courts are *de facto* obliged to follow it. Within civil law systems, legislation is more detailed, and is continuously updated. Under common law systems, judgements are interpreted with the aim of inferring universal rules, whereas in civilian systems the interpreter aims to identify individual rules.

5 Judge-Made Law

Other important characteristics of the common law include the range of techniques used by the courts in order to identify the reason for a decision within legal materials, the adjustment of legal precepts in line with new circumstances, the development of principles to address new cases, and the identification of precepts appropriate to a specific individual case (Pound 1937, p. 186). On the other hand, the civil law excels at interpreting, developing and applying written texts. By contrast, in common law systems, the body of judicial knowledge is drawn up in order to identify the reasons for a decision in a specific case. Roscoe Pound (1870–1964), the eminent American legal theorist and authoritative founder of the school of American legal thought known as legal realism, as well as sociological jurisprudence, states that "It is a technique of shaping and reshaping principles drawn from recorded judicial decisions" (Pound 1937, p. 186). The common law is a tradition based on the application of judicial experience in order to resolve disputes. While in civil law systems academics, codes, and commentaries on codes, serve as oracles on what the law is in any given case, in common law systems these oracles are judges and case reports, (text books by contrast are simply treatises on subjects developed through comparison and judicial experience) (Pound 1937, p. 186). Pound argues that "If we think of the common law as a taught tradition of decision, it is a tradition of applying judicial experience to the decision of controversies. If we think of it as a tradition of teaching and writing, it is one of teaching a systematic application of this technique and writing systematic expositions of the results of its application" Pound 1937, p. 186). The common law relies on the tangible and not on the abstract. It deals with problems as they arise instead of anticipating them through abstract formulas. Experience of life and experience of administering justice are the two features of the private and public aspects of the common law.

One of the advantages of the civil law is that the law is created by parliamentary assemblies because written rules provide a greater certainty and democratic control, and also ensure that people are aware which rules are applicable. In this way the courts are thus bound by the law. However, a disadvantage of civil law systems is that their normative response to new phenomena can be slower than it is in common law countries because the parliamentary assembly must first enact a new legislation. Moreover, the case law system of common law countries enables the courts to adapt rules more easily and quickly to the specific individual circumstances.

6 Roscoe Pound and the Spirit of the Common Law

Roscoe Pound emphasized the importance of social relationships in the development of law and vice versa, and undoubtedly recognized the important role of stable traditional aspects within American law. He also believed in the need for legal reform, saw the law in terms of organic growth, and affirmed that only those parts of the law should survive that were useful. Above all he considered the law as a coherent system and thus as more similar to the idea of civil law. He stated that the idea of relationship is central to the common law (Pound 1937, p. 185), for the idea of relationship reflects the very essence of human society whose inner order is the foundation of law. Moreover, he stressed that the doctrine of the supremacy of the law reflects the notion that the human nature is not subject to an arbitrary will.

Pound investigated the influence of the civil law on the common law in three main publications. The most extensive and important one was the book "The Spirit of the Common Law" (1921) (Pound 1921), followed by the article "What is the Common Law"" (1937) (Pound 1937), and finally the article "The Influence of the Civil Law in America" (1938) (Pound 1938). These three publications of Pound are best understood as part of Pound's broader efforts to defend the tradition of legal education, including the common law method of adjudication in particular, and the Anglo-American jurisprudential tradition in general, as the best guarantor of liberty (Presser 2002). He points out how the history of American law began in the seventeenth century and how the civil law developed in continental Europe out of roots in medieval study and in the teaching of Roman law in the Italian universities. The main features of civil law—according to Pound—are system, classification, the development of doctrine, the elaboration of codes, and the interpretation of the *corpus juris civilis* through glossators and commentators. Considered together, all of these elements called for new methods in legal science, a new juristic apparatus, and a different approach to philosophy of law. Being unrivalled Pound argues that Roman law was received and adopted on the Continent by a customary reception and not because it had been enacted by a sovereign. The reason lay in the rise of nations, and in the idea of nationality that broke down the political unity of Christian values that were rooted in the authority of the *corpus juris civilis*. Therefore, a new philosophical basis had to be found for the reception of Roman law. The new authority for legal precepts and the ultimate validity of the law was discerned in the concept of reason. The adoption of reason as the new paradigm for legal thinking led to a liberal, rational, and creative period guided by the philosophical ideas of natural law with the aim of ensuring that the legal coincided with the moral. The ultimate aim was to infer a complete legal system of legal precepts with universal validity, and to enact them in the form of a code. The civil law became thus systematized, more clear and coherent, and was eventually formalized in authoritative codes.

On the other hand, the development of the common law, which mostly occurred within the courts, was quite different. Its purposes were above all practical. Its focus lay mainly real property and procedure, and was further modernized by commercial and mercantile law. Thanks to a shared language, English law had the most significant influence on American law. For example, William Blackstone, Edward Coke and Matthew Hale were the main sources of legal information concerning the common law. With regard to civil law it was mostly based on great principles, whereas in common law there was almost no generalization or working out of broad principles.

For Roscoe Pound, the civil law influenced the development of American law in mainly three ways: (1) by setting out systematic ideas pertaining to the law, and by furnishing generalizations that both influenced common law precepts and introduced new precepts; (2) by referring to comparative law where common law authority or English law was lacking; and (3) by resorting to the French law on questions of commercial law and private law.

However, American law was undoubtedly influenced by the systematic ideas of the French civil law, by English analytical jurisprudence (John Austin), and especially by the Pandectists (Friedrich Carl von Savigny). Comparative law also exercised a strong influence, and especially judges and lawyers were influenced by natural law expressed through positive law. This view, according to which authority was derived from natural law with legal precepts derived through reason (Grotius, Pufendorf, Burlamaqui), also influenced the writings of Coke and Blackstone. In fact, English law books from the late eighteenth century and the nineteenth century referred to comparative law, to continental treatises and to Roman law.

The common law is a system of taught law, and a taught tradition of ideals, methods, doctrines and principles. Professional lawyers drew distinctions between oral rules, cases began to be distinguished, principles were expressed in the form of maxims, legal reasoning began, doctrines arose to unify principles, and logically interdependent precepts began to organize precepts. Law thus organized gave certainty of application, and stability, thereby satisfying the needs of change. Law thus became effective for its purpose of guiding relations and conduct (Pound 1937, pp. 180–181). Notwithstanding, local European nationalisms, the civil law of continental Europe developed in a real unity of spirit, technique and doctrine. New ideas of justice became common within civil law, and some of them were also adopted by common law (Pound 1937, p. 183).

In the United States the common law was established during the first 75 years of the country's history. Above all commercial law was adopted from continental treatises, and attained the status of binding rules for all courts. Mercantile law was considered as it *ought to* be, and this *ought to be* reflected the ideas both of what *was* and of what *ought to be*. Natural law became the rule of English law in the area of commercial law as well as American law. Subsequently, the tendency to rely on natural law spread from commercial law. Thus, based on a comparative law approach focusing especially on French law, the civil law exerted a general influence on American law during its formative period as a whole. Later, as English law increasingly came to be rejected, an American code based on the law of nature was elaborated. French law became the preferred paradigm, and the common law became a reflection of the French civil law. The courts of many states adopted various rules and the doctrines from French civil law. However, even though much had been absorbed from the French code, natural law and faith in reason were not completely absorbed. Despite its formal and systemic advantage, despite the idea of codification of the American common law, and despite the many cultural advantages of French law, the civilian French law was not comprehensively received.

In the United States a strong growth in the number of law schools started around 1870 and continued into the twentieth century. In continental Europe legal scholarship developed above all in the Italian universities with the drafting of codes and treatises. However, in America the civil law was not propagated by universities and the academic world, even later when university teaching of law became the rule in the United States. Law teachers and law schools as academic institutions only became widespread in the twentieth century because no translations of French law books were available in the United States, and English law books were not readily accessible. Moreover, at that time there were also no legal publishing houses. However, comparative law derived its entire schema and system from the civil law, especially from the Roman law books and the *corpus juris civilis*, although the influence of the civil law in the United States came to an end in the third quarter of the 18th century. Pound states "that the freeing of the science of law from the shackles imposed by the historical school, the economic globalization of the world, and the need of over-hauling 19th century law and reshaping it to the exigencies of justice in the twentieth century, repeat the conditions that made comparative law an instrument in the formative period of law in America" (Pound 1938, p. 16).

Roscoe Pound's "The Spirit of the Common Law" (1921) is his most important and extensive work on the common law. In this book Pound paints in eight chapters a suggestive picture of the evolution of the common law legal system paying particular attention to the formative developments of its evolution, as well as its ideological influence. The book contains the lectures delivered by Pound in 1921, and examines the legal tradition, the elements and the spirit of the legal development of the common law.

An examination of the common law legal tradition reveals two outstanding features; on the one hand, extreme individualism, and on the other hand, a tendency to impose duties and liabilities on people independently of their individual wishes. For Pound, these features were due primarily to seven factors. These were the

Germanic origin of legal institutions in America, the feudal law, Puritanism, the relations between the courts and the crown in the seventeenth century, the political ideas of the eighteenth century, the conditions under which American law developed between the Revolution and the Civil War, and the philosophical ideas about justice, law and the state that prevailed during this formative period. Six of these features were important for individualism; on the other hand, feudal law has given the American legal system a fundamental mode of thought, tempering individualism and providing the other distinctive feature of the legal tradition of America. These seven features are discussed in the first six lectures. The last two lectures, entitled "Judicial Empiricism" and "Legal Reason" deal respectively with the technique of legal development and the theory of the ends of law.

The method adopted by Pound in his lectures involves generalization and the suggestion of parallelisms drawn from legal history. Pound states that the key issue in Roman law and in the Middle Ages was the maintenance of the social *status quo*. Since the seventeenth century it has been the promotion of strong individualism as a means of self-assertion. This process determined what the law was for all actors involved: the jurist was required to analyse society in the light of a new legal order, the legislator to provide new premises for judicial decisions based on the jurist's analysis, and the courts to apply the new legal criteria to the existing rules.

In the nineteenth century common law courts incorporated social ideas into traditional law, and also imposed limits on individual interests in favour of broader social interests. Undoubtedly the law had to change in line with mutating social and economic conditions. In most of his writings Roscoe Pound clearly states his view that the function of the law is to fulfil individual, social and public interests as well as imposing social control. This flows from his view of the law as a social institution designed to satisfy social wants by giving effect to the needs of society as far as possible and with the least sacrifice, insofar as such wants can be satisfied by ordering human conduct through a politically organized society, and through social control securing social interests. Pound defined this process as "social engineering".

7 Common Features of Common Law and Civil Law

Although it might appear to be clear, today the distinction between the civil law and common law systems appears to be apparent more in terms of philosophy of law and for academics. This is because of the increasing commingling between the legal cultures of English-speaking countries and those of continental Europe which, starting from quite different positions, have in practice ended up with the same results. More specifically, civilian systems are experiencing a progressive rise in the recognition of a certain degree of binding force to judicial rulings, including in particular the decisions of the higher courts. At the same time, the binding force of precedent within common law systems seems to be diminishing to an increasing extent, while statutory law is being enacted with greater frequency. Thus, common law countries are in fact more inclined to enact legislation in order to regulate matters that are not governed at all, or to regulate better those that are already provided for by law.

8 Conclusion

The comparison between common law and civil law reveals that there are probably more similarities than differences between these two legal systems. Despite their very different legal cultures, history and traditions common law and civil law have displayed a remarkable convergence in the treatment of most of their legal issues. The fast globalization and the worldwide common interests of the last decades have propelled civil law and common law systems to show several signs of convergence. Many of the differences that used to exist between the two systems are now much less evident, mostly due to the changes which have occurred both in common law and civil law. For example, in common law regulatory law has achieved a greater importance leaving less space for the courts, while in civil law the role of the courts in creating law has increased.

Today we can affirm that the differences between common law and civil law are not very relevant and seem to have been overcome. But it is also important to note that differences on many issues still exist both in civil law and common law countries. Those differences are more formal, that is mostly in argumentation and methodology than in the content of legal norms. And this because both civil law and common law tend to reach the same goal, and similar results are often obtained also by applying different methods. The fact that common law and civil law, despite the use of different means arrive quite often at the same legal solutions, shows that the legal methods and the basic values in both legal systems are more or less the same.

The problem is not to judge which legal system is better. The task of legal institutions should not be to defend their own legal system, but to improve them. Each legal system has positive and negative sides. If any of the legal systems should determine that it has some advantages by taking legal issues from another legal system it should then incorporate them in his system. The resulting convergence of the different legal systems will so contribute to reach a common goal by creating a better and overall just system that would provide legal certainty for all subjects.

References

Pound R (1921) The spirit of the common law. Marshall Jones Company, New Hampshire
Pound R (1937) What is the common law. Univ Chicago Law Rev 4(2):Article 3
Pound R (1938) The influence of the civil law in America. Louisiana Law Rev 1
Presser S (2002) Roscoe Pound, the ideal element in law. In: Presser S (ed) Indianapolis, Liberty Found. Chapter: Foreword

Tree Diagram or Pyramid of Norms?

Michael Potacs

Abstract For Joseph Raz, the hierarchical structure of legal orders may be described more appropriately using a tree diagram than the model of a pyramid of norms. This view is tested in this chapter, paying particular attention to the differences between civil law and common law.

1 Introduction

One of the important teachings of the Vienna School of Legal Theory is the view of a hierarchical structure of legal orders. It has to be emphasized that this view was not developed by the founder of this school Hans Kelsen himself. In fact, it was generated by Adolf Julius Merkl (1967, pp. 252 ff) who was Kelsen's disciple (*See* Olechowski 2018, p. 354). However, Kelsen (2009b, pp. 221 ff) adopted this view and it became a solid ingredient of the Pure Theory of Law. As such, it was also the subject of a discussion in the book "The Concept of a Legal System" of Joseph Raz. Therein, the hierarchical character of legal orders was in principle not called into question. However, for Raz this hierarchical structure may be described more appropriately as a tree diagram than as a pyramid model of norms.

Making his case, Raz states:

> Some of the commentators on Kelsen's theory use the pyramid model of legal systems. I prefer the tree diagram, for it makes clear the hierarchical organization of the law, which is Kelsen's main object in using the pyramid model, while avoiding some undesirable implications of the use of the pyramid model. The tree diagram is free from the implication that one norm cannot authorize the creation of both general and individual norms, or that one authority cannot legislate both constitutional and individual norms. Perhaps the most important undesirable implication of the use of the pyramid model is that there is the same number of layers in the pyramid of every legal system (1997, p. 99 n. 1 fn 1).

M. Potacs (✉)
University of Vienna, Vienna, Austria
e-mail: michael.potacs@univie.ac.at

N. Bersier et al. (eds.), *Common Law – Civil Law*, Law and Philosophy Library 139,
https://doi.org/10.1007/978-3-030-87718-7_6

In the following, this statement will be examined a little more closely. Therefore, the question to be investigated is which image describes the structure of a legal order better: the tree diagram or the pyramid of norms. In particular, it shall be examined whether it makes a difference in answering this question if the legal order in question is a civil law system or a common law system.

2 Stairway Model

Before going into this, the teaching of the hierarchy of norms in general has to be recalled. It must be stressed that as far as can be seen neither Merkl nor Kelsen used the image of a pyramid of norms to describe the hierarchical structure of legal orders. In the German versions of their publications, they speak about a "stairway of the legal order" ("Stufenbau der Rechtsordnung") to illustrate their doctrines which was later translated into "hierarchical structure of the legal order" (Kelsen 2009b, p. 221). However, it must be admitted that other scholars also described this structure as a "pyramid of norms" ("Normenpyramide"; *See* e.g. Achterberg 1974, p. 454). This description of a pyramid of norms means a certain shape of the stairway model because stairs do not usually have the form of a pyramid. The idea of a pyramid of norms therefore presupposes the stairway model which is why first of all the main elements of the stairway model have to be described.

Such a description must be preceded by pointing out that according to Merkl the stairway model has two sides. One side is the "stairway model in terms of legal conditionality" ("Stufenbau nach der rechtlichen Bedingtheit") and the other side is the "stairway model in terms of derogatory power" ("Stufenbau nach dem Derogationszusammenhang") within a legal order. These different sides of the stairway model are largely connected with each other but do not completely coincide (Olechowski 2018, p. 361). In the present context it has to be noted that Kelsen in his considerations only dealt with the "stairway model due to the relation of legal conditionality". Kelsen's considerations were the subject matter of Raz's discussion when he proposed the idea of a tree diagram as a (more) suitable description of the hierarchy of norms. Therefore, the following considerations merely address the "stairway model with regard to the relation of legal conditionality". From here on, I will only address this model when referring to the "stairway model".

The starting point of this model is the consideration that it is characteristic of law that it regulates its own creation (Kelsen 2009b, p. 221). A norm belongs to a particular legal order only because it has been created in accordance with the empowerment of another norm of this order (Kelsen 2009a, p. 132). Norms which predetermine the requirements of the lawful creation of a norm are "higher" in relation to the created norm. A norm whose creation is not predetermined by such a "higher" norm cannot be considered as a norm created within the particular legal order and therefore cannot be a part of it (Kelsen 2009b, p. 235). The stairway model is based on the assumption that legal orders characteristically emerge in a step-by-step process.

In national legal orders the constitution forms the top of such systems. For its feature as the "highest level of positive law" (Kelsen 2009b, p. 222) it is not relevant whether the constitution is a written constitution or a constitution created by custom. Nor does it matter whether constitutional law can be created, abolished or amended just as ordinary law or under more rigid conditions (Kelsen 2009b, p. 222). The character of the constitution as the highest level is justified by the fact that all other norms of the particular legal system are finally based on it. In the stairway model, the relation between the constitution and other norms of the legal order appears in "different levels" (Kelsen 2009b, p. 221) and takes the form of a stairway.

The constitution contains the provisions for enacting statutory law. This regulation of legislation at the very least determines the competent organs and oftentimes also the procedural requirements for the enactment of statutes. Therefore, statutes can generally be described as the next level (step) subordinated to the constitution. If a legal order also acknowledges custom as a source of law, then this acknowledgement requires constitutional assent. Therefore, stating Kelsen, custom "has to be, like legislation, a constitutional institution" (2009a, p. 126). It depends on the particular legal order if customary law enjoys the same legal rank (i.e. whether it is to be considered on the same rank) as statutes. In any case, it is a feature of statutory law as well as of customary law that they provide legal foundations for other "lower" especially individual norms like judgements or decisions of administrative bodies (*See* Kelsen 2009b, p. 230).

Often, the constitution or subordinated legal acts like statutes authorize institutions to issue regulations ("ordinances"; Kelsen 2009b, p. 229) which regulate individual norms and may form a special level in the stairway model. In addition, it should be noted that it is a feature of the stairway model that the creation of law on all levels under the constitution is a combination of applying and creating law. Quoting Merkl (1917, pp. 425 ff), the law-making process is "two-faced" in this respect. This concerns the creation of statutes by legislators which have to consider the constitution as well as decision-making by judges within the framework of statutes or other legal norms (Kelsen 2009b, pp. 231 f).

This law-making process on different levels in the form of a stairway construction is somewhat at odds with the image of a tree diagram. While the stairway model assumes that legal orders have a systematic structure in the form of steps, the image of a tree diagram emphasizes the varied branches which might appear in legal orders and do not fit into a systematically structured model according to the pattern of a stairway. Before going into a more detailed discussion of the pyramid model and the tree diagram using the examples of civil law systems and common law systems, some basic objections to the stairway model have to be taken into consideration.

3 Objections

One objection to the stairway model is the fact that sometimes legal provisions govern their own amendments. The charter of an association for instance often contains rules about the requirements for its own renewal. Parliamentary rules of procedure have to be amended with due regard to their own requirements. It is argued that this would question the picture of a strict hierarchical structure of legal norms in accordance with the stairway model (Jakab 2005, p. 346). However, this objection is not really convincing because the stairway model does not preclude that a legal act contains legal provisions on different levels. Legal requirements about the amendment or abolishment of provisions, in fact, have a "higher" level than other provisions of the particular legal act. This does not change just because these requirements can themselves only be amended or abolished according to their own conditions. As requirements for the legality of other provisions of the particular legal act they have the quality of a higher priority to them and are therefore superordinate in terms of the stairway model.

Also, the objection that sometimes norms of a lower level determine the conditions for norms on a superior level proves to be unconvincing upon closer inspection. The enactment of a constitutional provision, for instance, often has to be in accordance with parliamentary procedural rules and publication requirements at the level of ordinary statutory law. At first glance, perhaps, this could be regarded as irrefutable evidence as to the deficiency of the stairway model but at second glance such phenomena may indeed be brought in line with it. Of course: Standards set by ordinary statutes or other subordinated legal acts can only be conditions for the legality of the constitution if the constitution itself explicitly or implicitly provides for this case. To put it in Kelsen's words: "The constitution authorizes the legislator, instead of the constitution, to determine the procedure of legislation" (2009a, p. 156). It is not incomprehensible why this view should contradict the stairway model.

Another objection to the stairway model might be raised with regard to "unlawful" legal acts. It is a well-known phenomenon of legal orders that they comprise legal acts which infringe superior legal norms. Although these acts are unlawful, they are valid within the particular legal order. Legal orders therefore to some extent accept (in the interest of finality and certainty) even erroneous acts as a valid part of the legal system. In the terminology of Merkl, this is called the "Calculation of Fault" ("Fehlerkalkül"; 1923, p. 293) of a legal order. An "unlawful" judgment for instance might be a valid part of the legal order until it is overruled by a higher court. The phenomenon of the "Calculation of Fault" demonstrates that we have to distinguish between the validity and the legality of legal acts. A norm might be valid even though it is not legal in terms of conformity with "higher" legal norms. However, also this phenomenon does not put the stairway model into question as this model only concerns legal conditionality and therefore the legality and not the validity of acts within a legal order. Despite the validity of "unlawful" legal acts the conditions of legality therefore might be described as a step-by-step relation.

Still, other possible objections to the stairway model have to be taken into consideration. One of them is the fact that some norms authorize the creation of general as well as of individual norms. A prohibition of discrimination in the constitution for example might empower to enact a law as well as to render a judgment in order to act on this interdiction. Furthermore, it has to be recognized that one authority can enact constitutional as well as individual norms. A parliamentary assembly may be authorized by the constitution to enact a constitutional law (by a simple majority or a super-majority) and to issue a norm that invalidates particular convictions.

Both arguments were raised, as indicated above, as objections to the pyramid model by Joseph Raz, but they aim at the stairway model in general. These objections can be supported with further examples such as a statute which empowers to issue an individual norm such as a judgment as well as general norms such as regulations. It is also not unusual that the constitution empowers an authority (such as the president) directly to issue an individual norm (such as the reprieving of criminals). Finally, it is also possible that the delivery of an individual norm like a judgement is predetermined by constitutional law (for example with regard to competences of the courts) as well as by statutory law (with regard to the procedure and questions of the content).

All these examples demonstrate that legal relations may take different forms. However, they do not call into question the stairway model as such. For none of these examples does seriously question the conclusion that the condition of the legality of an act would not be another "superior" norm. This superordination of norms in terms of legality is the essential feature of the stairway model. However, these examples illustrate at the same time that the stairway of legality within a legal system does not necessarily have equal and uniform levels. If an individual norm is based on a regulation which has its foundation in a statute enacted within the framework of a constitution, the stairway seems to be quite long. But it is in accordance, on principle, with the stairway model if in another field of the same legal system the stairway only consists of two layers like the constitution and the individual act which is based on it (Kelsen 2009a, p. 144; Kelsen 2009b, p. 224). Nor does it call the model into question if an act is predetermined by norms of two different levels such as the constitution and subordinated statutes. The examples merely demonstrate that the stairway model does not necessarily appear in a single form.

This provides an answer to another, aforementioned, objection raised by Raz to the pyramid model which could aim at the stairway model as such: the stairway model does not imply that there is the same number of layers in every legal system. It does not even require an equal and coherent design of the layers within the same legal system. The stairway model simply expresses the step-by-step character of legal conditionality.

4 Civil Law

This leads to the question whether the pyramid model is appropriate to describe the "stairway of norms" in its different expressions. This question will be answered here first with regard to civil law systems. These systems differ from common law systems in a certain organization of power distribution. Civil law systems are characterized by the fact that the regulation of social processes is primarily carried out by general norms adopted by centralized authorities (*See* Kelsen 2009a, p. 128). In democracies, these legislative bodies are in particular parliamentary assemblies while in authoritarian systems legislation may be enacted to a large extent by administrative bodies. However, also in democracies the statutes adopted by parliaments are quite often supplemented by government regulations. These regulations might be enacted in addition to parliamentary laws or in order to concretize them.

The main feature of civil law systems is, however, the binding force of judicial and administrative decisions executing general norms such as statutes or regulations. In principle, the binding force of these decisions applies only to the parties of a specific procedure. This is the result of the idea that society should be governed by general standards enacted by legislative institutions such as parliaments. It has to be admitted that this idea of centralization is mitigated in civil law systems within federal states. However, that only affects the state as a whole. The legal order on the federal level as well as on the state level are in those systems again characterized by the idea of regulation by centralized legislative institutions.

This idea has consequences for the organization of legal orders in civil law systems. Generally speaking, these systems are shaped by a systematic structure which expresses the centralization of regulation by general norms. At the head of this structure is the constitution with the basic provisions on the state organization. On the basis of the constitution, general standards such as statutes and regulations are then adopted by central legislative institutions. These general standards are finally implemented by means of individual legal acts such as judgements or administrative decisions which, however, only apply to litigants in particular cases. This structure can certainly be adequately described using the stairway model.

Of course, it also happens in these systems that in certain cases the image of such a stairway is affected. Examples such as constitutional authorizations for the president to pardon criminals or for parliament to annul judgments were already mentioned. However, these are exceptional cases that do not seriously question a description of these systems as largely consistent stairways. The systematic structure of the legal order in civil law systems may be explained by the fact that it enables a calculable planning of social organization. This is particularly important in complex societies. It is quite questionable if particularly in such societies a legal system designed according to the pattern of a tree diagram with a "rank growth" due to many different branches meets this requirement.

However, not only the stairway model, but also the pyramid model can be regarded as a basically appropriate description of the structure of civil law systems. First of all, it should be considered that constitutions are generally characterized by a relative scarcity of their instructions. This is because constitutions only provide the framework conditions of the state organization in principle. Further regulation of social coexistence must be carried out by other standards subordinate to the constitution. In civil law systems, this task is primarily accomplished by laws and regulations issued by central legislative authorities. Due to their decisive function in these systems, it is obvious that provisions in laws and regulations are far more numerous than the regulations of the constitution. Laws and regulations, in turn, are implemented through a variety of judgements rendered by courts and decisions handed down by administrative bodies.

It may safely be assumed that these judgements and decisions are ultimately far more numerous than the laws and regulations on which they are based. This seems plausible even if some laws and regulations (such as emergency laws) are applied to a very limited extent. However, in other areas like contract law, criminal law or public traffic law such frequent implementation is carried out by individual legal acts which make them appear far more numerous than general norms within the legal order. In civil law system, this displays not only a structure of legal conditionality which largely corresponds to the stairway model. This model also appears to correspond with a pyramid-shaped structure (small on top and wide at the end) which is why the description of civil law systems with the pyramid-model seems – at least in principle – appropriate. It expresses a systematic organization of the division of power, which is a prerequisite for a functioning society.

5 Common Law

This raises the question of whether this finding also applies to common law systems and their organization of power distribution. These systems differ from civil law systems by increasing the decentralization of the creation of law (Kelsen 2009a, p. 128). In common law systems, the decentralization takes place by authorizing courts to a larger extent to issue general norms (*See* Kelsen 2009a, pp. 149 f). In contrast to civil law, in common law systems courts decisions do not only apply to litigants in particular cases. The exact extent of the binding effect of judgements may vary in particular common law systems. Generally speaking, however, judgements of earlier cases (precedents) are conceived as "binding" on the court that decided the cases and on lower courts (*See* e.g., Schauer 2009, p. 180). Decentralization can increase even further in federal states with a common law system as the binding effect of precedents of state courts is limited to their local jurisdiction (Schauer 2009, pp. 36 f). However, it is an essential feature of any kind of common law system that basically all court judgements have a general effect beyond the specific case.

Judgements of common law-courts may concern the interpretation of statutes or may also refer to a field not regulated by statutes (*See* e.g., Sinclair 2007, p. 364). It is obvious that the power of courts to create law is particularly great in the latter case. That must be taken into account when describing common law systems based on the stairway model. First of all, even in common law systems the constitution can be regarded as the top stage of the legal order because it forms the basis for the legal creation in these systems.[1] Yet, an important question of common law systems concerns the sources of judicial decisions below the constitution. To the extent that judgements relate to statutes, these are, of course, the basis of court decisions. However, there seems to be no agreement on the basis of judgements in those areas that are not regulated by statutes. The main question is whether the constitution provides any guidelines for judgements in these "purely common law domains" (Sinclair 2007, p. 368). On the one hand, it could be assumed that a judge is insofar to a large extent "exercising his discretion" without further determinations[2] and acts, in this sense, as a more or less pure "law maker" (Greenawalt 2013, p. 180). On the other hand, however, it is considered that judges in common law systems have to "discover" law in the area not regulated by statutes (Greenawalt 2013, pp. 180 f).[3]

As guidelines for such a discovery, customary law (Kelsen 2009b, p. 254; Simpson 1973, p. 80), principles (Dworkin 1978, pp. 22 ff; Greenawalt 2013, pp. 247 ff) or moral standards (Perry 1987, p. 257) are taken into consideration. The crucial question in this context is that of the relationship between these guidelines and statutes within common law systems in terms of legal conditionality. It is conceivable to assume equal status, a priority of statutes or a priority of such guidelines. However, according to the predominant view it seems that statutes have at least in principle priority over precedents and thus over their guidelines (*See* e.g. Simpson 1973, p. 90; Sellers 2006, pp. 84 f), unless they are (like the principles of equality or fairness) also guaranteed by the constitution. As a consequence, first and foremost judges have to consider statutes. This primacy of statutes is not significantly questioned by the fact that statutes are considered to be interpreted as compliant as possible[4] with guidelines of common law judges like "justice or fairness" (Dworkin 1978, p. 22) or narrowly if they derogate precedents (Rheinstein 1952, p. 98; Eskridge et al. 2006, p. 298). Common law systems may, therefore, be described in a similar way to civil law systems by the stairway model.

The question remains whether common law systems have a pyramid-shaped construction. In this respect it should be remembered that court decisions in common law systems relate to a large extent to statutes. In this sense, the legal conditionality between statutes and court decisions does not differ from civil law systems. However, the situation is slightly more complicated with regard to what may be referred to as purely the "common law domain". If judges are considered "law makers" in this area, their discretion is only limited by "higher" norms such as statutes. It may be assumed that judgements in common law systems are generally more numerous than statutes or other "higher" norms which is why the image of a pyramid-shaped model is insofar fulfilled. Things look different if we take into account that in "purely common law domains" the view is taken that judges have to "find" the law based on

[1] *See* with regard to common law systems Kozel (2017), p. 791, pp. 834 ff.

[2] Criticizing this position Dworkin (1978, p. 17).

[3] Sinclair (2007, pp. 374 f) calls this position the "declaratory theory".

[4] *See* to this aspect Laws (2014, pp. 11 ff).

superior standards like custom or principles. As mentioned, it seems to be widely recognized that these guidelines must basically not contradict statutes. However, it is by no means certain that such standards in a common law system are more numerous than statutory provisions.

This may call the image of a pyramid-shaped construction of common law systems into question to some extent. However, it has to be considered that in common law systems regulation by statutes is advancing and an increasing part of the law relies on "precise, detailed, complex, and often very lengthy statutes" (Schauer 2009, p. 105). Furthermore, there is no doubt that in common law systems standards as well as statutes are implemented by countless judgements and administrative decisions. Finally, it may be assumed that precedents are narrowing a variety of other judgements. With good reason, there is talk of a "hierarchically ordered pyramid" ("hierarchisch geordnete Pyramide"; Schlüchter 1986, p. 72) of precedents in common law systems. Therefore, at least by and large also common law systems may be described as pyramid-shaped step-constructions. This structure expresses also in legal orders with a common law a systematic organization of power distinction as a prerequisite for a functioning society.

6 Conclusion

By way of conclusion, it may be summarized: It is a feature of legal orders in general that they have, at least in principle, not only a hierarchical but also a systematic structure. This applies to civil law systems as well as to common law systems. The reason for this structure is that legal orders require a systematic and hierarchical organization for regulation by division of power. Associated with the idea of tree structures is generally (last but not least with regard to the possible "rank growth" of trees) a less stringent structure than with the idea of a stair construction shaped as a pyramid. The image of a tree diagram can therefore also obscure the systematic structure of legal systems. In contrast, the image of a pyramid of norms better fits the systematic nature of legal orders even though the tree diagram may indeed be instructive in other disciplines.

References

Achterberg N (1974) Hans Kelsens Bedeutung in der gegenwärtigen deutschen Staatsrechtslehre. DÖV 74:445–454

Dworkin R (1978) Taking rights seriously. Harvard University Press, Cambridge

Eskridge W, Frickey P, Garret E (2006) Legislation and statutory interpretation, 2nd edn. Foundation Press, New York

Greenawalt K (2013) Statutory and common law interpretation. Oxford University Press, New York

Jakab A (2005) Probleme der Stufenbaulehre. ARSP 91:333–365

Kelsen H (2009a) General theory of law and state. The Lawbook Exchange, Clark

Kelsen H (2009b) Pure theory of law. The Lawbook Exchange, Clark
Kozel R (2017) Precedent and constitutional structure. Northwest Univ Law Rev 112:789–837
Laws J (2014) The common law constitution. Cambridge University Press, Cambridge
Merkl A (1917) Das doppelte Rechtsantlitz, JBl:425–427:444–447:463–465
Merkl A (1923) Die Lehre von der Rechtskraft entwickelt aus dem Rechtsbegriff: eine rechtstheoretische Untersuchung. Franz Deuticke Verlag, Vienna
Merkl A (1967) Prolegomina einer Theorie des rechtlichen Stufenbaus. In: Verdross A (ed) Gesellschaft, Staat und Recht, pp 252–294
Olechowski T (2018) Legal hierarchies in the work of Hans Kelsen und Adolf Julius Merkl. In: Müßig U (ed) Reconsidering constitutional formation, pp 353–362
Perry S (1987) Judicial obligation, precedent and the common law. Oxford J Leg Stud 7:215–257
Raz J (1997) The concept of a legal system, 2nd edn. Oxford University Press, New York
Rheinstein M (1952) Common law and civil law: an elementary comparison. Revista jurídica de la Universidad de Puerto Rico 90:90–107
Schauer F (2009) Thinking like a lawyer. Harvard University Press, Cambridge
Schlüchter E (1986) Mittlerfunktion der Präjudizien. de Gruyter, Berlin
Sellers M (2006) The doctrine of precedent in the United States of America. Am J Comp Law 54: 67–88
Simpson A (1973) The common law and legal theory. In: Simpson A (ed) Oxford essays in jurisprudence, pp 77–99
Sinclair M (2007) Precedent, super-precedent. George Madison Law Rev 14:363–411

The Invisible Foundations of Originalism

Alessio Sardo

Abstract Legal scholars have made many efforts to compare non-originalist models of constitutional adjudication with non-positivistic models of legal orders. Surprisingly, the opposite holds true for the relation between originalism and positivism; their relation and, indeed, their complementarity remain, to this day, largely unexplored. Although originalism and positivism have been the dominant models in the US and in Europe, they have never been an object of comprehensive comparison. This essay aspires to fill, in part, that gap. Focusing on methodological issues, on the one hand, I will suggest that, in principle, originalism and positivism overlap and, to a very considerable extent, might complement each other. On the other, I will argue that, whereas many originalists are inclined to endorse legal positivism at the justificatory level, the new versions of legal positivism defended by Raz, Marmor, and Shapiro reject originalism.

1 Introduction

The necessity of undertaking a wide-ranging, comparative analysis of originalism and positivism arises first and foremost from the fact that these two approaches have much in common. The task has become even more urgent now, for two main reasons. *First*, European constitutional courts have recently endorsed an originalist approach in leading cases by ascribing a key role to historical arguments. Here, I will mention *same-sex marriage* cases, which opened a discussion on the original meaning of the Constitution both in Germany (*see* Volkmann 2017; Möller 2017) and Italy (s*ee* Massa Pinto and Tripodina 2010). *Second*, the recent appointments of Neil Gorsuch, Brett Kavanaugh, and Amy Coney Barrett to the US Supreme Court have already begun to promote a return, in the States, to discussions over natural law versus positive law.

A. Sardo (✉)
University of Genova, Genova, Italy
e-mail: alessio.sardo@unige.it

N. Bersier et al. (eds.), *Common Law – Civil Law*, Law and Philosophy Library 139,
https://doi.org/10.1007/978-3-030-87718-7_7

This essay will be developed along the following lines: Sect. 2 offers a reconstruction of originalism as a (prescriptive) model for legal interpretation. Section 3 introduces the central tenets of legal positivism *qua* theory of the concept of law, with an eye to the relations between law and morals. Turning to the core of the theoretical proposal, Sect. 4 adduces evidence to show that many originalists endorse or, at least, presuppose a positivistic conception of the law. Section 5, in particular, deals with the so-called "positive turn", the recent development of the originalist paradigm that establishes an explicit connection between originalism and legal positivism. Instead, Sect. 6 shows how several first-generation positivists (John Austin and Jeremy Bentham, for instance) endorsed the jurisprudence of text and intentions, whereas new positivists such as Joseph Raz, Andrei Marmor, and Scott Shapiro surprisingly reject an originalist approach, although they are still inclined to define the concept of law as a product of a law-making authority's intent. Section 7 contains a few concluding remarks. On the one hand, I will suggest that, in principle, originalism and positivism overlap and, to a very considerable extent, might complement each other. On the other, I will suggest that, while many originalists are inclined to use positivism as a justification for originalism, the new (post-Hart) versions of legal positivism frequently reject this association.

Although a wide-ranging analysis of originalism and positivism has not yet been undertaken, several authors have suggested the thesis of a possible (or even necessary) connection between the two, and still others have vigorously opposed the idea. Among them, we have some of the leading American constitutionalists, and some of the most influential European legal philosophers.

Larry Alexander considered that there is a strong bond between originalism and positivism:

> If law is a human artifact, and if legal norms are posited by those persons with the authority to do so, as legal positivism would have it, then it follows that the job of those who must interpret the texts promulgated by the authorities [. . .] is to discover just what norms those texts convey (2015, pp. 4–5; *see also* Himma 2019, pp. 66 ff).

Still more concisely:

> originalism is nothing more than the corollary of the legal positivist's claim that law consists of norms chosen by human authorities [. . .]. Originalism and positivism are thus a package deal. (Alexander 2015, p. 5)

At the beginning of the 1980s, no less an authority than John Hart Ely (1980, p. 1) equated "interpretivism" (alias "originalism") to legal positivism.[1] "Interpretivism", he writes, "*is* about the same thing as positivism, and natural law approaches are surely one form of noninterpretivism." Ely (1980, p. 39) shows convincingly how the framers themselves defended the separation between law and morals, conceiving natural law as a "ghost".

[1]Dworkin (1981), p. 472: "Any recognizable theory of judicial review is interpretive in the sense that aims to provide an interpretation of the Constitution as an original foundational legal document." *See also* Berger (1986), p. 1.

A decade later, James A. Gardner argued that originalism could be understood as a form of "consent-based positivism" (1991, p. 1). Gardner's essay suggests that originalism "provides a ready explanation for the authority of the original understanding" (1991, p. 1), not only a doctrine of legal interpretation; such an explanation is based on the ultimate justification of authority as derivative from a *legitimizing social fact*: a purely contingent, historical consent of the governed. Also, Gardner underlines that this social fact *per se* entails a sacrifice of natural rights. It turns out that both ideas belong to the core of legal positivism. André LeDuc adds some fuel to this debate, showing how convincingly Scalia and Bork defended a positivist version of originalism (*see* generally LeDuc 2016).

Conversely, two leading figures in contemporary legal positivism stood against the positivism/originalism association. Eugenio Bulygin (*see* generally 2015) considered the claim that originalism and legal positivism cannot be pried apart as an "overstatement" and, for conceptual reasons, there cannot be any implication between the two. In the same vein, John Gardner (2001, p. 218) dismissed the claim that legal positivism must favor particular methods for legal interpretation.

To be sure, Gardner and Bulygin are right: adherence to positivism does not *entail* (in a logical sense) any commitment to a specific theory of legal interpretation, let alone the endorsement of originalism as a doctrine. But what happen if we try turning the relation the other way round, an option that has never been considered yet? Does originalism *presuppose* a positivistic conception of the legal order? Moreover, what happens if we endorse a comparative perspective (a dimension which is absent in the studies mentioned above), considering both Europe and United States; both doctrinal contributions, and case law? Can we identify a specific variety of originalism, defended by constitutional scholars and judges in flesh and bones—that is tied to originalism? According to my perspective, if we read the debates on originalism and positivism through a comparative inquiry, focusing on methodological issues, we can identify both a positivist version of originalism, and an originalist version of legal positivism.

A methodological clarification is in order. One of the main objectives of this essay is to shed light on the philosophical foundations of originalism. This task can be accomplished only through a comparative analysis. I will not directly borrow solutions from one system to try to solve the problems of another—a risky move, which might produce undesirable consequences (e.g., questionable decontextualized conclusions) (*see* Weiler and Trachtman 1997, p. 355). On the contrary, the current inquiry is oriented to the descriptive identification of deeply rooted similarities between two prominent paradigms for the analysis of legal materials: originalism and positivism. This essay will search for specific (that is: not broad) similarities within an actual sub-group of American constitutional scholars and judges, and another actual sub-group of European legal scholars. I expect to identify a common argumentative pattern, which shows the increasing convergence of European and U.S. views on constitutional adjudication.

I will not assume that American constitutional lawyers have overlooked some key-points in their own field of inquiry, or in their legal tradition—an assumption that no-one could take seriously. Instead, I will introduce comparative considerations taken from an apparently unrelated field—the more abstract debate over legal positivism and, more broadly, *die Rechtswissenschaft*—to produce a series of adjustments on the theoretical, "invisible" foundations of originalism. Thus, this essay does not propose any modification of the accepted canons and sources for the interpretation of the U.S. Constitution. Rather, it deals with the relations between certain presuppositions of the originalist method and the positivistic concept of law, focusing the possible connections between law and morals.

My inquiry might be considered, to a certain extent, as an exercise in *general jurisprudence.* According to John Austin and Alf Ross, this discipline is nothing other than a linguistic and conceptual analysis that abstracts from a set of different legal systems.[2]

Jurisprudence plays a variety of functions: creating conceptual maps, elucidating concepts, developing normative theories, building bridges with other disciplines and "most important, critically examining the underlying assumptions of different kinds of discourse of and about the law". To be also "general", jurisprudence shall develop abstract models that are valid for a set of legal systems (more than one, and possibly many different systems), starting from an empirical analysis of existing legal systems (*see* generally Van Hoeke 1985). General jurisprudence is thus responsive to relevant aspects of legal scholarship and practice.

The result of my analysis on originalism and positivism is expected to foster the discussion between North American and European constitutional scholars on the common foundations of the constitutional legal order, thereby developing a synthesis that captures the variety of the phenomena involved. Coming full circle, the broader purpose of this essay is to improve our understanding of one prominent approach to the law, namely positivism coupled to originalism, and, more broadly, to rethink—based on new data and, correspondingly, a new conception—the boundaries between theories of interpretation and concepts of legal orders.[3]

2 Originalism: The American Paradigm for Constitutional Interpretation

Originalism has been the object of a long-running debate and includes a constellation of theories whose core tenet holds that the main task of judges is to identify and give effect either to the *intentions of the Framers and Ratifiers*, or to the *original public meaning* of the Constitution (Colby and Smith 2009, p. 244). Originalism claims that the communicative content of the U.S. Constitution is "fixed" at the time in which

[2] *See generally* Austin (1954); Ross (1959). The agenda of the approach of general jurisprudence has been revived, in recent times, by leading authors such as Tamanaha (2001): "Jurisprudence is the theoretical part of law as a discipline.

[3] Shapiro (2011), p. 283: "Debates about proper interpretive method pose an even greater difficulty for legal positivism."

each provision was adopted (namely, framed or ratified) (Colby and Smith 2009, pp. 244–245; Solum 2013, p. 456). A few authors suggest that the fixed meaning is also the *true* meaning of the Constitution (Whittington 2010, p. 121). Others, like Antonin Scalia (1989), raise a more modest claim: originalism is only "the lesser evil", compared to other interpretive methodologies.

Although the term "originalism" was introduced by Paul Brest (1980), expressions such as "original intentions", "original understanding", and "original meaning" had been widespread, much earlier, both on and off the bench. In the (in)famous decision *Dred Scott* (1857), Justice Taney invoked the notion of original intent to justify his normative conclusion,[4] and in *South Carolina v. United States* (1905), Justice Brewer professed his belief in the originalist dogma: the Constitution—he remarked—is mainly a written instrument.[5] As such, its meaning does not change: that which it meant when adopted is what it means now. As early as in 1900, the constitutional scholar Arthur W. Machen's published the article 'The Elasticity of the Constitution' (1900, pp. 200 ff): this seminal work offered one of the first detailed analysis of the opposition between a fixed constitution and the society's evolution.

After a decline during the *Lochner Era*, originalism reemerged as a reaction to the Warren Court's activism and became the dominant model for constitutional adjudication by the 1980s. Now, in 2020, the originalist method is still prominent in the Supreme Court's jurisprudence, also due to the long presence on the bench of two of the nation's leading proponents of originalism and most influential judges: Associate Justice Clarence Thomas and the late Associate Justice Scalia (Sutton and Whelan 2020). For the originalist, the Constitution is, so to speak, a "static" document that can be amended only through the process prescribed under Art. V of the U.S. Constitution. The original meaning is legally binding. Some authors maintain that this directive necessarily leads to a form of textualism (Scalia 1997, p. 22): at least when the text is clear, original meaning can be obtained solely by looking at old dictionaries and grammars (Scalia 1997, p. 16; Manning 2010, p. 1288; Rubin 2010, pp. 167 ff.). Antonin Scalia's use of dictionaries in *Heller* (2008) is a case in point.[6]

The greatest challenge faced by proponents of originalism is to be able to argue that original intentions and original public meaning, *first*, are ascertainable and, *second*, can be fruitfully applied to most contemporary constitutional issues (Brest 1980, pp. 214 ff; Bennett 1984, p. 456). According to *intention-based originalism*, we are justified in assuming the existence of genuine collective intentions (or collective will), which can be ascribed to the Framers taken as a whole. For *public-meaning originalism*, instead, original meaning is a semantic function of the standard linguistic conventions of Old American English.

Both versions of originalism share a common core-principle, which corresponds to the so-called "fixation thesis" (Solum 2015, pp. 1 ff): the original meaning has

[4] *Dread Scott v. Sandford*, 60 U.S. 393 (1856).

[5] *South Carolina v. United States,* 119 U.S. 437 (1905).

[6] *District of Columbia v. Heller,* 554 U.S. 570 (2008).

binding force: so, for instance, the Equal Protection Clause might forbid LGBTQ+ discrimination only if the Framers, ratifiers, or the reasonable citizens that lived at the time of enactment would recognize this possibility (Berger 1977, pp. 403–405; Bork 1986, p. 823). In the eyes of the critics, originalism is therefore committed to a "dead Constitution" (Siegel 2009, p. 1408; Samaha 2008).[7]

The theoretical construct of the *reasonable, informed (or well-educated) person* is front and center in the public meaning method (Lawson and Siedman 2006, pp. 48 ff): the original meaning is not a sheer combination of the single words' semantic meaning; public meaning, instead, is the product of complex reasoning that takes into account several contextual elements through a reasonability standard (Barnett 2011, p. 66).

Intention-based originalism was the major paradigm of constitutional interpretation until the late 1980s, notably endorsed by Justice Southerland, Justice Rehnquist, and Judge Robert Bork. For instance, in *Blaisdell,* Justice Southerland wrote that "The whole aim of construction, as applied to a provision of the Constitution, is [. . .] to ascertain and give effect to the intent of its framers and the people who adopted it."[8] Similarly, Judge Bork declared that "the Framers' intentions [. . .] are the sole legitimate premise from which constitutional analysis may proceed" (*see* 1985, p. 171; Rehnquist 1976, p. 695 raises altogether similar claims). As hinted above, intention-based originalism struggles to justify the possibility of ascribing collective intentions to the framers: the Philadelphia Convention members lacked genuinely shared intentions, for each member acted with diverse goals, beliefs, and reasons. Plausibly the Framers ascribed to the same provision different communicative contents. These objections are quite difficult to counter.

Instead, the new versions of originalism advocate a peculiar form of textualism (Whittington 2004, pp. 599 ff), the public meaning theory, which is much more technical than the old fashion forms of "strict constructionism". The starting point of the public meaning theory is the assumption that only the Constitution's written text is binding, not the intentions of the Framers (s*ee* generally Monaghan 1981; Kay 1990). Thus, the public meaning aims at identifying the ordinary, textual meaning of a constitutional provision (e.g., whether the ordinary meaning of "using a firearm" includes *trading a gun with drugs*).[9] The textualist approach stretches back to the early nineteenth Century: for instance, in his *Commentaries*, Joseph Story claimed that "[n]othing but the text itself was adopted by the people" (1873, p. 300). However, this new form of textualism is radically different: the public meaning theory relies on the technical notion of "ideal" or "reasonable" speaker to identify the class of relevant linguistic conventions that determine the original meaning of the U. S Constitution (Lawson and Siedman 2006, p. 73; Barnett 1999, p. 621).

---

[7] McConnell (1998), p. 1127: "The first question any advocate of constitutionalism must answer is why Americans today should be bound by the decision of people some 212 years ago."

[8] *Home Bldg. & Loan Ass'n v. Blaisdell*, 290 U.S. 398, 453 (1934) (Southerland J., dissenting).

[9] *Smith v, United States,* 508 US 223 (1993).

The defenders of the public meaning approach generally reject intention-based originalism. For instance, Antonin Scalia claimed that:

> [I]t is simply incompatible with democratic government, or indeed, even with fair government, to have the meaning of a law determined by what the lawgiver meant, rather than by what the lawgiver promulgated [. . .]. Government by unexpressed intent is similarly tyrannical. It is the *law* that governs, not the intent of the lawgiver (1997, p. 17).

Both versions of originalism use a specific set of sources for ascertaining original meaning, which an originalist judge normally considers authoritative and legal. Interpretation is thus conceived as a source-based, cognitive activity. The list includes *The Federalist Papers,* the records of the Philadelphia Convention, the records of the ratifying debates, and top-rated dictionaries from the eighteenth and nineteenth centuries.

For the originalists, the rule of law is a law of rules: the fidelity to the US Constitution requires adhering to its original meaning, and this, so the argument goes, is the only democratic way to bring into effect the separation of powers. The Constitution is regarded as a *gag-rule*, which binds what Alexander Bickel (1986) portrayed as the least dangerous branch. As Philipp Bobbitt (1982, p. 26) points out, under the originalist's view, the Constitution's authoritative force is grounded on the contingent fact of consensual adoption, not on some "on-going" consensus, eternal moral principle, or purely philosophical argument. Original meaning controls constitutional interpretation because, under normal conditions, it prevails on ethical, prudential, and economic considerations.

Among the paradigms of constitutional interpretation, originalism is precisely the antagonist of the *Living Constitution approach*. The term "Living Constitution", too, is associated with a whole variety of different theories that share the idea that constitutional meanings are mostly the result of a dynamic update of the Constitution. The very idea of a contextual update of the original meaning(s) flies in the face of the fixation thesis. The variety of living constitutionalism comprises, for instance, Ronald Dworkin's moral reading, David A. Strauss's common law method, Richard A. Posner's pragmatic approach, and Philip Bobbitt's eclectic theory (Dworkin 1986, pp. 355–399; Strauss 2010, pp. 1–5; Bobbitt 1982, pp. 9–119). In the eyes of most originalists, these constitutional theories cannot be considered, strictly speaking, as *theories of interpretation*: Dworkin, Strauss, and Posner's methods do not even attempt to identify the meaning of the Constitution, for they are rather aimed at creating new meanings through subjective value judgments.

The most contemporary versions of originalism acknowledge a certain degree of indeterminacy of original meanings: on many occasions, the historical inquiry is not sufficient for dissipating the ambiguity and vagueness that affect any constitutional provision due to the open texture of language. Hence, one should distinguish between *interpretation*, which amounts to discovering the original meaning, and *construction,* that is, determining the legal effect (or the doctrine) for a case (*see* generally Whittington 1999).[10] The construction zone involves judicial discretion and value-laden judgments that cannot be reduced to a sheer linguistic analysis. In Madisonian jargon, reducing the level of indeterminacy in the construction zone is a form of judicial "liquidation" of the original meaning otherwise ambiguous or vague (*see* also Madison 1999, pp. 197–198).

Now—and this is the central question I shall address in this inquiry—does originalism have a European counterpart? Might legal positivism be *the* candidate?

3 Legal Positivism: A European Tradition

It turns out that legal positivism has never been all that popular in the United States, and according to many authors, it has also suffered from misconceptions (*see* generally Sebok 1995; Eisgruber 1993; Purcell 2015). By contrast, in Europe, legal positivism has always represented one of the intellectual bedrocks of modern legal studies, and it is still the dominant approach in this field. Early positivist theories were primarily autonomous creations of the public and private lawyers such as Carl Friedrich Wilhelm von Gerber, Paul Laband, and Georg Jellinek. Nevertheless, positivism is still a dominant approach among contemporary authors: for instance, in Germany, Norbert Hoerster (2006) has recently developed one of the most robust defenses of positivism.

Defining legal positivism is no easy task: the word 'positivism' is shorthand for a multitude of ideas. Legal positivism can be described as a broad intellectual tradition distinguished by an emphasis on what we might call the *factual dimension* of law (Alexy 2002, pp. 14 ff), by a sharp separation between law and morals, and by the rejection of natural law: the law is a combination of authoritative force and social efficacy, not a combination of human law-making and sempiternal principles—or "higher" values—that belong to an ideal morality or the natural law. The label "legal positivism" (*Rechtspositivismus*) is traditionally used to distinguish the law that originates from some human activity—either an act of the legislation or customary law—from natural law. Thus, the word "positive" conveys precisely the idea that (positive) law is entirely contingent and essentially set down by men.

Law is essentially a human artifact, and natural law is regarded as "nonsense on stilts", as an "anarchical fallacy", or, at best, as a form of critical morality (*see generally* Bentham 1970). Legal norms lack an ideal dimension and come into existence only through *authoritative enactments*, a species of institutional acts. To put it in Dubislav's and Kelsen's words: *kein Imperativ ohne einen Imperator.* What is more, all laws are based on social sources, which can be identified through

[10] See also Solum (2013), p. 483: "Originalism may be tempted to argue that the original meaning of the constitutional text provides an answer to every constitutional question. Once they understand the distinction between interpretation and construction, originalists become open to the possibility that the linguistic meaning of the constitutional text may sometimes undermine the outcome of constitutional cases."

value-free research (Raz 1985, pp. 296 ff). In this connection, it is worth noticing that the great ambition of the German positivists was to develop a scientific approach to the analysis of legal materials. To reach that goal, they thought that the starting point was to eradicate every sort of speculation over natural law (the "veil of mystery" that surrounds the law) (Olivecrona 1978), and promote a genuine knowledge of positive law (*die Wissenschaft vom positive Recht*) (Bergbohm 1892, p. 49).

Under the positivist view, fundamental rights have no logical priority over norms; rather, rights *must* be defined as privileges, immunities, and liberties ascribed to classes of individuals by positive law norms. Jellinek and other nineteenth-century German and Austrian positivists used to say that *subjektive öffentliche Rechte* were the "reflex" (*Reflexrechte*) of legislative supremacy (Jellinek 1892). The factual dimension of the law comprises two elements: authoritative force and social efficacy (Alexy 2002, pp. 3 ff).

The second key-feature of positivism is the denial of the *necessary* connection between law and morals: the law is a closed system of norms or, at least, it can be conceptualized as a closed system of norms (Austin 1954, p. 175; Raz 2003, pp. 1 ff). A morally defective law is still law or, to put it in Buckland's ironical terms, "[t]o introduce goodness into the definition of law is like introducing the ability to trot into the definition of a horse. A horse which cannot trot is still a horse, though a bad horse. A law ignoring justice is still a law, though a bad law" (Buckland 1945, p. 33).

Legal norms do not have to raise any claim to correctness (*Anspruch auf Richtigkeit*), let alone satisfy that claim (Alexy 2002, pp. 35 ff). On the contrary, as Joseph Raz (1983; *see* Himma 2019, pp. 121 ff) maintains, they only raise a claim to (legitimate) authority. The idea that law is a "special case" of moral discourse (*Sonderfallthese*)—a landmark of the German discursive theories—shall also be considered as mistaken. Legal positivism aspires to offer a value-free, "morally inert", theoretical enterprise (Hart 1958, pp. 601–602; Gardner 2001, p. 213). To put it in Charles Eisenmann's words, "*la tâche en question est de pure description, de pure relation des données de fait*" (1959, p. 208; *see also* Raz 1979, p. 41). For this very reason, positivism stands in an excellent position to provide an instructive theoretical foundation to purely descriptive sociological approaches for the analysis of legal materials.

We can distinguish various kinds of legal positivism. Following a fundamental taxonomy, we can distinguish between the *will theory* and *customary positivism*. The early forms of legal positivism proposed by Jeremy Bentham and John Austin connect the binding force of legal obligations to the subordination of the law addresse(s) to the will of a sovereign authority. The idea of binding force, in turn, can be explained as a restraint on the liberty of the legal subjects, based on the disclosed will of the sovereign. For these reasons, the approaches of Bentham and Austin are generally identified as "will theory". Bentham, for instance, attempted to explain the law as a set of empirical facts tied to the authoritative will of the sovereign. The sovereign—the person or assembly that holds supreme power within a political community—possesses supreme authority (and binding force, thereof) under a habit of obedience of its subjects. According to Bentham (1945, pp. 104, 243 ff; *see* generally Schofield 1991, pp. 58 ff), the sovereign's authority and binding force are not dependent on moral justifications. The very notion of command captures this asymmetry between authority and legal subject: following the will theory: following the will theory, the law is the set of commands of the authority. As we shall point out in due course, this view bears a striking resemblance with intention-based positivism, which considers constitutional law as a set of norms that correspond to the Framers' will.

However, the will theory is not the only form of legal positivism: the idea that law is a set of (social) norms accepted by legal officials within legal practices, too, boils down the concept of law to a set of institutional facts that can be separated from moral considerations. This is the core principle that inspires H.L.A. Hart's (2012) customary positivism: law derives from the officials' social, rule-following practices. Many legal positivists, first and foremost Joseph Raz (1977, p. 210; 1982, pp. 927 ff), claim that judges have the general obligation to obey the laws as they judge. This obligation is a requirement of the principles of legal certainty and predictability that are constitutive elements of the legal system itself (*see* also Moore 1989).

The next question is: can we isolate some originalists that endorse positivist claims? Before answering this question, further clarification is in order. In this essay, legal positivism is mainly understood as a *normative* and *conceptual* theory for reading legal materials, not as a descriptive enterprise. To be sure, the head 'legal positivism' also descriptive and empiricist approaches, such as the legal realist model proposed by Alf Ross. According to Ross (1958), legal science is mainly aimed at elaborating a predictive model for future judicial decisions based on social norms accepted within legal practice and grounded on *opinion juris*. Legal validity is tied to an idea of (perceived) competence; legal norms are directives that acquire normativity (i.e., binding force) through a subjective act of acceptance of the addressee(s). Natural law is "like a harlot", "at the disposal of everyone" (1958, p. 261): there are no objective criteria of justice, independent from human will. The realist, empiricist, and attitudinal/predictive models fall outside the scope of my inquiry: I am here mainly interested in the relation between originalism and legal positivism *qua* normative and conceptual theories, proposing top-down a specific conception of the legal order, which is not necessarily based on or confirmed by empirical observation.

Furthermore—as it will be explained in due course—legal positivism is not necessarily committed to a theory of legal interpretation. Still, several positivists in flesh and bones have often tied their theories of legal interpretation to several positivist assumption about the legal order. I am mainly interested in these contingent connections.

4 Originalism Coupled with Legal Positivism

The main aim of this essay is to show that a strand of originalism and legal positivism overlap on several points: *first,* the rejection of natural law; *second,* the idea that law can be identified through a value-free judgment; *third,* the claim that law is grounded on an institutional fact: the act of enactment; *fourth*, the idea that the semantic content of the law derives entirely from text and intentions. Robert Bork, William Rehnquist, Antonin Scalia, Akhil R. Amar, and many other acclaimed originalists presuppose and, in some instances, explicitly defend something that squarely corresponds to a positivist conception of law. I shall now offer textual evidence of their commitment to the purely factual dimension of the law, the sources thesis, as well as a rejection of natural law. Once more, I am not claiming that *every* originalist is also a legal positivist: in fact, several originalists defend natural law theories (*see* e.g. Strang 2019). The domain of this comparative claim is limited to a sub-group of originalists that share common argumentative patterns.

The first step is to show that, according to originalism, giving judges the power of making determinations based on natural law counts as granting them the power to decide as they wish, as any consistent positivists would argue. One of the main aims of originalism is to offer a value-free model of constitutional interpretation: the Federal Judiciary should bow to the original meaning of the Constitution, which can be identified through an objective, historical investigation that suspends moral considerations.

"[J]udges' personal [...] values should not be part of their constitutional interpretation", said the originalist President Ronald Reagan (1987, p. 761). This conception of legal interpretation is generally tied to a specific conception of legal authority: striking a moral balance between competing practical or moral reasons is a prerogative of parliaments and constitutional assemblies, not of the judicial power. In other words, the originalist paradigm is committed to a specific form of judicial deference towards Framers and legislatures (Bennett 1985, pp. 58 ff). The commitment to a fact-finding, historical analysis into the original meaning of the U.S. Constitution prevents the excesses of an exuberant judiciary that decide based on subjective moral considerations. But why many originalists are so skeptical towards a moral reading of the Constitution? Simply because, like several legal positivists, they endorse *the separation thesis*: law and morals must be separated, either at the conceptual level or the level of the content of the U.S. rule of recognition. Thus, with a few exceptions, most originalist reject the moral rights-based characterization of the law, such as the one notably endorsed by Ronald Dworkin (1996, pp. 7 ff).

A couple of examples can be useful to illustrate this point. The former Chief Justice William Rehnquist—a prominent figure within the originalist tradition—considered value judgments as matters of pure individual preference; it is the sheer "fact of their enactment that gives them whatever moral claim they have upon us as a society", and not "any intrinsic worth" or "someone's idea of natural justice" (1976, pp. 402 ff). Here Rehnquist relies on a positivistic argument. In a similar vein, Antonin Scalia, a Roman Catholic who explicitly professed his belief in a universal principle of justice, was accustomed to relying solely on strictly legal, not philosophical, arguments, when he had to strike down what he considered an obvious violation of fundamental rights, understood as human-made law.[11] Under the

[11] *See* e.g. *Oregon v. Smith*, 494 U.S. 872 (1990) (where Scalia limited the scope of the Free Exercise Clause).

originalist's view, self-evident moral truths are unenforceable unless they are expressly codified in statutory law or the written Constitution.

The claim that the Federal Judiciary is not entitled to a balance of moral reasons has been raised by many originalist judges. The moral reading of the Constitution is the "the main danger in judicial interpretation", for judges might mistake their subjective moral ideologies for the (positive) law.[12] In *Bowers v. Hardwick*—a case involving a statute sanctioning sodomy—the Supreme Court underscored that "[the] case does not require a judgment on whether laws against sodomy [...] are wise or desirable."[13] Accordingly, the Court avoided any form of substantive, moral reading of the Due Process clause, and decided the case based on the intent of the Ratifiers: there was no fundamental right to engage in sodomy, simply because sodomy was prohibited by the laws of the States that ratified the Constitution and the Fourteenth Amendment.

The second step is to demonstrate that originalists also rely on positivistic arguments to justify their theory of interpretation, and ascribe legitimacy, validity, or binding force to the US Constitution. Many originalists consider the Constitution as a human act that transforms a simple multitude into *We, the People*, a proposal of the Philadelphia Convention into *the Supreme law of the land.*

For instance, Raoul Berger (1977, pp. 283–299) contends that the binding force of the original understanding comes directly from the authoritative statute of the Constitution as (positive) law, and not from other kinds of normative arguments. Similarly, Robert Bork (1990, pp. 144–145, 176 ff, 209 ff, 251–259) claims that a norm is valid not because it is correct, just, or consistent with some moral consideration, but only because it corresponds to the Constitution's meaning. The adoption of the U.S. Constitution is a social fact and not a reflection of natural law.

Justice Hugo Black, one of the most controversial figures of the Supreme Court and, at the same time, one of the most prominent defenders of a textualist form of originalism, "embraced a positivist conception of the judicial role" (Hall 2005, p. 86). He generally rejected balancing and reasonableness as legitimate constitutional interpretation methods, especially in *First Amendment* and *Interstate Commerce* cases. According to his view, the Constitution should not be regarded as a system of objective values or natural rights, but as a law enacted by the American people.

Even a contemporary, liberal constitutional scholar such as Akhil Amar sounds like a Scandinavian radical positivist: constitutional law stems from an act of enactment of *We, the People*, namely, a collective sovereign. In his volume "America's Unwritten Constitution", Amar (2012, p. 55) describes the U.S. Constitution as an *act of establishment*, which was the result of a process of

---

[12] Scalia (1989), pp. 863–864: "[T]he main danger in judicial interpretation of the Constitution – or, for that matter, in judicial interpretation of any law – is that the judges will mistake their own predilections for the law." And originalism "does not aggravate the principal weakness of the system, for it establishes an historical criterion that is conceptually quite separate from the preferences of the judge himself."

[13] *Bowers v. Hardwick,* 478 U.S. 186, 190.

adoption by the States. According to Amar, the text unveiled on September 17, 1787, in Philadelphia, was only a *proposal,* which became law only after an act of *deed*, carried out through a long democratic process. That very act, which turned the Constitution into law, can be described (borrowing from philosophers) as a "performative", a '*fiat*' Constitution that transformed a *de facto* power into the ultimate source of a legal order. It turns out that this claim squarely corresponds to the thesis that the Scandinavian positivist Karl Olivecrona spelled out in the second edition of his classic *Law as Fact* (1971, pp. 96–105, 115–133, 217–233): the performative-based explanation of legal validity.

Third, as a final step, I will now isolate further overlaps in the originalist way of characterizing legal norms as specific semantic entities based on text and will, as first-generation positivists used to do. Let me begin with a general remark: originalists suggest that the meaning of the U.S. Constitution depends on a set of linguistic facts—or sources—that can be used to identify the correct meaning of a constitutional provision (Lawson 1997, pp. 1823–1824). Now, the very idea of interpretation presupposes the concept of meaning. As explained above, originalists conflate the Constitution's legal meaning either with its ordinary, public meaning, or with the intended meaning. In both cases, the notion of original meaning interacts with the context of promulgation: thus, the identification of original meanings proceeds through inferences that take into account situational elements—and written documents, too—that account for the semantic and pragmatic ideas, beliefs, and expectations held at the time of promulgation. Hence, to a certain extent, the historical context determines the meaning of a constitutional provision.[14]

Now, it turns out that both originalists and—as we shall see in due course—first-generation legal positivists conflate legal meaning with the intended or textual meaning for the very same reason: this is the most obvious way of understanding the content of an act of authoritative stipulation *qua* human act of institutional communication.[15]

For instance, Richard Kay—a prominent defender of intentioned-based originalism—characterizes legal norms precisely as semantic entities that express the "exercise of human will" (1988, p. 209). Similarly, Raoul Berger tied intention-based originalism to a fundamental claim about "the essence of communication": "It is for the writer to explain what his words mean" (1988, p. 353).

Both Kay and Berger are reluctant to rely on a natural law justification of intention-based originalism. In general, intention-based originalism ascribes priority to the real intentions of the framers, not to a hypothetical intent of a reasonable law-maker (Ely 1980, p. 3). This choice is further evidence of the positivistic commitment to a fact-based characterization of the law. It turns out that Kay and

[14] Scalia and Garner (2012), p. 20: "*Nail* in a regulation governing beauty salons has a different meaning from *nail* in a municipal building code."

[15] Soames (2013), p. 603: "[s]ince the paradigmatic aim of legal speech is authoritative stipulation, its natural counterparts include ordinary commands firm requests, or action-guiding directives, rather than cooperative exchanges of information."

Berger's definitions of what we might dub "original meaning norms" squarely correspond to the standard definition of a legal norm provided by the legal positivists that endorsed the will theory: the claim that the commands of sovereign *qua* "assemblage of signs declarative of a volition" constitute law (more on this *below*) (Austin 1954; Bentham 1970, p. 1). For the originalists, *We, the People* is the sovereign lawgiver whose commands must stand as the Supreme law of the land.

Therefore, we are entitled to conclude that there is a striking overlap between intention-based originalism and a specific version of positivism: the will theory. In both cases, the law's content is ascertained according to either the contextually enriched semantic meaning (Manning 2006, pp. 79 ff), or the semantic intentions of the lawgiver, and not through a moral reading, case by case balancing, purposive interpretation, economic assessment, or any other value-laden approach.

I would like to conclude this section with a *caveat.* The consideration that many originalists endorse—or, at least, presuppose—several elements of the positivist conception of law does not entail that they are committed to the specific positivistic conception of legal authority proposed by Joseph Raz. The conception of authority advocated by Raz seems too demanding for legal positivism. The Razian concept of authority requires full deference towards framers and lawmakers: the law is a peculiar example of practical authority in which certain subjects (the addresses) endorse the (contents of) the utterances of other subjects (lawmakers) as sufficient, content-independent reasons to act (Raz 1990, pp. 35 ff). According to Raz, this asymmetric relation between two subjects (or, more precisely, two sets of subjects) is precisely the core of the positivistic conception of authority. The addresses shall consider legal norms as second-order *exclusionary reasons* for action (Raz 1990, p. 185). This means that judges and citizens must necessarily defer to the balancing of reasons performed by legislatures and constituent assemblies: the commands of the normative are *definitive*, for they always rule out any other conflictive practical reason for action.

It turns out that no originalist would endorse such a demanding account. To be sure, original meanings normally prevail on other (moral or prudential) practical reasons. However, the original meaning of the Constitution is *defeasible*; namely, it is subject to several (either implicit or explicit) exceptions.[16] For instance, Antonin Scalia has always recognized that settled precedents might trump original meanings (Scalia and Garner 2012, pp. 413 f), by the same token, Calabresi and Rickert, instead, concede that originalism does not apply to new cases and applications that were not foreseeable at the time of enactment (e.g., GPS devices, social networks, aircraft, and so forth). Hence, it would be simply mistaken to assume that originalism is committed to the account of authority proposed by Joseph Raz.

Under this respect, originalism is much closer to Schauer's (1991) theory of "presumptive" authority. The norms that reflect the original meaning are not sufficient reasons for action. Sure enough, legal norms have binding force. The binding

[16]Some versions of the originalist paradigm defend a form of wide discretion, as noticed by Kay (1990), p. 1202.

force of legal rules is, to a great extent, independent from the feelings, desires, and beliefs of the law-applying officials (and the other addressees, too). However, the binding force has different strength levels, because legal norms are defeasible. Schauer characterizes legal rules as partially entrenched reasons for actions, and this is precisely how an originalist would consider an original meaning norm. In contrast with Raz (1990, pp. 210–219), originalism denies that judges are *necessarily* "preempted" from reconsidering first-order reasons derived from original meaning, although this reassessment would be exceptional.

This shows *inter alia* that Schauer's model has a greater explanatory capacity if applied to originalism. Original meanings provide, most of the time, contend-independent reasons for action based only on pedigree; however, in exceptional cases, other, competing reasons might prevail.

What is more, unlike Schauer, Raz (1990, pp. 3, 34, 179–190) is inclined to consider legal norms as *moral* (or, at least, as *morally relevant*) reasons for action. This assumption, too, is incompatible with the standard originalist view, which generally considers original meaning norms as *legal* reasons for action, and not as *moral* reasons for actions. In other words, a prominent strand of originalism is committed to the Separability Thesis (i.e., law and morals can be, or even must be, separated), but rejects the Preemptive Thesis (i.e., judges must not reconsider the balance of reason prescribed by the lawgiver).

In this section, I have isolated several examples of originalists that endorse *implicitly* originalist claims. The next section, instead, deals with a recent version of originalism that assumes an *explicit* connection between originalism and positivism as a starting point.

5 The Positive Turn

The so-called "positive turn", recently proposed by William Baude and Stephen E. Sachs, is a new version of originalist that is explicitly tied to legal positivism. The positive turn does not endorse anything that comes close to the will theory. Instead, it turns to a different form of legal positivism: H.L.A. Hart's "customary" or "practice-based" positivism. The central intuition that underpins the positive turn might be summarized as follows: originalism is the American paradigm for constitutional interpretation not because legal officials in general—and the Federal Judiciary in particular—*must* implement the will of *We, The people*, but simply because the originalist method *can* be traced back to the U.S. rules of recognition.

H.L.A. Hart (2012) understood the rules of recognition as social norms effectively endorsed at the level of adjudication: rules of recognition are the projection of the nested practices of the law applying officials. Officials tacitly apply specific substantive and—according to a possible reading of Hart's legal philosophy—interpretive rules because they (intentionally) consider them binding. The positive turn claims that the originalist interpretive canon is *de facto* recognized as a set of binding rules in the American interpretive practice(s).

Baude and Sachs assume that originalism must (necessarily) presuppose a legal philosophy (positivism) that defines the ultimate criteria for identifying valid legal norms. The positive turn's ambition is precisely to show that the ultimate criteria for the validity of the U.S. law entail originalism. Therefore, the positivist turn reshapes the debate over originalism in terms of a factual analysis customary practices: to answer the question 'Is Originalism our law?', a value-free survey on the social sources and practices of recognition of the U.S. Federal Judiciary must be undertaken. Baude and Sachs maintain that originalism is justified because it is actually endorsed by the American law at the constitutional level: this is an observable social fact (Sachs 2015, pp. 823–835). This claim presupposes that the law is determined by social facts and morality is not a truth-maker for legal statements (Baude 2015, p. 2351).

Baude and Sachs claim that, if it turns out that the American constitutional system is committed to originalism, then there are strong reasons to be originalists, although these reasons are *contextual* rather than *absolute* (Pojanowski and Walsh 2016, p. 98). In other words, the Positive Turn claims that originalism is the primary method for constitutional interpretation because its primacy is grounded on *well-established legal practices* that provide the ultimate sources of the legal system. Originalism is part of the U.S. constitutional law: after all, American lawyers and judges rely on originalism as the primary method for interpreting the law (Baude 2015, p. 2351). The qualifier 'positive' should grasp the idea that this new approach connects originalism to a factual account of the legal order as a set of first-order and second-order legal practices understood as *social facts* (Baude 2015, p. 2351). Mostly in response to their critics, the proponents of the 'positive turn' tend to weaken their claims, both by suggesting that their argument does not prove "once for all" that U.S. law is originalist (Sachs 2015, p. 874; Baude and Sachs 2017, p. 1147).

What would be the payoff of coupling originalism with Hartian positivism at the grounding level. According to Baude and Sacks, the positive turn can dissolve the dead-end argument (Baude 2015, p. 2048; Sachs 2015, p. 847), and "justify a form of originalism that does not derive from the dead hand" (Baude 2015, p. 2353). What is more, the positive turn yields simplicity at the justification level: one should not tackle an inquiry into the puzzles of moral and political philosophy to seek a justification for originalism. If we agree that legal officials should obey the (positive) law and that the (positive) law includes originalism, then we have good reasons to endorse originalism, although these reasons are "contingent", for they are based on "actual commitments" (Baude 2015, p. 2352). More broadly, the combination of originalism and legal positivism should reorient the current debate on originalism (Baude 2015, p. 2353).

In the eyes of the positive turn's critics, the belief in the positivist axioms sounds pretty much like an assertion concerning the American rule of recognition based on pure speculation. This leads nowhere. Charles L. Barzun, for instance, contends that it "fails under every approach considered", for "each approach either leads to obviously false conclusions or fails to produce the normative and methodological payoff the positive turn promises" (2017, p. 1323): 'the promise of the positive turn—he declares—"is more apparent than real" (2017, p. 1330). What is more, the positivist turn might sacrifice the originalist promise of offering a useful source of judicial constraint and a powerful safeguard against arbitrary decisions (Kessler and Pozen 2016, pp. 1846 f). Due to the reconstructive and neutral approach endorsed in my essay, I will avoid comments on the dispute between the defenders of the positive turn and their critics.

6 Two Kinds of Positivism: For and Against Originalism

As mentioned above, positivism encompasses a whole set of heterogeneous theories, a large spectrum that ranges from those versions of the theory least interested in legal interpretation to those views that are most interested. Sure enough, from a purely conceptual point of view, legal positivism is not necessarily committed to a proper theory of adjudication. Still, if we give close attention to positivism as a socio-legal phenomenon, we can appreciate that several legal positivists—for instance, Bentham and Austin—advocated an account of legal interpretation that is very close to intention-based originalism. Hence, a specific strand of positivism stands for fidelity to legislative or Framers' intent. What is more, even those legal positivists that overly rejected originalism—Joseph Raz, Andrei Marmor, and Scott Shapiro—characterize law-making in terms of collective intentions. Therefore, a constitutional scholar might use this conceptual claim about positive law as a justification for a jurisprudence of original meanings: if law is simply a set of intention-based legal norms, then it seems reasonable to interpret these norms through an originalist canon, aimed at discovering the textual and intentional meaning of a constitutional provision. Still, Raz, Marmor and Shapiro explicitly reject originalism.

As hinted above, the early versions of positivism defended by Bentham and Austin embraced the so-called will theory of legal norms. Legal norms are *binding* commands. In turn, these binding commands are understood as either prescriptive propositions (imperatives), or proposition-like entities that express a wish or will backed up by the threat of a sanction. The will theory has three corollaries: (a) the law is a set of commands; (b) the commands reflect the will of the lawgiver; (c) the sovereign's commands have binding force.

The will theory partially overlaps with intention-based originalism: both approaches characterize legal provisions as the expressions of the lawmaker's will and intentions. Iintention-based originalism presupposes a conception of law that is quite close to the imperativist account: as McConnell explains, intention-based originalism is grounded in the assumption that "[a]ll power stems from the sovereign people, and the authority of the Constitution comes from their act of sovereign will in creating it" (1998, p. 1132). It is precisely on this "voluntarist" premise that originalism calls for obedience to the Framers' understanding of the Constitution. This is only the beginning: there are further overlaps.

The will theory generally rejects non-originalist approaches to legal adjudication. For instance, Jeremy Bentham's attack on the common law method resembles Scalia's more contemporary criticism (*see* 1982, pp. 8 ff; 1977, pp. 165 ff): both

Bentham and Scalia maintain that the common law is artificially created by the judges, and not simply discovered. Precisely as an originalist would do, Jeremy Bentham (1988) stressed that law can be identified without using moral criteria.

At a prescriptive level, Bentham, who was a supporter of the codification movement, suggested that the law applying officials shall adhere to the jurisprudence of text and intentions (Schauer 2015, pp. 167 ff). When Bentham deals with institutional design matters, he becomes a convinced supporter of a reform program that contains judicial discretion, and enhances the public understanding of the law (1843; 2010). In this respect, his goal is not so distant from the promises of the public meaning theory:[17] the exposition of the (positive) law ascertains what the law *is*, without determining how law *ought to be* according to moral standards (Bentham 1982, pp. 293 ff; Bentham 1988, pp. 7 ff). The law-maker, and not the judge, is the authority that "causeth it [the law] to be so" (Bentham 1982, p. 294).

Similarly, in his *Lectures*, John Austin proposed a method for the correct interpretation of the law that grants priority to the textual and historical meaning of the law over the moral reading: in particular, according to Austin's positive methodology of interpretation (1885, pp. 624 ff), interpretation is not aimed at restating the law as it is, but at discovering the lawgiver's intention based on the usual, literal, plain meaning of the text, and legislative history. Austin's method bears a striking resemblance with the originalist methodology's core: Austin, too, advocates fidelity to the historical meaning of the law.

Still, the proposition that legal norms are authoritative orders does not entail that interpreters must follow either the intention of the authority, or stick to a public meaning canon, although this conclusion would seem reasonable. Hence, two leading figures in the positivist tradition—Joseph Raz and Andrei Marmor—accept, on the one hand, that legal norms are intentional commands of legislators and framers and, on the other, reject originalism.

On the one hand, Joseph Raz (2009, pp. 230, 298) recognizes the public and conventional nature of the legal meaning, ascribed to the intentional acts of the legal authority; he emphasizes also the central role that stability and continuity with the past play in legal interpretation (Raz 2009, p. 233). These two values are systematically related to the very concept of authority (Raz 2009, pp. 235 f). On the other hand, Raz (2009, pp. 239 ff) denies the priority of the original, intentional meaning straightforwardly: interpretation shall not be conflated with the retrieval of the original meaning; there is plenty of room for innovative, dynamic interpretations of any legal document, constitutions included (Raz 2009, pp. 265 ff).[18] According to Raz (2009, p. 224), legal interpretation is always a dialectical process between the

[17] Within the current debate, the philosopher Scott Soames is both an outspoken defender of legal positivism, and a defender of intention-based originalism. *See* Soames (2011), p. 43: "Textualism may well be a plausible theory of legal content [... when it] recognizes the importance of the illocutionary intentions of law-makers."

[18] Raz stands for the limited binding force of legislative intent. He qualifies the view that all interpretations are necessarily aimed at discovering intentions as "contrived and unhelpful" (2009, p. 272): "There is a lot wrong with this doctrine", he says (2009, p. 273).

identification of existing law and the creation of new law: on many occasions, an evolutionary, "dynamic", reading of the law based on equity is required, also for securing the coordinating capacity of the legal system, especially when laws are ancient (Raz 2009, p. 290). The Framers' "original" recognition is not sufficient to bind future generations (Raz 2009, pp. 335, 338 ff).

Marmor is even more explicit and trenchant: the goal of *any* constitution is to establish an inter-generational commitment, but the collective actions of past majorities "do not purport to have authority over future generations" (2005, p. 145). Marmor concedes that "by following the constitutional prescriptions we are more likely to follow the correct moral reasons that apply to us than by trying to figure out those reasons for ourselves", but he hastens to add that "the argument clearly fails" because it ascribes to framers a sort of quasi-absolute moral authority that they did not possess (2005, pp. 146, 156). Under Marmor's perspective, originalism is not a sensitive method for constitutional interpretation:[19] originalism "makes no moral sense" (2005, p. 159) and "there is no substitute for sound moral reasoning" (2005, p. 160).

Scott Shapiro, too, has endorsed a more holistic method for interpretation, which is quite distant from originalism. Shapiro defines the content of the law as a combination of plans that a law-making authority endorsed intentionally. The planning theory is committed to the legal positivism: "moral facts *never* determine the content of law" (Shapiro 2011, p. 302). Consistently with the core positivist thesis, Shapiro argues that only institutional facts determine the content of the law. Based on the premise that questions about the nature of law provide answers to fundamental questions about legal interpretation and interpretive methods, Shapiro (2011, p. 331) claims that the plans of a law-making authority *might* constrain legal interpretation, and Scalia's originalism is—Shapiro says—an example of the "Planners" method of interpretation:

> Scalia's argument, on the other hand, is an instance of what I will call the 'Planners' method. According to this approach, a meta-interpreter should not assess her own trustworthiness, but rather defer to the views of the system's planners regarding her competence and character. (2011, p. 345)

If the normative authority does not betray her fundamental commitment to rational planning, breaching the underlying element of trust with the citizens, then the Planners method prescribes fidelity to the plan's designers. However, quite surprisingly, Shapiro argues that the Planners method does not entail a commitment to originalism:

> This privileging of the attitudes of constitutional designers does not entail that originalism is the proper methodology for constitutional interpretation; nor does it mean that only the

[19] Marmor (2005), pp. 146, 157: "Just as it makes no sense to bind the constitutional interpretation to application intentions of 'old' framers, because they could not have predicted the kind of concerns we face today, it would make no sense to bind any constitutional interpretation for the future by the application intentions of framers in our generation."

> framers' attitudes matter. The entrails of a legal system are messy and evolving, and their interpretation no simple matter. (2011, p. 352)

Reliance on the originalist methodology is contingent upon a more general and broad assessment: "the economy of trust"; this (meta-)principle establishes when the law applying official shall depart from the authoritative rules promulgated by the Planners (lawmakers and constituent assemblies) (Shapiro 2011, pp. 354 ff), and update the legal system through interpretive methods that are not necessarily aimed at identifying original meanings.

Sure enough, Shapiro's theory ascribes much weight to the Planners' "original" intent, but the economy of trust yields a peculiar form of interpretive eclecticism that is altogether different from intention-based originalism.[20] The economy of trust grants the law-applying official a wider discretion in evaluating the reasons that justify a choice of the law-making authority. The interpreter "grades the interpretive methodologies according to their performance in imagined circumstances" (Shapiro 2011, p. 370). By the admission of Shapiro himself, this methodology is incompatible with originalism.[21]

To wrap it up, we can say that the will theory justifies and originalist approach to interpretation. By contrast, the most recent version of legal positivism defended by Raz, Marmor, and Shapiro, on the one hand, accept the idea that law is an intentional act of the law-giving authority and, on the other hand, reject originalism as a method for legal and constitutional interpretation. Also in this case, there is (only?) a partial overlap between originalism and legal positivism. There are two types of positivism: for and against originalism.

7 Tacking Stock

The connections between originalism and positivism are not necessary but contingent. Still, there is a high number of incidental, overlapping similarities between a strand of originalism and the positivist view. Many originalists have endorsed positivistic arguments against the moral reading of the Constitution. Both the will theory, and intention-based originalism considers (the content of) law as "an

[20] Shapiro (2011), p. 370: "Because the Planning Theory treats legal systems as planning systems that are designed to achieve certain political and moral ends, it ranks interpretive methodologies according to their capacities to advance those ends. In assessing their potential, though, the Planning Theory adds a crucial proviso: it insists that the evaluation of methodologies be conducted against the background of trust extracted from the current institutional arrangements. An interpretive methodology is appropriate for an interpreter just in case it best furthers the goals that legal actors are entrusted with advancing on the supposition that the interpreter and certain other actors have the extracted competence and character."

[21] Shapiro (2011), p. 376: "As I have argued, the textualisms of Scalia and Easterbrook are both based on a cynical reading of the American economy of trust. Strict construction is appropriate, they claim, because certain officials are deemed to be deeply disingenuous."

assemblage of signs declarative of a volition" of the sovereign authority. A few originalists (e.g., Akhil Amar) would also be inclined to present the original Constitution in radical positivistic terms, as a follower of Bentham or Olivecrona would do: the "power of imperation" of *We, The People* transformed the proposal of the Philadelphia Convention in the supreme law of the land through a performative act (namely, a speech act with constitutive effects) (Bentham 1970, pp. 18–20, 139). In other words, the will (and the inclination to obey, too) of *We, The People* is the "constitutive cause" of the U.S. Constitution authoritative nature. The most recent versions of positivism defended by Raz, Marmor, and Shapiro reject originalism as a dominant paradigm for constitutional interpretation.

References

Alexander L (2015) Legal positivism and originalist interpretation. San Diego Legal Studies Paper 15-200:1–24
Alexy R (2002) The argument from injustice: a reply to legal positivism. Clarendon Press, Oxford
Amar A (2012) America's unwritten constitution. Basic Books, New York
Austin J (1885) Lectures on jurisprudence, or the philosophy of positive law, 5th edn. Murray, London
Austin J (1954) The province of jurisprudence determined (1832). The Noonday Press, New York
Barnett R (1999) An originalism for nonoriginalists. Loyola Law Rev 45:611–654
Barnett R (2011) Interpretation and construction. Harv J Law Publ Policy 34:65–72
Barzun C (2017) The positive U-turn. Stan Law Rev 69:1323–1388
Baude W (2015) Is originalism our law? Columbia Law Rev 115:2349–2408
Baude W, Sachs S (2017) The law of interpretation. Harv Law Rev 130:1079–1147
Bennett R (1984) Objectivity in constitutional law. Univ Pa Law Rev 132:445–496
Bennett R (1985) The mission of moral reasoning in constitutional law. South Cal Law Rev 58: 647–660
Bentham J (1843) Scotch reform. In: Bowring J (ed) The works of Jeremy Bentham, vol 5, pp 1–54
Bentham J (1945) The limits of jurisprudence defined (1782). Columbia University Press, New York
Bentham J (1970) Of laws in general (1782). The Athlone Press, London
Bentham J (1977) A comment on the commentaries and a fragment on government (1776). The Athlone Press, London
Bentham J (1982) An introduction to the principles of morals and legislation (1789). Meuthen, London
Bentham J (1988) A fragment on government (1776). Cambridge University Press, Cambridge
Bentham J (2010) On the limits of the penal branch of jurisprudence (1789). Clarendon Press, Oxford
Bergbohm K (1892) Jurisprudenz und Rechtsphilosophie. Duncker & Humblot, Leipzig
Berger R (1977) Government by judiciary. Liberty Fund Books, Indianapolis
Berger R (1986) Some reflections on interpretivism. Geo Wash Law Rev 55:1–16
Berger R (1988) Originalist theories of constitutional interpretation. Cornell Law Rev 73:350–358
Bickel A (1986) The least dangerous branch, 2nd edn. Yale University Press, New Heaven
Bobbitt P (1982) Constitutional fate. Oxford University Press, Oxford
Bork R (1985) Tradition and morality in constitutional law. In: Cannon M, O'Brien D (eds) Views from the bench: the judiciary and constitutional politics, pp 186–194
Bork R (1986) The constitution, original intent, and economic rights. San Diego Law Rev 23:823–832

Bork R (1990) The tempting of America. MacMillan, New York
Brest P (1980) The misconceived quest for the original understanding. Boston Univ Law Rev 60: 204–238
Buckland W (1945) Some reflections on jurisprudence. Cambridge University Press, Cambridge
Bulygin E (2015) Comments on Larry Alexander "Legal Positivism and Originalist Interpretation". Revista Argentina de Teoría Jurídica 16:39–44
Colby T, Smith P (2009) Living originalism. Duke Law J 59:239–307
Dworkin R (1981) The forum of principle. N Y Univ Law Rev 56:469–517
Dworkin R (1986) Law's empire. Harvard University Press, Cambridge
Dworkin R (1996) Freedom's law. Harvard University Press, Cambridge
Eisenmann C (1959) Le Droit Naturel. Presses Universitaires de France, Paris
Eisgruber C (1993) Dred again: originalism's forgotten past. Const Comment 10:37–65
Ely J (1980) Democracy and distrust. Harvard University Press, Cambridge
Gardner J (1991) The positivist foundations of originalism: an account and critique. Boston Univ Law Rev 71:1–45
Gardner J (2001) Legal positivism: 5 ½ myths. Am J Jurisprud 46(1):199–227
Hall K (2005) The Oxford companion to the Supreme Court of the United States. Oxford University Press, Oxford
Hart HLA (1958) Positivism and the separation of law and morals. Harv Law Rev 71(4):593–629
Hart HLA (2012) The concept of law, 3rd edn. Oxford University Press, Oxford
Himma K (2019) Morality and the nature of law. Oxford University Press, Oxford
Hoerster N (2006) Was ist Recht? Beck, München
Jellinek G (1892) System der subjektiven öffentlichen Rechte. Mohr, Freiburg
Kay R (1988) Adherence to the original intentions in constitutional adjudication: three objections and responses. Northwest Univ Law Rev 82:226–292
Kay R (1990) The Bork nomination and the definition of "the constitution". Northwest Law Rev 84: 1190–1202
Kessler J, Pozen D (2016) Working themselves impure: a life cycle theory of legal theories. Univ Chic Law Rev 83:1819–1892
Lawson G (1997) On Reading Recipes. . .and Constitutions. Georgetown Law J 85:1823–1836
Lawson G, Siedman G (2006) Originalism as a legal enterprise. Const Comment 23:47–80
LeDuc A (2016) Paradoxes of positivism and pragmatism in the debate about originalism. Ohio North Univ Law Rev 42:614–704
Machen A (1900) The elasticity of the constitution. Harv Law Rev 14(3):200–216
Madison J (1999) The Federalist No. 37. Signet Classics, New York
Manning JF (2006) What divides textualists from purposivists. Columbia Law Rev 106(1):70–111
Manning J (2010) Second-generation textualism. Cal Law Rev 98:1287–1318
Marmor A (2005) Interpretation and legal theory. Hart Publishing, Oxford
Massa Pinto I, Tripodina C (2010) Le unioni omosessuali non possono essere ritenute omogenee al matrimonio. Diritto Pubblico 1(2):1–18
McConnell M (1998) Textualism and the dead hand of the past. Geo Wash Law Rev 66:1127–1140
Möller K (2017) Eine Frage der Würde. Sueddeutsche Zeitung, 04.07.2017
Monaghan H (1981) Our perfect constitution. N Y Univ Law Rev 56:353–396
Moore M (1989) Authority, law, and Razian reasons. South Cal Law Rev 62:827–896
Olivecrona K (1971) Law as fact, 2nd edn. Stevens & Sons, London
Olivecrona K (1978) Bentham's "Veil of Mistery". Curr Leg Probl 31(1):227–237
Pojanowski J, Walsh K (2016) Enduring originalism. Geo Law J 105:98–157
Purcell E (2015) A democracy, the constitution, and legal positivism in America: lessons from a winding and troubled history. Fla Law Rev 66:1457–1511
Raz J (1977) Promises and obligations. In: Hacker P, Raz J (eds) Law, morality and society: essays in honour of H L A Hart 2010, pp 210–229
Raz J (1979) The authority of law. Oxford University Press, Oxford
Raz J (1982) Promises in morality and law. Harv Law Rev 95(4):916–938

Raz J (1983) The authority of law. Clarendon Press, Oxford
Raz J (1985) Authority, law, and morality. The Monist 68(3):295–324
Raz J (1990) Practical reasons and norms, 2nd edn. Clarendon Press, Oxford
Raz J (2003) About morality and the nature of law. Am J Jurisprud 48(1):1–15
Raz J (2009) Between authority and interpretation. Oxford University Press, Oxford
Reagan R (1987) Remarks announcing the nomination of Robert H. Bork to be an associate justice. Weekly Comp Pres Doc 23:761
Rehnquist W (1976) The notion of a living constitution. Tex Law Rev 54:693–706
Ross A (1958) On law and justice. University of California Press, Berkeley
Ross A (1959) On law and justice. University of California Press, Berkeley
Rubin P (2010) War of the words: how courts can use dictionaries consistent with textualist principles. Duke Law J 60(1):167–206
Sachs S (2015) Originalism as a theory of legal change. Harv J Law Publ Policy 38:817–888
Samaha A (2008) Dead hand arguments and constitutional interpretation. Columbia Law Rev 108: 606–680
Scalia A (1989) Originalism: the lesser evil. Univ Cin Law Rev 57:849–865
Scalia A (1997) Common law courts in a civil-law system: the role of the federal courts in interpreting the constitution and laws. In: Gutmann A (ed) A matter of interpretation, pp 3–49
Scalia A, Garner B (2012) Reading the law: the interpretation of legal texts. West, Eagan
Schauer F (1991) Playing by the rules. Clarendon Press, Oxford
Schauer F (2015) The path-dependence of legal positivism. Va Law Rev 101:957–981
Schofield P (1991) Jeremy Bentham and the nineteenth-century English jurisprudence. J Leg Hist 12:58–88
Sebok A (1995) Misunderstanding positivism. Mich Law Rev 39:2054–2132
Shapiro A (2011) Legality. Belknap Press, Cambridge, MA
Siegel R (2009) Heller and originalism's dead hand – in theory and practice. UCLA Law Rev 56: 1399–1424
Soames S (2011) What vagueness and inconsistency tell us about interpretation. In: Marmor A, Soames S (eds) Philosophical foundations of language in the law, pp 31–58
Soames S (2013) Deferentialism: a post-originalist theory of legal interpretation. Fordham Law Rev 82:597–617
Solum L (2013) Originalism and constitutional construction. Fordham Law Rev 82:453–537
Solum L (2015) The fixation thesis: the role of historical fact in original meaning. Notre Dame Law Rev 91:1–78
Story J (1873) Commentaries on the Constitution of the United States, 4th edn. Little Brown, Boston
Strang L (2019) Originalism's promise: a natural law account of the American constitution. Cambridge University Press, Cambridge
Strauss D (2010) The living constitution. Oxford University Press, Oxford
Sutton J, Whelan E (2020) The essential Scalia: on the constitution, the courts, and the rule of law. Random House, New York
Tamanaha B (2001) A general jurisprudence of law and society. Oxford University Press, Oxford
Van Hoeke M (1985) What is legal theory? Acco, Leuven
Volkmann U (2017) Warum die Ehe für alle vor dem BVerfG nicht scheitern wird. Verfassungsblog, 02.07.201
Weiler J, Trachtman J (1997) European constitutionalism and its discontents. Northwest J Int Law Bus 17:254–397
Whittington K (1999) Constitutional interpretation: textual meaning, original intent, and judicial review. University Press of Kansas, Lawrence
Whittington K (2004) The new originalism 2. Geo J Law Publ Policy:599–613
Whittington K (2010) Constructing a new American constitution. Const Comment 27:119–137

Presumption(s) of Correctness(?): Comparing the Methodological Relevance of *Precedents* in Civil Law and in Common Law Systems

Ana Margarida Simões Gaudêncio

Abstract Though invoking different foundations and generating distinct methodological and normative consequences(-results), the diverse structures presented by *civil law* and *common law* systems share a partially common tradition in what concerns the methodological relevance of *judicial jurisprudence*, thus conferring a specific normatively constitutive meaning to the roles played by *Juristenrecht*, and, within it, *Richterrecht*, in *adjudication*. Establishing a dialogue between *common law* and *civil law* systems, and, within it, comparing the roles of *legal norms* and *judicial jurisprudence* in adjudication—therefore, debating the construction of judicial adjudication as *logical deduction* and as *analogical judgment*—, the essay proposes an understanding of *judicial jurisprudence* not only as an effective *source of law*, but also—and mostly—as a methodologically constitutive juridical criterion, emphasizing a normatively constitutive *juridically binding presumption of correctness* (*Richtigkeit*).

1 Introduction: Facts, Norms and Adjudication—The Methodological Stake

The present reflection intends to discuss contemporary comparisons on the methodological relevance of judicial adjudication in *civil law* and in *common law* systems. In order to accomplish this proposal, two main steps will be taken: *firstly, a brief historical comparative analysis of the role played by judicial jurisprudence in the construction of adjudication in* civil law and in common law systems, contrasting formal *and material* juridical reasoning approaches; and, secondly, a discussion on the meanings of bindingness and correctness of judicial jurisprudence, and the

This essay has been prepared within the framework of the research project "Societal Challenges, Uncertainty and Law: Plurality | Vulnerability | Undecidability" [University of Coimbra Institute for Legal Research (UCILeR), Coimbra, Project I&D, UIDB/04643/2020].

A. M. S. Gaudêncio (✉)
University of Coimbra, Institute for Legal Research (UCILeR), Coimbra, Portugal
e-mail: anagaude@fd.uc.pt

N. Bersier et al. (eds.), *Common Law – Civil Law*, Law and Philosophy Library 139,
https://doi.org/10.1007/978-3-030-87718-7_8

assumption of the practical effect of precedents, as exempla for the construction and development of the juridical system, as the rational structure of juridical content.

In order to expound such an approach, this reflection will be focused on a critique of the consideration of reality as a multitude of *facts* and of the juridical system as a set of *norms*. Historically, and intentionally, this consideration has allowed for the understanding of *logical deduction* as the *ideal* rationalization of adjudication, meaning a deductive *modus operandi* connecting the generality and abstraction of *norms* and the particularity and concreteness of *facts*—consequently requiring syllogistic reasoning and the absence of the normatively constitutive relevance of *facts* in adjudication. In the perspective proposed, however, the judicial decision will be considered as an *analogical* connection between the *juridical problem* and the *juridical system*. This involves adopting a different perspective on the role of *norms*, and even of other *criteria*, such as *precedents* and *dogmatic models*, and ascribing a different understanding to *juridical reasoning*—specifically featured as *practical*, *material*, *axiological*, but also *teleological*, and, though not essentially, *argumentative* reasoning.

Accordingly, adjudication will be acknowledged as an *analogical judgment*—beyond *adjudication* as a strictly *theoretical-deductive application*, and as a sternly *practical-finalistic decision*—, comparing the problem stated *in concrete* by the case *sub judice* and the problem solved *in abstract* by the juridical criterion, and, in tandem, proposing an *analogical juridical reasoning*.

Such a proposal will involve, on the one hand, an understanding of juridical *criteria* as *strata* of that *juridical system*—whether they be *legal norms*, *precedents*, *dogmatic models*, or even *juridical reality*. And, on the other hand, the assumption of an axiological horizon, settled in another *stratus*, of *normative principles* (as foundational *warrants*, meaning specifically juridical foundational *values*), which are designed to support the *normative adequacy* of the concrete judgment of the *realization of law* as a *judicative decision*.

2 The Role of *Judicial Jurisprudence in the Construction of Adjudication in* Civil Law and in Common Law Systems

Though invoking different foundations, and generating distinct methodological and normative consequences, the historically and intentionally diverse structures presented by *civil law* and *common law* systems share a partially common tradition in terms of the methodological relevance of *judicial jurisprudence*. This assertion implies, thus, conferring a specific normatively constitutive meaning to the roles played by *Juristenrecht*, and, within it, *Richterrecht*, in *adjudication*—whether they state this latter primarily as the *logically correct application of law* (*inductively* and/or *deductively* acknowledged), as the *finalistically adequate decision* (*instrumentally* moulded), or as the *normatively constitutive realization of law* (*analogically* reflected).

Establishing a dialogue between *common law* and *civil law* systems, and, within it, directly comparing the roles of *legal norms* and of *judicial jurisprudence* in adjudication, the present reflection relies on an understanding of *judicial jurisprudence* not only as an effective *source of law*, but also as a methodologically constitutive juridical criterion, emphasizing a specific *juridically binding presumption of correctness* (*Richtigkeit*). Such roles may be recognized, after all, even in the contemporary (re)construction of European Community Law, restating common law and civil law as ordinary experiences in the European Community context, understood as a *community of law* (*Europäische Union als Rechtsgemeinschaft*). And this represents an illustration of the historical dialogue between *common law* and *civil law* systems, directly comparing *normative principles*, *legal norms*, *judicial jurisprudence* and *dogmatic* in adjudication, in the increasing "continentalization" of English law and "insularization" of continental law (Bronze 1982), mostly through the overcoming(s) of the normativistic heritage(s).[1]

The *traditional-historical* distinction between *civil law* and *common law* systems, as the mirror of a relationship between *law* and *power*, in its different forms, may be synthetically illustrated through Giovanni Orrù's reflection in his *Lezioni di storia del pensiero teorico-giuridico Moderno* (1988), pointing out that in continental Europe judges used to be instruments of regal absolutism, looking for law's certainty, while in England judges would be able to act even questioning the sovereign power.[2] It should however be emphasized right away, also exemplarily, with Orrù, within that *diagnosis* of the past, that that distance is no longer recognizable in the same way from the second half of the nineteenth century onwards. In fact, exemplarily, it was not only by Bentham's and Austin's codification proposals, but also by the development of the techniques of *distinguishing* and *overruling,* that the *bindingness* of precedents changed, progressively allowing the judge to supersede the *rationes decidendi* of a judicial precedent, when manifestly presented as *plainly unreasonable*.[3]

---

[1] *See*, for instance, about the construction of European Community Law, Schulze and Seif (2003), pp. 7–8. On the crescent "'continentalization' of English law and 'insularization' of continental law", *see* Bronze (1982), pp. 123 ff, specially pp. 165 ff, 174 ff. *See* also Núñez Vaquero (2013); Gaudêncio (2019a).

[2] "Sul continente I giudici erano per lo piú strumenti dell'assolutismo regio, ed in questo va vista la causa dell'esigenza della certezza del diritto, che doveva costituire un argine all'arbitrario imperversare del sistema contro il cittadino. Ben diversa e quasi opposta era la situazione in Inghilterra: qui il diritto prodotto dai giudici, detto *common law*, era sempre andato in direzione contraria alle tendenze del pottere sovrano, il quale invece cercava di consolidare la sua influenza proprio attraverso le leggi".—Orrù (1988), p. 191.

[3] "In questi ultimi tempi, nel mondo anglosassone, la dottrina del precedente à andata via via perdendo quel rigore que à stato inpassato una sua caratteristica. Il precedente, infatti, non à piú in realtà strettamente vincolante, ma lo è quasi solo presuntivamente. L'idea della vincolatività assoluta ha avuto il suo momento di auge, nella dottrina e nella prassi della *common law*, solo nella prima metà del secolo scorso, più o meno durante il periodo della propagazione dell'idea di

In fact, nowadays, as in the past, the distance between *law* and *reality*, meaning the connections between the *judicial precedent* or the *legal* statute and the *problem-case*, on the one hand, and the topic of judicial mediation, which allows for the realization of law through adjudication, on the other, emphasize the essential differences between *common law* and *civil law* systems. Therefore, understanding judicial adjudication and its methodological and dogmatic relevance in practice is a decisive step on the path to the presentation of the differences and resemblances between these systems.

2.1 Formally Juridical Reasoning in Adjudication: Deductive Decisions

From the point of view of formal-deductive juridical reasoning, not only in the past, but also in the present, the consideration of the juridically relevant reality as a multitude of *facts* and of the juridical system as a set of *norms* allowed for the understanding of *logical deduction* as the *ideal* rationalization of adjudication—as a deductive *modus operandi*, entailing the generality and abstraction of *norms* vis-à-vis the particularity and concreteness of *facts*.[4] Such an understanding requires a syllogistic form of reasoning and the absence of the normatively constitutive relevance of *facts*—and so, of *reality*—in adjudication. Concomitantly, in normativistic-positivist proposals, mostly from the nineteenth century on, *rules* should be understood as *norms*—meaning *general* and *abstract* normative *criteria* for action, commanded by the authority of the institutionalized instance to establish them.

In civil law systems, a normativistic *intentional dualism* has established a counterpoint between the practical character and intention of the *law*—created and instantiated as *legal norm*—and the theoretical, apophantic character and intention of *juridical thinking*—understood and instantiated as *positivistic science*. . .—, which was meant to consider *legal norms* as *cognoscible objects* (Neves 1999a, pp. 57–69).

codificazione ad opera di Bentham e Austin. Le technique del *distinguishing* e del *overruling* permettono al giudice inglese di liberarsi da un precedente, se giudicato manifestamente irragionevole (*plainly unreasonable*)".—Orrù (1988), p. 192. On the doctrine of codification by Bentham an Austin, *see* Orrù (1988), pp. 195–198. *See* also Bronze (1982), pp. 177 ff.

[4]As Reiner Schulze and Ulrike Seif refer—though not actually following such an approach—, considering the contemporary relevance of *Richterrecht* in the building of European law's systems, the *methodological* distinction between continental *civil law system* and *common law system* rests, *traditionally*, mostly on the *deductive* character of the former and the *inductive* nature of the latter. In fact, in such a distinction, the *continental* civil law would be understood as mainly *deductive*, for a systematic codification is composed by abstract norms, this way providing the basis for solving cases, whereas *English* common law would be mainly *inductive*, for in the ???latter general rules would derive from cases, so that decision-making in common law systems would be typically determined by *stare decisis*. *See* Schulze and Seif (2003), pp. 8 ff, mostly pp. 22–23.

Jhering's proposal, within the so called *Begriffsjurisprudenz*, illustrates such an assertion, through his quasi-*chemical* understanding of the *juridical system* as a *formal-abstract structure* logically constructed through *concepts*, the significances of *legal thinking*, and *dogmatic*, as *science* (1883, pp. 379–414). The scientific construction of the juridical concepts would, in this context, be wrought by a logical inductive production of progressively more general and abstract logical formulations, normatively *simpler* and logically *clearer*. The *juridical bodies—Körper* (Chiassoni 2016, pp. 590–597)—would, then, represent the logical purification of juridical *data* (whether *consuetudinary* or *legal* criteria, translated by *normative propositions*), in order to construct *objective* law. This implies proposing a kind of *chemistry of concepts*, consisting of a progressive logical induction from the juridical materials to the formal and logical links between concepts as the definition of the different juridical figures. Concomitantly, the pyramidal structure of Puchta (1838) would illustrate the inductive/deductive *rationale*, by logically relating *criteria* and *concepts* to each other, at different hierarchical levels (Larenz 1995, pp. 17 ff, 263 ff).

In common law systems, however, the relevance of criteria *inducted* from *rationes decidendi* was decisive, and the dogmatic was also invoked even within formalist approaches (Ibbetson 2003, pp. 27 ff, 37; Peczenik 2007, pp. 17 ff), corresponding to the ways it could be considered in *civil law* systems. This shows that in *civil law* systems it would also be essential to conjoin case-law with doctrinal reasoning, not only in the Middle Ages, but also in the early Modern and in the Enlightenment periods, though in different ways. In fact, in the Middle Ages, the multidimensional character of the juridical system would correspond to the hermeneutical-practical rationality and the dialectical structure of juridical thinking. And in the early Modern and in the Enlightenment periods, while legal statutes were increasingly considered to be the main source of law, the juridical system was progressively constructed and thought as unidimensional, constituted by legal statutes and assuming an axiomatic rationality and a theoretical structure to dogmatic (Ibbetson 2003, pp. 29 ff; Bronze 1982, pp. 123–142).

Of course, it must be kept in mind that the characteristic *inductive* construction of English Common Law, represented by the creation of *criteria* by selecting *rationes decidendi* and *obiter dicta* (Schulze and Seif 2003, p. 8; Bronze 1982, pp. 156 ff), would also allow for a *deductive* construction of *juridical solutions* in subsequent *analogous* cases, as the criterion thus mobilised would be considered as a *norm*.

Such an understanding of law as *norm*—whether in *civil law systems* or in *common law systems*—would indicate that *deduction* would always take place in judicial decision-making. And that would be so for the reason that the approach to *juridical reality*—meaning the juridically relevant reality—would be understood as a relationship between *norm* and *fact*. Which is to say that *law* would contemplate *reality* through the lens of its presuppositions, denoting that the *juridical system* would define *a priori* which and on which terms *reality* would be relevant: juridically relevant reality would, then, be the factual correlative of normative propositions. This shows the relevance of a *paradigm of application* in judicial decisions, which is not exclusively emphasized in nineteenth century juridical thinking, since it appears nowadays, in several, mostly formal-argumentative, approaches (Lege 2012, pp. 259–280).

Considering adjudication as a deductive application, and, as such, stressing a *paradigm of application*, the *legal norm* would then be taken as the major premise for the *deduction*, and the minor premise would be itself built through a *subsumption*. This requires consideration of the *fact* under analysis as a *species* corresponding to the norm, and more precisely in its general and abstract *hypothesis*, as a prescribing *gender*. If the fact corresponded, in this sense, to the norm's hypothesis, a logical deduction would determine the application of the legal consequence stated by the norm to the fact(s) in question. And it would presuppose that there would be no normatively constitutive contribution of reality (as facts) to juridicity, once the juridical system was presupposed as a politically and scientifically complete structure of norms (Neves 1999a, pp. 102–110; Neves 1995c, pp. 301–308; Bronze 2019, pp. 370–376, 763–775).

In such normativistic understandings, law should be specifically stated in *legal norms*, thus set as the primary relevant *criteria* of *juridicalness*—as constitutive juridical *criteria*, mostly in the creation of statute law, but also as adjudicating/ judicial deciding juridical *criteria*—, placed on a logically organized one-dimensional *system*. Judicial jurisprudence and dogmatic would represent, in such approaches, external, logical and reflective consequences of the logical-deductive application of legal norms.

And this would also be a fundamental question regarding the construction of common law systems; on the assumption of judicial jurisprudence as a source of law. In fact, in representing an effectively institutional *auctoritas*, the binding force of *stare decisis* would rest on the *rationes decidendi*. And the *rationes decidendi* would represent constitutive practical *memories* of valuation, which would be institutionally binding as *criteria* to future decisions in *analogous* cases, according to *stare decisis*, both when considering, as well as when overcoming, *obiter dicta*. The distinction between *interpretation* and *application* would then be crucial. And, therefore, the core question in this field would be the distinction between *precedents* as *concrete case decisions*—and their eventual *normative bindingness*—and as *normative general and abstract criteria*—inductively obtained from those decisions—; and, in this last sense, taken as the formal *schemes* to be assumed as major premises for future deductive applications, proposed by the analogy between the *sub judice* case and the judicial precedent expressed by its *ratio decidendi* (Larenz 1995, pp. 252–261, especially p. 253; Peczenik 2007, mostly p. 26).

The formalist application paradigm that was predominantly subscribed to in the nineteenth century is, then, represented by a subscriptive syllogism, summoning the essential major premise—translated into the universally rational statement expressed in the hypothesis of the norm and to which the conditional structure of the norm would be constructed—, the minor premise—as an effective subsumption of (discrete) facts to the norm hypothesis—, and the conclusion—the logically deductive correspondence of the application of the legal consequence to that subsumption. This would assume reality as a field of application of norms, and these latter as rational statements assembled in a self-subsistent and complete system, which would remain unscathed before and after its mobilization through that syllogism (Neves 1999a, pp. 102–110; Neves 1995c, pp. 301–308; Bronze 2019, pp. 370–376, 763–775).

In common law systems, *analogy* represents a fundamental connection between successive cases and rationes decidendi, within the *stare decisis* system, even if after this the formalist proposition would require the elaboration of a syllogism to state a *deductive application* of law. Traditionally, also from a formalist point of view, in civil law systems, *analogy* would be stated as a logically operative mechanism, acceptable, under specific circumstances, if and when there would not be the possibility of *subsumption*—through *syllogism*—of the *facts* under analysis to the interpretative (literally) admissible meanings of the *legal criteria*. And this would be so mostly when there would be no connection between the literal selected meanings of the legal text (*grammar*) in association with the meanings admitted by the other *intra-textual* elements (*logic*, *history*, *system*)—and, when acceptable, the *extra-textual* element (*teleology*)—and the *empirical factuality* in question (Neves 1995d). *Analogy* would then signify, firstly, comparing *facts*—the fact without literal connection to the juridical criterion, and a fact with such a connection, within the literal prevision of a juridical criterion—, and, secondly, inductively identifying and deductively applying this juridical criterion to the omitted fact. Which implies that the dogmatic completeness of the juridical system would only admit the *integration of omitted facts*—the gaps—through elements internal to the juridical system. Therefore, though the omitted fact could be subsumed to the literal relevance of that juridical criterion, such a subsumption would be the result of the so called *analogia legis*. And, if it were not possible to achieve, there would still be the possibility of subsumption of the omitted fact to the *general principle(s) of law* in force on the matter in which such omission could be subsumed, which would be called *analogia juris*. Beyond these two operations, the fact would be considered juridically irrelevant (Neves 1999a, pp. 108–110).

2.2 *Materially* Juridical Reasoning in Adjudication: From Finalistic to Judicative Decisions

Overcoming the nineteenth century dominant legal *positivism* allowed for, among many other possibilities, an alternative *paradigm* of judicial realization as a *practical-finalistic decision*—it could be said a *paradigm of decision* (Neves 1999a, pp. 102–105); even mobilizing *rational theories of decision* to configure adjudication as an effective option, taken between alternatives considered as means to an end which would be stated as objectives in law—whether in judicial decisions or in statutory law—, and law itself as a *final program*. In such a perspective, the selection of alternatives and the viability and adequacy of judicial decisions would be determined by their effective consequences, as objectives transformed into effects-*results*, both in common law and in civil law systems. This would illustrate that law should be pragmatically evaluated (as in American Legal Realism and in Law and

Economics, for instance), in relation to—and as a function of—the objectives to whose accomplishment it could be used as an instrument, and, concomitantly, the effective results obtained through judicial performance on the social stage (Neves 1993, pp. 205 ff; Gaudêncio 2012, p. 101; Gaudêncio 2019b).

Under its consequentialist approach, considering Oliver Wendell Holmes (1881) as a reference point, American Legal Realism (Tarello 1962), mostly considering the view inspired by Karl Llewellyn, assumed that formal criteria, pragmatism and prediction should conjoin in adjudication, so that it should simultaneously provide formal certainty and finalistic social adequacy, both considering the literal and scope binding reference of criteria within the results (Tarello 1962, p. 4; Llewellyn 1962, pp. 42–76).

This is also, just as an example, now in the Law and Economics field, an essential reference to Posner's proposal on judicial decision-making, for Posner (1998; Posner 1999, pp. 393–395; Minda 1995, pp. 149–166; Linhares 2001, pp. 664–670) states that in interpreting the legal text, the legislator's will must be taken into account, whilst pragmatically conjoined with the decisive consideration of the effects of adjudication.

Such a decision paradigm—or paradigms (Kuhn 1962, pp. 10–51, 208–210), rather, considering that they are, after all, very different from one another, though they join pragmatism and finalism together—presents a rationally oriented option taken from different possible alternatives, in order to achieve specific predefined objectives whose availability to produce effective results would be measured concretely, through probability judgments, if and when possible, and through their readiness to assume reality as a determining factor of the option (Neves 1999a, pp. 176–191; Neves 1999b, pp. 25–28; Wälde 1979; Kilian 1974).

Beyond that paradigm, but still under the influence of Legal Realism, two examples may be considered in order to represent a different construction of adjudication, both still within common law systems.

A first example is given by Dworkin, who assumes the construction of judicial adjudication as the decision that can best suit the specific case, the "correct" and "coherent" solution/answer within the framework of the system—the "integrity": the activity which must be coherent in normative terms and valid in the light of principles, for the interpreter of a text is in the position of a chain writer, within a *chain novel* (Dworkin 1981, pp. 469–518; Dworkin 1986, p. 52: "Creative interpretation, on the constructive view, is a matter of interaction between purpose and object", pp. 52–68, 225 ff, 228–232; Dworkin 1985, pp. 154–158).

Interpretation, whilst referring to such a "chain novel", would count on a practical inertia, in terms of argument, which would guarantee the solution's coherence—"coherence as integrity"—, not strictly normative, and nor strictly narrative, as in the literary text.[5] The community of lawyers would have an experience built up over time, inserted into this chain; thus, the jurist-interpreter, integrated into a community,

[5] *See*, in particular, Stefan Arnold's contribution to this volume.

would be in permanent positive and negative dialogue with that experience, in the course of the interpretative activity (Dworkin 1986, pp. 225–275).[6]

The interpreter would be subject to some constraints that the legislator would not have to deal with, due to the requirement of consistency. Thus, in the first place, and in principle, the requirement for the resolution should be adapted to the "body of legal materials"—*rectior*, the requirement for consistency—which would ordinarily decide the case. However, when this were not possible, the judge would have to choose between competing versions of possible coherent solutions, and then develop his "personal political theory", but under two other constraints: the justification of his "personal political theory" as the most coherent for the explanation of legal materials, and its application to the sub judice case (Dworkin 1986, pp. 65–68).

A second example is offered by MacCormick, somewhat differently from Dworkin's proposal, actually disagreeing on the possibility of the weighting of principles—in which one prevails whilst the other or others do not lose their validity—but not of conflicting "rules" (*See* MacCormick 1997, pp. 155–156; Dworkin 1984, pp. 14–45, in particular pp. 26–27, 46–80, in particular pp. 71–80).

MacCormick asserts that such legal rules aim to ensure a certain end considered to be valid, or a general mode of conduct considered to be desirable, and that the expression of that end through "a general normative statement" translates the enunciation of the principle—"the principle of the law" which underlies them.[7] Therefore, justification of the decisions in the usually said "hard cases" is not so much a question of the weighting of principles, but of the interaction of arguments of principle with arguments of consequentiality (MacCormick 1997, pp. 197, 227–228).

When the "rules" are not sufficiently clear or the qualification of the facts themselves debatable, or even when the question of the existence or absence of a juridical basis for a certain case is controversial, then there would be a "second-order justification", in conjunction with the directives on coherence and consistency (MacCormick 1997, pp. 100–101).[8]

---

[6] "[. . .] I think that the popular idea, that some legal questions have no right answer because legal language is sometimes vague, does not depend on any argument from vagueness at all, but rather on the different argument, [. . .], that there can be no right answer to a legal question when reasonable lawyers disagree about what the right answer is".—Dworkin (1985), p. 131 (*see* mostly chapter 5, *'Is There Really No Right Answer in Hard Cases?'*, pp. 119–145). See also Linhares (2001), pp. 670–671, 673–679; Pintore (2000), pp. 156–160.

[7] "(. . .) legal rules (. . .), singly, or much more commonly, in related groups may be conceived of as tending to secure, or being aimed at securing, some end conceived as valuable, or some general mode of conduct conceived to be desirable: to express the policy of achieving that end, or the desirability of that general mode of conduct, in a general normative statement, is, then, to state 'the principle of the law' underlying the rule or rules in question".—MacCormick (1997), p. 156.

[8] "(. . .) second-order justification in the law involves testing rival possible rulings against each other and rejecting those which do not satisfy relevant tests – the relevant tests being concerned with what makes sense in the world, and with what makes sense in the context of the system".—MacCormick (1997), p. 103. "(. . .) second-order justification involves two elements, consequentialist argument and argument testing proposed rulings for consistency and coherence with the exiting legal

Consequently, the judicial decision, as a constitutive, and not merely a declarative, act, should be delimited not by deduction from "rules" but by the justifying reasons for the mobilization of the "rules". Which, when affirming consequentialist considerations—and, thus, as dimensions of "policy"—are susceptible to determination by the content of the "rule" itself, constituting the normative expressions of such reasons—"policies" justifying or rationalizing statements of "legal principles" (MacCormick 1997, p. 166).

The judicial decision is therefore subject to restrictions, not freely constitutive but interstitially constitutive, and, thus, restrictively innovative, distinct from the legislative constitution of law (MacCormick 1997, pp. 188–191).[9] On the other hand, the analogical mobilization of "rules" in the field of "case law", as a system of binding precedents, would itself be analogous to the analogical mobilization of "rules" of "statutory law".[10] And, as such, both would be subject to the double requirement for valuing argumentation, and, therefore, coherence—and of the justification of the admissibility of the mobilization of arguments by analogy or of legal principles as the support for future decisions (MacCormick 1997, pp. 186–187).

A different requirement, then, is stated by consistency, *stricto sensu*, as a limit to the convocation of consequentialist arguments when they contradict fundamental norms of the system, which is relevant for the interpretation, and also for the identification of "easy" ("clear") and/or "hard" cases, though there is no effective contradiction in this point (MacCormick 1997, p. 106): the former would be decided by deduction, while for the latter interpretive rules could be instituted that would not (always) allow the selection of the meaning closest to literality, in order to reach other meanings, in the light of principles and, under specific circumstances, of consequentialist arguments (MacCormick 1997, pp. 199–200).

Like Dworkin, MacCormick (1997, p. 251) asserts that judges do not convoke (or are not burdened with) "strong" discretion" before "hard" cases, but only "weak" discretion, though not in exactly the same direction. In fact, while for Dworkin "strong" discretion would imply a decision in the light of the arguments that the judge considers most appropriate, for MacCormick discretion would always be

---

system".—MacCormick (1997), p. 107. *See* also MacCormick (1997), pp. 105, 111–112, 115–116, 129–151 (*see* mostly chapter VI '*Consequentialist Arguments*'). "It is the interaction of arguments from principle and consequentialist arguments which fully justifies decisions in hard cases – and even at that we have yet to consider the important matter of 'consistency' (...)".—MacCormick (1997), p. 194 ("*The Requirement of 'Coherence': Principles and Analogies*", pp. 152–194); MacCormick (1988), pp. 99–112, specifically pp. 105–106.

[9] "The highly desirable recognition of a judicial power to make law must be restricted by recognition of a duty to make it only 'interstitially'. Therefore there must be a criterion for distinguishing interstitial from architectural legislation. One possible criterion is that either a relevant analogy or an established principle is a necessary element of justification of an innovative decision".—MacCormick (1997), pp. 187–188.

[10] "(...) it is false to suppose that there is any essential difference between statute and common law as to the force and function of arguments by analogy and from principle, even though we may assent to the proposition that perhaps the most characteristic use of such arguments is in the elaboration and concretization of doctrines from case to case (...)".—MacCormick (1997), p. 194.

limited by the argumentative requirements of the system—principles, consequentialist arguments and the "consistency test". Furthermore, and unlike Dworkin, MacCormick proposes that the possibility of presenting different possible solutions for hard cases does not give rise to a primarily "speculative" and, consequently, "practical" disagreement, but to a primarily practical one—not purely and simply practical, but boundedly practical, in the light of the bindingness of rules—argumentatively concluding with the "right answer" for the case (MacCormick 1997, pp. 246–250).[11]

Thus, against Dworkin's theory of the weighting of principles, MacCormick states, in addition to the notion that that thesis leaves the analogical application of "rules" unexplained, that, in terms of interpretation, "rules" effectively compete with "principles", and will not be rendered invalid in case of non-application, because it is possible to distinguish the delimitation of the scope and the field of application of a rule in a given context from the determination of its validity or invalidity. And this is also considering that a "rule" may imply the delimitation of the sense of a principle and be applied to the detriment of it, when contextually justified (MacCormick 1997, pp. 230–232).[12]

Rejecting both the previous formulations, and specifically presupposing the civil law system's structures, the judgment paradigm followed in the present reflection focuses on the specific requirements of the sub judice case, and from this point it invokes the criteria and the principles normatively available in an open and multidimensional system, in order to assume reality in its normatively constitutive relevance, and, thus, establishes a (re)constituting dialectical relation (Neves 1999b, pp. 93–94; Linhares 2017, pp. 171 ff; Gaudêncio 2019b). So, mostly assuming juridical thinking as *a*nalogical reasoning, *adjudication* has been developed in this approach as a *judicative analogical decision*—beyond a sternly *theoretical-deductive application* or a strictly *practical-finalistic decision*. And such a statement presupposes adjudication as an effectively *practical, concrete* rationally dialectical-dialogical *realization of law*, to which the whole *juridical system* is convoked, within a *judicative paradigm*. In contrast to the previous views, such a *practical, concrete realization of law* requires a specific *analogical relation* between the *case-problem* presented and the (constituting) *juridical system* (Neves 1993, pp. 159 ff; Neves 1995b).

[11]"The important truth that there are genuine disagreements about the proper solution of legal problems is explicable otherwise than by reference to the "one right answer" theory".—MacCormick (1997), p. 249; *See* also Dworkin (1984), pp. 31–32, 68–71; "(...) a disagreement which it is in principle impossible to send to any theoretical "Hercules" for objective resolution by delivery of the right answer".—MacCormick (1997), pp. 254, 265–274.

[12]"'If we are to achieve a clear conceptual distinction between' rules and principles (and it is a necessity both for the present thesis and for the 'rights thesis'), we shall have to look elsewhere than in the rights thesis. (The idea that principles identify rights wouldn't do either – so do many rules, as I have recently argued at some length)".—MacCormick (1997), p. 232; *See* Linhares (2017), pp. 55 ff, 157 ff.

So, it is not a matter of *subsumption* of *facts* to the *hypothesis* of *norms*, or of *finalistic selection* between *alternatives*, it requires a specific practical *judgment*—materially founded and constituted, and, nonetheless, normatively and argumentatively enounced. Consequently, the *judicative decision* is progressively built within a *methodical scheme* in which the distinction *question-of-fact/question-of-law* is only allowable as an analytical tool. This indicates that what is at stake in this proposal is the dialectical link constructed between the concrete *case-problem*—the case-*thema*—, in its specific juridical relevance—as the interpellation it addresses to law in its intention and normativity—and the juridical system as a whole (or, in some specifications, the case solved in abstract by the juridical criteria—the case-*foro*, or *exemplum*—), in its distinct dimensions, or *strata: normative principles*, *legal norms*, *precedents*, *dogmatic models*, and *juridical reality* (Neves 1993, pp. 196–197, 205; Bronze 1993; Bronze 1994, pp. 139 ff; Bronze 1998, pp. 110–122; Bronze 2008, pp. 335–373).

As proposed by Castanheira Neves, under this approach to the juridical system as a materially autonomous structure, and therefore considering the jurisprudentialist assimilation of the comprehension of law, as far as the foundation of law is concerned, a normative suprapositivity is assumed. Such a normative suprapositivity means bringing together a historical and civilizational determinant edification, in a materially constitutive historicity that allows the law to assume a normative content by and for itself in that historically constructed and civilizationally coined sense, and a materially densified, normatively practical, and shaping historical-concrete praxis. And, therefore, law affirms a constituting communally assimilated and normatively filtered sense, intrinsically related to the changes in reality, simultaneously as a critical instance of and in the conformation of intersubjectivity. And, so, in such a normative suprapositivity the assimilation of juridicity is densified into founding principles, hence called normative principles, autonomously constituted, and filtered by the juridical system (Neves 1999b, pp. 88–90; Bronze 2019, pp. 627–650; Linhares 2012, pp. 413–421).

The configuration of normative principles proposed by Castanheira Neves (1999b, pp. 93–94; Bronze 2008; Bronze 2020, pp. 175 ff) is outlined in a practical-normative conception of the realization of law—neither a strictly logical formal operation, on one extreme, nor a finalistically determined choice on the other, but a specifically assumed decision-judgment, as a practical-rationally-based consideration. Thus, taking a multi-stratified, densified and densifying system as its normative horizon of reference, to admit the juridical relevance of the controversy—whose elements are the subjects, a shared situation and the context-order.

The juridical relevance of the shared situation, as a specific case, will be assessed, within the *question-of-fact* point of view, considering the distinction between *question-of-fact* and *question-of-law* as Castanheira Neves (1993, pp. 162–286) proposes: in order to acknowledge if the concrete problem can be admitted as juridically relevant, in the light of the presupposed juridical system (and with the respective qualification of that problem, that is, the inclusion of the case, once its juridical relevance is verified, in a given dogmatic field) and of proof (as the determination of the truth of the facts alleged in the sub judice case, not a theoretical-scientific demonstration of *truth*, rather a practical and intersubjectively significant construction of normative relevance) (Neves 1993, pp. 163–165).

And this implies, still, analytically, a specific distinction within the *question-of-law*: the *question-of-law in abstract*—whose object is the determination of the legal criterion that will guide, and contribute to substantiating, the juridical solution of the case *sub judice*—and the *question-of-law in concrete*—whose object concerns the problem of the concrete decision-making judgment that will decide the case (the specific *question-of-law* regarding the resolution of the case through the mediation of this norm, as its criterion, or, if this is not the case, providing, finally, a concrete judgment by autonomous normative constitution, within the intentionality of the juridical system) (Neves 1993, pp. 165–286).

This shows that the decision-making judgment crucially assumes the juridical system as its normative reference horizon (Neves 1993, p. 159; Neves 1995b, p. 276). More precisely, in the context of the specific question-of-law, the realization of the law through the mediation of a norm (whilst considered as practically adequate in order to solve the case) may occur under different forms, depending on the relation between the normative relevance of the norm selected and the problematic relevance of the case sub judice. If there is a practically and normatively analogy—if there is such a correspondence between the material relevance of the norm (the hypothetical relevance) and the material relevance of the case (the concrete relevance), the realization of the law occurs by assimilation as concretization. But, if there are some differences, through there is still an analogy, there can be an assimilation as adaptation or an assimilation as correction. This mean that the sub judice case-problem is still intended by the normative relevance of the norm, but there are some differences between the way the norm intends the problems and the way the concrete problem is presented: on the one hand, in an extensive or in a restrictive way—if the concrete relevance of the problem posed by the case is more restricted or is wider than the hypothetical relevance and intention of the norm (assimilation as adaptation—extensive or restrictive); or, on the other hand, in a synchronic or diachronic way—if the relationship between the concrete relevance of the problem posed by the case and the hypothetical relevance and intention of the norm requires a correction of this latter, considered since the original moment of its bindingness or specifically in the moment of adjudication (assimilation as correction—synchronic or diachronic).

However, there may also be considered an effective non-assimilation of the concrete relevance of the case by the hypothetical relevance the norm—a situation that will lead to a normative overcoming of the norm due to its obsolescence. And, differently, by reference to the relationship between the normativity of the nom and its foundations of validity, the normative principles, there may, differently, be necessary the correction (synchronic or diachronic) or to the preterition or the overcoming of the norm according to those principles (Neves 1993, pp. 176–195).

Therefore, by considering adjudication as a *practical-normative rationalization*, *interpretation* will be encompassed *in adjudication*, not as a logically autonomous operation, but as an operative step within the methodological construction of the *concrete realization of law*—as such, it makes sense towards the mobilization of a legal criterion to the resolution of a concrete problem-case. Concomitantly, *interpretation* will involve integrative moments, thus overpassing the formal-logic scission between *interpretation* and *integration*. Which requires recognizing that there is no intentional distinction between *interpretation* and *application*, but an intentional continuity from *interpretation* to *application*, and also, consequently, that there is no intentional distinction between *application* and *integration*, but an intentional continuity from *application* to *integration*.

Hence, *interpretation*, *application* (not deduction) and *integration* will be methodological steps within the construction of the *judicative decision*, with or without the mediation of a *legal norm*—and, so, decisively constitutive elements of the normatively dialectical relation settled between *problem* and *system*. The juridical problem is then considered as the concrete situation of reality requiring a juridical answer, and the system as the juridical intentionality and content structurally proclaimed, considering the *normative principles* as axiological foundations, and the *legal norms*, the *precedents* and the *dogmatic models* as practical-normative criteria intentionally joining together in *judicative decision* (Neves 1993, pp. 238 ff; Bronze 2007, 2012). And *analogy* will, therefore, be considered as the specific juridical *rationale*, whilst interpretation in adjudication should not be affirmed any more as a logical and abstract operation accomplished in an autonomous methodical hermeneutical moment, for the normative sense of a juridical criterion is to be understood in the moment of and by the mediation of the concrete relevance of the case-problem *sub judice* (Bronze 2020, pp. 175 ff, 223 ff).

Analogy translates, here, then, a distinct judgment, recalled from its Aristotelian terms, representing a *comparison* between two terms, as *relata*—not implying a transition from the particular to the general and back to the particular—, through a *tertium comparationis*, which is *juridical normativity*. This means the consideration of the core of adjudication as a dialectic exercise, establishing the correspondence between the case and the system, a correspondence understood as Arthur Kaufmann (1982) proposes it, and, thus, considering analogy as the noetic construction and development of practice. Consequently, the *judicative decision* will be constructed by stating the similarities and differences between those *relata*, thus analogically relating the problem stated by the case sub judice and the problem purposely intended by the criteria and the principles within the juridical system. And, therefore, an argumentatively structured adjudication results from such ponderings, able to be considered in future decisions as *exempla* (Bronze 1993; Bronze 2012, pp. 345 ff; Bronze 2020, pp. 196 ff).

3 Judicial Jurisprudence and the Presumption(s) of Correctness(?)

Reflecting on the institutional and, mostly, on the methodological value of judicial jurisprudence and on its presumption(s) of correctness, as proposed here, requires the acknowledgement of the specifically different methodological roles assumed by precedents in the construction and development of the juridical system(s) in common law and in civil law systems.

Understanding the practical and normative relevance of precedents will require bearing in mind James Kent's (1832, pp. 475–476) consideration of *correctness*, stated in the *common law* systems context, as a *presumption* in favour of a mature deliberation, which would translate a methodological and institutional requirement for adjudication.[13] Stating judges' adjudication as being *correct* would, then, be, and, it might be said, still is, understanding its *reasonableness* as a key point, in the adequacy of judicial decisions both to reality and to the juridical system. This means a guarantee of *security* of and, also through it, but, maybe, even beyond, a certain *justice*.

Notwithstanding, in the *civil law* systems context, such a *presumption of correctness* has been differently considered, though in the last century it has assumed a specific practical relevance in juridical methodology, mostly considering its practical effect within the perception of adjudication not as a mere deductive judgment, but as an analogical judgment, based on the comparison of the problems posed concretely in reality and the problems solved abstractly within the juridical system.

Significantly, for Martin Kriele (1976, pp. 253–254; Kriele 1979, pp. 91 ff), it would be a *presumption* of (*non-absolute*) *justness/correctness—Richtigkeit*. And, yet, for Karl Larenz, and, subsequently to him, Robert Alexy, this *justness/correctness—Richtigkeit*—would be taken as a specific characteristic of judicial decisions, though not necessarily as a *presumption of bindingness* on future decisions (Larenz 1995, pp. 252–261, in particular pp. 254–255, note pp. 165–166; Alexy 1983, pp. 334 ff). This indicates that precedents, as practical judgments of the realization of law, should be understood as normatively constituting decisions offering the specific normatively adequate answer of the law to a concrete case-problem. And, thus, taken as effective normatively constitutive solutions to juridically relevant problems, precedents are upskilled to be considered as *criteria*—meaning as practical operators which confer, with more or less generality and abstractness, a normatively intentional orientation towards the resolution of a concrete problem, able to be directly convoked, within the juridical system, along with legal norms, normative principles and dogmatic models, to provide the practically and normatively adequate judgment required by the concrete problem.

So, beyond the formally *institutional bindingness* ascribed to precedents in common law systems, and presupposing the differentiation of the relationship established between precedents and legal norms, the consideration of precedents as normative *criteria* with *presumptive bindingness* in civil law systems implies that this substantially *presumptive bindingness* may be contested on different terms, and

[13] "A solemn decision upon a point of law, arising in any given case, becomes an authority in a like case, because it is the highest evidence which we can have of the law applicable to subject, and the judges are bound to follow that decision so long as it stands unreversed, unless it can be shown that the law was misunderstood or misapplied in that particular case. If a decision has been made upon solemn argument and mature deliberation, the presumption is in favour of its correctness (...)".—Kent (1832), pp. 475–476.

under different circumstances of the terms and circumstances required to contest the *stare decisis* in *common law* systems (Bydlinsky 2005, p. 107).

Therefore, and simultaneously, what has been said about the relevance of the *presumption of correctness* of judicial decisions in *civil law* systems presupposes recognizing the influence of Chaïm Perelman's (1976 : II, 2.; Perelman 2002, p. 93; Urbina 2010, pp. 8, 75; Bodenheimer 1985, pp. 391–417) *principle of inertia* (or, as in Robert Alexy: "*Trägheit – Trägheitsprinzip*" [Alexy 1983, p. 336]) and the correlative *burden of contra-argumentation*, as proposed by Perelman, and by Giovanni Orrù (1983, pp. 109–111).[14] Methodologically, this entails the *presumption of correctness*, understood as the normative adequacy of adjudication, both to the problem *sub judice* and to the *juridical system*. Such normative adequacy requires a specific relationship between system and problem and constrains a methodological bindingness, based on the presumption that the judge elaborated a judgment which was pondered over, fitting the problematic characteristics and normative specificity of the case and the normative intentionality and problematic setting of the system.

That said, it must be argued that, in future analogue problems, the judge must take into account former judgments, as *criteria* to ponder. And, therefore, after a concrete judgment on the relationship between the case-problem and the juridical system, meaning the criteria—and within these the precedents—and the principles in force within the juridical system, there must be a substantively and argumentatively sustained conclusion on whether the precedent should be upheld or overruled: upheld under the substantial confirmation of the normative and practical adequacy of the former judgment, argumentatively invoking the reference of the *principle of inertia*; overruled due to the substantial justification of the normative and practical inadequacy of the former judgment, argumentatively invoking the reference of the *burden of contra-argumentation*.

Besides, understanding this *presumptive bindingness of justness/correctness* presented by precedents may also require recognizing it as an effective methodologically constructed *source of law*, from a *phenomenological-normative perspective* whether it is stated or not in positive *legal norms* concerning *the sources of law*; and it is also presupposed by the present proposal (Neves 1995a). But this does not mean, of course, formally ascribing institutionally authoritative *formal bindingness* to judicial decisions in civil law systems. This *presumption of bindingness*—considering the different roles discussed above, for Martin Kriele, and, yet distinctly, for Franz Bydlinsky, Karl Larenz, or Robert Alexy—states a materially and argumentatively based point of reference for a judge's decision. Accordingly, ascribing a *presumption of correctness* to a previous judicial decision is to confer on it a specific kind of methodological bindingness, in order to guide the judge on the path to

[14] "Differenze relativamente minime tra *common law* e *civil law*". "In ogni caso, sia il giudice continentale, sia quello inglese sono obligati a consolidare le loro decisioni inserendole nel sistema: possono essere diversi i modi in cui questa coerenza viene cercata e dimonstrata, ma il risultato cui si deve arrivare è sostanzialmente il medesimo...".—Orrù (1983), p. 111.

judicial adjudication, by relating the juridically relevant reality and the binding juridical system. While constituting a normatively and practically adequate example of this dialectical relationship, each judicial adjudication must be convoked for the following judgments on analogical problems. Thus, judicial decisions constitute—substantially and institutionally—judicial jurisprudential criteria included within the juridical system, forming a specific stratum within it, and, concomitantly, establishing normatively constitutive sources of law.

All this implies, consequently, that, when facing a future analogous problem-case *sub judice*, the criterion constituted by judicial jurisprudence is to be considered as an effective source of law, as well as a strict criterion (as an example of the previous normatively adequate resolution of an analogous problem)—meaning a practical operator suitable for guiding the judge's reflection on the construction of the judicative decision. And this is so, in a *civil law* system, whether there is or there is not a *legal norm* which might be methodologically employed as a *criterion* for the construction of the judicative decision (Linhares and Gaudêncio 2015, *in particular* pp. 185–186, 195 ff). This requires, in turn, that the legal norm is interpreted and mobilised as a criterion within the whole juridical system, within all the *strata*, and, therefore, considering the judicial jurisprudence's criteria already constituted—whether to follow them or to refuse to follow them, due to the dialectical relationship stated between the problem *sub judice* and the normativity of the juridical system. So, the *presumption of bindingness* accorded to judicial jurisprudence is understood here as methodologically refutable, if this refutation is justified, that is, when the judge, concluding that the specific decision contained in the judicial precedent convoked is not adequate to be invoked as a foundational normative argument for the construction of the present judicative decision, through that *burden of contra-argumentation*.[15]

Precedents must, then, both in common law and in civil law systems (besides the institutional distinctions), be methodologically taken as effectively constitutive *judicative criteria*. They represent effectively operative mechanisms to judicial adjudication, both materially normative and dialogically argumentative. And all these features contribute to the corresponding *presumption of correctness* of judicial jurisprudence, which decisively denotes an essential distinction from *legal norms*—as *criteria* which assert a general and abstract determination and its *potestas*—and the corresponding *presumption of authority*.

[15] "The (...) judgments in question will benefit from a *presumption of justness* or *correctness* ('*Richtigkeit*'), meaning that they should be understood as substantially adequate according to the juridical significances inscribed in the legal system they presuppose. This presumption is, however, refutable: if the judge contemplates refuting it, he must normatively and methodologically justify this change in orientation, complying with a *burden of contra-argumentation* (*Argumentationslast)*".—Linhares and Gaudêncio (2015), pp. 191–192.

4 Beyond Institutional Bindingness, the Methodological Correctness of Judicial Jurisprudence

Institutionally, both within common law and civil law systems, *legal norms* and *precedents* play specifically different roles, with also distinct normative *relevance* and *bindingness*, constituting different operating *judicative criteria*, based on different theories on the sources of law and on the historical constitution of the juridical system.

Beyond institutional bindingness, the methodological *presumptions of bindingness* which *legal norms* and *precedents* undertake—*authority* and *correctness*, respectively—allow for the presupposition of the *juridical system* as a set of normative meanings. The juridical system is then understood in its complexity and in its multidimensionality, including the essentially founding *normative principles*, in their *validity*, also taken as a *presumption of bindingness*. In fact, the juridical system represents a set of foundations and of criteria normatively available for the effective construction and realization of law, between *abstractness* and *concreteness*. And *judicial jurisprudence*, assuming within that juridical system specific methodological relevance, is mobilised as a constitutive juridical criterion in the *normatively constitutive realization of law*, supporting the specific *juridically binding presumption* of *correctness* it holds, not merely *de facto*, but actually *de jure* (Peczenik 2007, pp. 25–28).

From this jurisprudential point of view, as proposed, the juridical system conjoins and states a substantial sense, in continuous development through the dialectic between normativity and reality, which guides the normative delineation and the substantial determination of the law. And such features are fundamental to the understanding of the juridical system as the materially grounding and normatively stabilizing horizon of reference for judicial decisions.

This axiological-material and practical-normatively described jurisprudential option, built upon the basis of an autonomous reflection on the practice of the law and the specifically juridical content it mobilizes, directly produces practical implications arising from the autonomy of normative principles as described above, and the determinant meaning of the dialectic (re)construction of the juridical system itself. This latter implies that the consideration of judicial decision-making—the realization of the law in practice—is a singular moment of reflection and articulation between system and problem.[16] And, more specifically, between the problem stated in abstract in the criteria and principles convoked and the problem present in the reality, concretely requiring an answer from law, which will, in space and time, link the essential valuations that the law brings to the reality which challenges it.

These are the meanings with which this normatively dialogical perception of juridical construction is to be assimilated. And as such, this approach is effectively

[16]The effects of adjudication regarded here are its specifically juridical effects, meaning the effects that the *Tatbestand* of the normative criteria assume as juridically assimilated by the juridical system. *See* Neves (1993), pp. 196–205.

far from analytical contemporary positivisms—whether exclusive or inclusive—, and from the corresponding debate about the determination of and the distinction between "clear cases" and "hard cases". And, therefore, far from the consequent deductive and/or non-deductive assimilation of the concrete decision, and also far from the argumentatively determined selection criteria which are finalistically oriented within the judicial decision.

So, methodologically, judicial jurisprudence's normatively and methodologically constitutive correctness expresses this specific dialectical connection between juridical problem and juridical system in adjudication, both in common law and in civil law systems, despite the institutional differences. It is a connection which constitutes the core of the judicial realization of law, and which also leads to a different comprehension of the role of legal norms, and of other criteria, such as precedents and dogmatic models. Such an approach on adjudication, and on its *analogical judgment*, establishes a comparison between the problem stated *in concrete* by the case *sub judice* and the problem solved *in abstract* by the juridical criterion, without *inductive* and/or *deductive* exercises. Therefore, judicial jurisprudence assumes a dialectical and practical mode of juridical reasoning, with its axiology and its teleology, and through its argumentative structure. Concomitantly, it states an *analogical juridical reasoning*, through the mediation of a materially constitutive, autonomous *normativity of law*. And all this establishes the normative acquis which confers on precedents the *presumption of correctness* expounded.

References

Alexy R (1983) Theorie der juristischen Argumentation. Suhrkamp, Frankfurt

Bodenheimer E (1985) Perelman's contribution to legal methodology. North Ky Law Rev 12:391–417

Bronze F (1982) "Continentalização" do direito inglês ou "insularização" do direito continental? Coimbra Editora, Coimbra

Bronze F (1993) Breves considerações sobre o estado actual da questão metodonomológica. Boletim da Faculdade de Direito da Universidade de Coimbra LXIX:177–199

Bronze F (1994) A metodonomologia entre a semelhança e a diferença (reflexão problematizante dos pólos da radical matriz analógica do discurso jurídico), Stvdia Ivridica 3. Coimbra Editora, Coimbra

Bronze F (1998) O jurista: pessoa ou andróide? In: Varela J (ed) AB UNO AD OMNES – 75 anos da Coimbra Editora, pp 73–122

Bronze F (2007) O problema da analogia iuris (algumas notas). In: de Albuquerque R, Cordeiro R (eds) Estudos em homenagem ao Professor Doutor José Dias Marques, pp 147–162

Bronze F (2008) A metodonomologia (para além da argumentação) In: de Figueiredo Dias J, Canotilho J, de Faria Costa J (eds) Ars Ivdicandi – Estudos em Homenagem ao Prof. Doutor António Castanheira Neves, Stvdia Ivridica 90, Ad Honorem – 3, vol I – Filosofia, Teoria e Metodologia, pp 335–373

Bronze F (2012) Pj → Jd: A equação metodonomológica (as incógnitas que articula e o modo como se resolve). In: Bronze F (ed) Analogias, pp 311–391

Bronze F (2019) Lições de Introdução ao Direito, 3rd edn. Coimbra Editora, Coimbra

Bronze F (2020) Metodologia do Direito. Imprensa da Universidade de Coimbra, Coimbra

Bydlinsky F (2005) Grundzüge der juristischen Methodenlehre. Wien Universitätsverlag, Wien
Chiassoni P (2016) 21.4.1. Rudolf von Jhering. In: Pattaro E, Roversi C (eds) Legal philosophy in the twentieth century: the civil law world, vol 12. Tome 2, pp 590–597
Dworkin R (1981) The forum of principle. N Y Univ Law Rev 56:469–518
Dworkin R (1984) Taking rights seriously. Harvard University Press, Cambridge
Dworkin R (1985) A matter of principle, a matter of principle. Harvard University Press, Cambridge
Dworkin R (1986) Law's empire. Harvard University Press, Cambridge
Gaudêncio A (2012) From centrifugal teleology to centripetal axiology(?). Boletim da Faculdade de Direito da Universidade de Coimbra LXXXVIII, Tomo I:91–103
Gaudêncio A (2019a) Correctness and rationality as presumptions of bindingness in adjudication: on the methodological relevance of precedents and dogmatic models in European civil law and common law systems. In: Linhares J, Gaudêncio A, Godinho I (eds) Jurists' law and European Identity: dogmatic-institutional, methodological and legal-philosophical problems, pp 291–308
Gaudêncio A (2019b) 'Jurisdictional Realization of Law' as Judicium: a methodological alternative, beyond deductive application and finalistic decision. Int J Semiot Law - Revue internationale de Sémiotique juridique 33:133–146
Holmes O (1881) The common law. Little, Brown and Co, Boston
Ibbetson D (2003) Case-law and doctrine: a historical perspective on the English common law. In: Schulze R, Seif U (eds) Richterrecht und Rechtsfortbildung in der Euröpaischen Rechtsgemeinschaft. Mohr Siebeck, pp 27–40
Jhering R (1883) Geist des römischen Rechts auf den verschiedenen Stufen seiner Entwicklung, zweiter Teil, zweite Abteilung, 8th edn. Benno Schwabe § Co, Basel
Kaufmann A (1982) Analogie und "Natur der Sache". R.v. Decker & C.F. Müller, Heidelberg
Kent J (1832) Commentaries on American Law I, 2nd edn. O. Halsted, New York
Kilian W (1974) Juristische Entscheidung und elektronische Datenverarbeitung. Toeche-Mittler, Darmstadt
Kriele M (1976) Theorie der Rechtsgewinnung. Duncker und Humblot, Berlin
Kriele M (1979) Recht und praktische Vernunft. Vandenhoeck und Ruprecht, Göttingen
Kuhn T (1962) The structure of scientific revolutions. The University of Chicago Press, Chicago
Larenz K (1995) Methodenlehre der Rechtswissenschaft, 3rd edn. Springer, Berlin
Lege J (2012) Subsumtion pragmatisch: Deduktion, Induktion und Abduktion. In: Gabriel G, Gröschner R (eds) Subsumtion, pp 259–280
Linhares J (2001) Entre a reescrita pós-moderna da modernidade e o tratamento narrativo da diferença ou a prova como um exercício de "passagem" nos limites da juridicidade (imagens e reflexos pré-metodológicos deste percurso). Coimbra Editora, Coimbra
Linhares J (2012) Na 'coroa de fumo' da teoria dos princípios: poderá um tratamento dos princípios como normas servir-nos de guia? In: Correia F, Machado J, Loureiro J (eds) Estudos em Homenagem ao Professor Doutor José Joaquim Gomes Canotilho, STVDIA IVRIDICA, 106, Ad Honorem – 6, Volume III – Direitos e interconstitucionalidade: entre dignidade e cosmopolitismo, pp 395–421
Linhares J (2017) O binómio casos fáceis/casos difíceis e a categoria de inteligibilidade sistema: um contraponto indispensável no mapa do discurso jurídico contemporâneo? Imprensa da Universidade de Coimbra, Coimbra
Linhares J, Gaudêncio A (2015) The Portuguese experience of judge-made law and the possibility of prospective intentions and effects. In: Steiner E (ed) Comparing the prospective effect of judicial rulings across jurisdictions, pp 185–201
Llewellyn K (1962) Jurisprudence: realism in theory and practice. The University of Chicago Press, Chicago
MacCormick N (1988) Le raisonnement juridique. Archives de Philosophie du Droit 33
MacCormick N (1997) Legal reasoning and legal theory. Oxford University Press, Oxford
Minda G (1995) Law and literature. In: Minda G (ed) Postmodern legal movements, pp 149–166
Neves A (1993) Metodologia Jurídica. Coimbra Editora, Coimbra
Neves A (1995a) Fontes do Direito. In: Coimbra Editora (eds) Digesta, vol II, pp 7–94

Neves A (1995b) O actual problema metodológico da realização do direito. In: Coimbra Editora (eds) Digesta, vol II, pp 249–282
Neves A (1995c) Método Jurídico. In: Coimbra Editora (eds) Digesta, vol II, pp 283–336
Neves A (1995d) Interpretação Jurídica. In: Coimbra Editora (eds) Digesta, vol II, pp 337–377
Neves A (1999a) Teoria do Direito. mimeo, Coimbra
Neves A (1999b) Apontamentos complementares de Teoria do Direito. mimeo, Coimbra
Núñez Vaquero A (2013) Five models of legal science. Revus 19:53–81
Orrù G (1983) Richterrecht: il problema della libertà e autorità giudiziale nella dottrina tedesca contemporanea. Giuffré, Milan
Orrù G (1988) Lezioni di storia del pensiero teorico-giuridico Moderno. Giappichelli Editore, Torino
Peczenik A (2007) Scientia Juris: legal doctrine as knowledge of law and as a source of law, vol 4. Springer, Dordrecht
Perelman C (1976) Logique juridique: nouvelle rhétorique. Dalloz, Paris
Perelman C (2002) L'empire rhétorique: rhétorique et argumentation. Vrin, Paris
Pintore A (2000) Law without truth. Deborah Charles Publications, Liverpool
Posner R (1998) Law and literature (revised and enlarged edition). Harvard University Press, Cambridge
Posner R (1999) The problems of jurisprudence. Harvard University Press, Cambridge
Puchta G (1838) Lehrbuch der Pandekten. Johann Ambrosius Barth, Leipzig
Schulze R, Seif U (2003) Einführung. In: Schulze R, Seif U (eds) Richterrecht und Rechtsfortbildung in der Euröpaischen Rechtsgemeinschaft, pp 1–27
Tarello G (1962) Il Realismo Giuridico Americano. Giuffré, Milano
Urbina S (2010) Reason, democracy, society: a study on the basis of legal thinking. Kluwer, Dordrecht
Wälde T (1979) Juristische Folgenorientierung. Athenaeum, Frankfurt

Profiling the American Judge: A Comparative Argument About Ideological Conceptions of Judging

Patricio Nazareno

Abstract Most comparative legal scholarship about judging focuses on institutional disparities among legal systems and downplays ideological differences. This essay pursues the opposite emphasis. It explores some traits of the ideological conception of judging typically associated with the American culture so as to show that remarkable differences in the judicial practice between systems may actually persist regardless of the similarities on the institutional plane.

1 Introduction

What accounts for the differences in judging among different legal cultures? Why is certain judicial behavior tolerated or even praised in some systems but criticized in others? These are standard questions for the discipline of comparative law. For the most part, comparative studies of judging attempt to account for disparities in judicial practice among legal systems by underscoring institutional differences: judicial organizational structure, procedural rules, systems for the recruitment of judges, the professional background of the candidates for judgeships, etc. Such a focus on institutional factors does not openly deny that there are ideological disparities as well, yet it tends to push these 'softer' dimensions into a secondary role, at best. This essay pursues the opposite emphasis: it is centered on the premise that each community's judicial practice is to a large extent shaped by (mainstream) ideological conceptions about judging. Conceptions like these of course cover many aspects; yet we will focus on two. One concerns the amount of discretion that judges enjoy as decision-makers given the extent to which the authoritative legal materials constrain them (i.e., the issue of legal indeterminacy); the other advances views about the kind of issues that judges must take into consideration in deciding,

P. Nazareno (✉)
Universidad de San Andrés Law School, Buenos Aires, Argentina

New York University School of Law, New York, NY, USA
e-mail: pnazareno@udesa.edu.ar

N. Bersier et al. (eds.), *Common Law – Civil Law*, Law and Philosophy Library 139,
https://doi.org/10.1007/978-3-030-87718-7_9

given the political role courts supposedly perform. This is a comparative argument insofar as it explores the contrast between systems with respect to the (prevalent) ideological views on these issues and suggests that discrepancies on this dimension account for a great deal of the differences in judicial practice between systems. The aim of the analysis, accordingly, is to help advert the importance of ideology in shaping practices with relative independence from the institutional configurations in place. The idea is to show that, against what some accounts seem to suggest, ideological conceptions are not necessarily tied to certain institutional platforms. As a testing stage for this claim, we will explore the conception of judging developed in the American legal culture.

The present volume is inspired by a challenge to the traditional contrast between civil-law and common-law systems. A seemingly ongoing trend toward institutional convergence seems to cast doubt on whether it is still fitting to think in terms of such a great divide, if there ever was one. Yet, this observation seems to apply to only one of the possible dimensions of a comparative project, namely, one centered on the institutional platform. This chapter's focus on differing ideological conceptions of the judicial practice eludes such challenges on the assumption that these conceptions are to a large extent independent of institutional factors. Consequently, even if institutional features are in a process of convergence, there are reasons to believe that some stark ideological differences persist. The more general purpose of this essay is therefore to invite us to deepen our understanding of the ideological dimension of comparative studies.

2 Comparative Arguments

This essay advances one standard kind of comparative argument. Comparative studies focus on the differences among legal systems and cultures and seek to account for them so that they make sense to observers who are less familiar with some of the systems being compared. One way to achieve this is by revealing contextual connections. Comparative-law scholars thus present the idiosyncratic practices of a given legal system as an anthropological upshot of the particular circumstances of context within which that practice flourishes. The underlying idea is that we understand alien practices, however strange they may look to us at first, by *relating* to them on the basis of our own experience. This occurs when we are able to picture these practices as the byproduct of historical and systemic circumstances that, given our knowledge of comparable social experiences, we believe may have plausibly created the conditions for such traits to develop. Following this template, when it comes to differences in the judicial practice among systems, a standard strategy to make them intelligible to observers is to correlate the features of each practice with underlying, yet more graspable factors that ostensibly vary from one national system to another.

These factors come in two basic kinds. (1) One first group may be referred to as each system's 'hardware' and is made up of the tangible institutional features that demarcate the overall conditions for the exercise of the judicial function (e.g., mechanisms of judicial appointment, incentives for career advancement within the judiciary, judicial bureaucratic organization, rules of procedure, etc.). (2) The other kind of factor concerns each legal culture's 'software,' so to speak, and alludes to the general beliefs about how judging can and should be carried out that inform the participants' engagement in that practice (e.g., the dominant ideological conceptions about how the law actually works and what counts as a proper exercise of the judicial function). Needless to say, both types of components, institutional and ideological, are inseparably tied and interdependent within every legal system—just like hardware and software in computing, to follow the analogy. Institutional arrangements inspire ideological conceptions and, in turn, ideology guides the practices that institutions are set to channel and serves as a source of ideas for institutional reform. We conceive the legal practice as a historical product because we understand it as the result of this synergic dynamic throughout time. Hence, sophisticated comparative law explanations are generally complex enough as to incorporate factors of both kinds, or at least not to dismiss any of them as irrelevant. Nevertheless, in the present Section I want to draw attention to the way in which these (holistic) explanations typically negotiate the balance between factors of each kind, since this might turn problematic. As we shall see, the fact that most comparative accounts accentuate 'hardware' factors over 'software' factors introduces a noticeable slant regarding the connection between ideology and institutional features.

2.1 *Accentuating* Hardware*: Institutional Differences*

The prevalent form of argument in comparative studies about judging explores the connections between this practice and underlying *institutional* factors. The basic assumption is that in every given system the judicial practice and the role of courts are highly dependent on the institutional framework that serves as their foundation. Accordingly, comparativists aspire to illuminate a fair amount of the differences between the judicial practices in two systems through an account of whatever it is that distinguishes these systems on the institutional plane. Comparative studies that advance these arguments contribute to our knowledge in two ways. First, they make legal cultures understandable by sketching and characterizing them in relation to one another, which is especially useful for observers who are familiar with at least one of the cultures compared. Second, yet equally as important, studies like these provide insights into *our own* legal culture by shedding light on correlations between our practice and particular institutional features that would probably go unnoticed were it not for the contrast with other systems. Although comparative scholars that explore the institutional dimension have made major contributions on both accounts, I am of the view that arguments that focus heavily on institutional factors present downsides in relation to each one of these aims.

First and foremost, emphasizing 'hardware' actually provides a somewhat distorted picture of legal culture. This comes via the misleading notion that this perspective conveys about the role of ‘software,’ even when it does not explicitly address the impact of this other factor. Of course, accounts that underscore institutional differences among legal systems do not deny (and occasionally acknowledge) that there are ideological dissimilarities playing their part as well. Still, because both kinds of factors are intertwined, disregarding ideology as peripheral to the explanation amounts at minimizing its actual influence on the legal practice. In fact, accentuating institutional features suggests that the agents’ ideological conceptions emerge in connection with, and stay attached to, institutional configurations—the implicit assumption being that if institutional features were to vary, ideology would eventually follow. The institutional-centered focus is thus problematic because it obscures the fact that ideological conceptions are to a significant extent independent from institutional arrangements, which leads to neglecting the twist that ideology puts on legal practices regardless of the institutional platforms in place. A brief review of some classic examples will help clarify the point.[1]

Patrick Atiyah and Robert Summers have written the single most influential book comparing the legal cultures and systems of England and the United States (Atiyah and Summers 1987). Their main thesis is that the legal practices in these countries can, all in all, be characterized fairly differently within a ‘formalistic/substantivistic’ spectrum, which largely confirms the “widespread, and [in their opinion] well-founded, view that the English legal system is more formal than the American” (Atiyah and Summers 1987, p. 32).[2] Although Atiyah and Summers frequently engage ideological aspects, these can always be traced to institutional features. Indeed, many of the differences they report with respect to courts and judges are presented in terms of ideology: for example, the fact that “American judges in courts of last resort actually perceive their function differently from English judges,” that “American courts are willing to perform many functions which in other countries would fall to the legislature,” and that “English courts would certainly reject the idea that courts ought to be initiators of social change” (Atiyah and Summers 1987, pp. 268, 270, 275). However, in the view of the authors, these attitudes emerge in correlation with institutional features, like the kind of individuals that become judges, their social and professional background, the incentives that dictate their career advancement, and the design of the bureaucratic structure in which they work (Atiyah and Summers 1987, pp. 267–297, 336–354). Atiyah and Summers’ findings on legal indeterminacy provide a concrete example. The authors report that “the indeterminacy of rules in the English system is far less acute than it is in the United States” and attempt to explain why this is the case (Atiyah and Summers 1987, p. 355). Atiyah and Summers begin by drawing a connection between this disparity and a strong ideological factor, namely, that “English judges believe in rules more

[1] Of course this brief review does not purport to cover the extensive literature on the topic in a couple of paragraphs. I selected only a few examples—to which I cannot even do justice—that are quite influential and that I believe illustrate the institutional-centered perspective and its difficulties.

[2] Nonetheless, the authors add the following caveat: “The English legal system is not nearly as formal as many American lawyers think, and the American system relies far more on formal reasoning than many English lawyers believe” (Atiyah and Summers 1987, p. 32).

than American judges [do]" (1987, p. 355). Now, at the same time, the authors also underscore institutional features, most notably, that in England the "[l]aw is more often formulated in terms of rules" and "[t]here is wider agreement about the criteria for determining the validity of rules" than in the American legal system (Atiyah and Summers 1987, p. 355). Therefore, when the argument is considered globally, the conclusion seems to be that institutional factors alone account for the differences regarding legal indeterminacy, and that the judges' beliefs about how indeterminate the law is are simply a foreseeable effect of such institutional arrangements.

Mirjan Damaška's landmark study on comparative legal process advances an argument with a similar slant (Damaška 1986). As part of his comprehensive exploration of legal cultures, Damaška seeks to account for the fact that (mainstream) practices of judicial decision-making found in comparative law assign different roles —and, in a way, also different weight—to legal norms. Indeed, as the author reminds us, while "[c]ontinental judges are ideally still expected to anchor their decisions in a network of outcome-determinative rules," American courts are "expected to consider 'the equities' of cases so that the door remains open to the consideration of various extralegal factors" (Damaška 1986, p. 68). Damaška believes that these differences can be captured with a distinction between "two modal variations of legalism"—namely, "logical" and "pragmatic" (1986, pp. 22–23). Surely enough, this classification brings to light a contrast that largely concerns ideology, as it reveals that lawyers in different latitudes hold different working conceptions of the role of legal norms in judging (Damaška 1986, pp. 8–9, 28, 31). Nonetheless, in Damaška's account, modes of reasoning like these are presented as if they emerged as a consequence of—or at least in direct connection to—institutional platforms. The core of the explanation hinges on alternative designs for the organization of state authority, especially regarding the coordination of state officials, and there are also references to institutionally defined practices, like the systems of civil-law legislation and common-law precedent, which either constrain or foster judicial creativity (Damaška 1986, pp. 9–10, 22–23, 42–43, 46). For an additional example, Mitchel Lasser (2004) has tackled the drastic differences in judicial argumentative style that stand out when comparing the opinion writing by American and French courts. And here again, although such a stark contrast would suggest a major ideological gap separating both cultures, most of the explanation rests on institutional pillars like the judiciary's organization, its modes of professional control, and the judges' position either as part of a bureaucratic elite or not, which set in motion different legitimation-seeking arrangements (Lasser 2004).

Yet there is another major drawback of accounts that accentuate 'hardware.' Arguments along these lines have become trendy in comparative legal scholarship to the point where one can claim that the slanted view they advance has restricted our chances of learning from, and being challenged by, comparative observation. In order to grasp this second difficulty we must bear in mind that, besides informing about foreign systems, comparative studies also contribute—somehow indirectly—to our general views on legal culture. Indeed, comparative insights into alien systems have an impact on how we come to see our own system (even when not featured in the comparison) because they open our eyes to the fact that legal practices are contingent. This challenges an intuition that is common among participants in every practice, according to which the features of one's own system are seen as more deeply engrained than they really are. The more sophisticated view of legal culture comes as a natural consequence of having enriched our understanding with the addition of a comparative perspective. Now, there is no doubt that comparative arguments that draw heavily on institutional factors may very well induce this comparative experience. Take the simplest of examples. Through comparative exploration we may eventually realize that some foreign institutional arrangements provide better solutions than ours to similar issues; one would then hope that such a finding would have us wonder whether our institutions are worth maintaining or if we should strive for their reform, perhaps even via legal transplants (Langbein 1985). Still, accounts that emphasize 'hardware' are problematic in one general sense: in portraying legal practices as primarily in connection with institutional factors, the literature within this trend confines the comparative experience to the institutional plane alone. To me, this looks like a missed opportunity. Imagine that we are confronted with the fact that alien legal cultures are characterized by ideological conceptions about the law different from the ones we hold, should this not trigger some questioning over our own conceptions analogous to the one described for our legal institutions? Well, the truth is that emphasizing 'hardware' inadvertently prevents an equivalent comparative experience in relation to ideology. As noted earlier, one of the effects of downplaying 'software' is to suggest that ideological conceptions are for the most part dependent on institutional configurations. This means that whenever comparative studies come up with intriguing findings regarding ideology that are felt especially disruptive, these can be conveniently dismissed if there are also institutional differences to account for. In fact, one may venture to say that one of the reasons why comparative accounts gravitate toward arguments where institutional factors outshine ideology is that these reaffirm the suitability of the observers' own ideological conceptions. Avoiding ideological comparisons seems reassuring to participants of any practice, as it seems natural that we try to shield our own ideological commitments from questioning.

2.2 *Attentiveness to* Software*: Contrasting Ideologies*

Focusing on ideology as a main factor (i.e., as explanans) to account for cultural variations provides an alternative twist to comparative arguments that may solve the two difficulties mentioned. But make no mistake: paying proper attention to 'software' neither neglects the role of institutional factors, nor ignores that ideology can itself be accounted for (i.e., as explanandum) by some other factors, institutional ones among them. Still, the fact that one can surely draw connections between ideological conceptions and institutional developments—as in, say, noting how the latter have inspired the former—does not entail a commitment to the view that ideology's influence on the legal practice is somewhat redundant, as if 'hardware' configurations rigorously dictated the conceptions that practitioners hold. It is precisely this institutionalist bias that the accent on 'software' strives to avoid. The first step in this direction is to conceive of the legal practice as the result of the steering of a specific institutional platform by ideologically informed agents. Certainly, this standpoint may encourage us to hypothesize that the impact of ideology—vis-à-vis that of 'hardware' factors—should be most noticeable when accounting for the differences between the judicial practices in systems that share similar institutional settings. And perhaps it is indeed the case that some comparative case studies lend themselves better to underscoring the impact of 'software.' (For instance, comparisons that consider systems like some in Latin America, whose judicial institutions are similar to those in the United States, and yet the ideological conceptions that lawyers hold seem closer to those dominant in Europe). Still, because legal cultures are inherently complex and unique, any attempt to isolate the impact of ideology through some ideally set case study appears hopeless. My suggestion is much more subtle. I only wish to warn against the prevalent impulse to account for every comparative disparity by means of an institutional contrast, so as to avoid depictions where ideological factors appear crowded out by institutional ones.

The ideological dimension comes up routinely, even if not in a fully articulated manner, when comparing the characteristic legal cultures of different systems. Reviewing the reactions of American observers to foreign legal cultures will help provide some flavor. American scholars frequently use the label "formalist" to characterize legal reasoning, scholarly styles, legal culture, and even ideology. The notion, however recurrent as a term of criticism, is hard to define with precision (Hart 1992, p. 297), and at times it is difficult to present examples from within the American legal culture that fit the description (Dworkin 1977, pp. 15–16). Still, its use in connection with the comparative cultural context tends to be fairly accepted among American observers and comparative scholars, since many believe it "helps make sense" of what goes on in other major jurisdictions (Leiter 2010, p. 128).[3] As has been pointed out, any "ordinary American lawyer is likely to find European solutions to classic legal problems blatantly formalist, in the sense of overestimating the power of deduction, and to find European culture in general formalist in the same sense" (Kennedy 1997, p. 107). For the same reason, American academics seem for the most part surprised that the approach to legal scholarship "as an internally valid, autonomous, and self-justifying science" embodied in doctrinal legal studies, which "is rarely seen in current American legal education," "still has much vitality" among "those trained in certain European and other foreign legal systems" (Pildes 1999, p. 609).

Some speculate that the foundation for such a stark contrast is a form of "skepticism about taking rules and their formulations too seriously" that is a "central theme of American legal thought [and] distinguishes [it] not only from a central

[3]This is thought especially helpful when contrasting American legal culture with those foreign cultures "where the law is still standardly taught from black-letter treatises written by the leading scholars" (Leiter 2010, p. 129).

aspect of civil law ideology . . ., but from the more formal . . . legal thinking in most common law countries not located in North America" (Schauer 2011, pp. 26–27). Something similar to this "skeptical" view can be traced back to O.W. Holmes Jr.'s writings in the late nineteenth Century (Holmes 1881, 1897) and seems to have peaked in the early decades of the twentieth Century with the arrival of Legal Realism. At the core of these ideas is the rejection of a strand of legal thought that believes that the law regulates social life rather comprehensively, that it is the job of judges to find the legally correct solution to cases (even when this might be hard to do) by reasoning down from legal rules and principles, and that the mission of scholars is to identify and articulate legal doctrine as clearly as possible to assist lawyers and judges in this task. Some American scholars curiously believed that these "formalistic" views were alien to the American legal tradition (even if held by quite a few prominent scholars back in the day) and that they had been transplanted from continental Europe. For instance, Herman Oliphant, a prominent Legal Realist, considered orthodox legal thought to be "nearer to the work of continental theorists than that of the patient particularists who were [American] early judges and scholars" (1928, p. 221). It is interesting that he thought this scholarly style had appeared in the United States as the result of "[g]reat cargoes of continental speculations . . . imported and thrown in" after "[a] wave of continental learning [had] swept over England, leaving a thick deposit of its obscurant abstractions" (Oliphant 1928, pp. 221–222). Along these lines, in recent times, some have advanced revisionist views about the Realist attack on formalistic thought that make the comparative dimension even more relevant. The claim is that the very accounts of what the Realist Movement presented as American "formalism" actually relied largely on fragments by European authors describing civil-law systems (Tamanaha 2010, pp. 4, 24–26).

Again, my point is not that comparative accounts have been entirely oblivious to the importance of such a strong ideological component. The difficulty arises, rather, from the secondary role that is too often assigned to it. Atiyah and Summers' work provides a case in point. In fact, these authors do hypothesize about the importance of ideological "visions" of law and conclude their study by succinctly speculating that these conceptions may have shaped legal practices in multiple ways (Atiyah and Summers 1987, pp. 4–5, 411–415).[4] However, as discussed before, this only comes as a marginal addendum to a lengthy analysis that prioritizes institutional explanations throughout (Atiyah and Summers 1987, pp. 3–4, 32–35), and presents institutional contrasts as absorbing the ideological disparities that recurrently pop up. Arguments that focus more directly on the ideological dimension may prevent

[4] Atiyah and Summers even present their work as an attempt "to explain the relationship between Realism and various institutional aspects of the American legal system" (1987, p. vii). The ideological dimension is most central in their consideration of the role of legal academia. Indeed, these authors acknowledge that the leading American law schools "ha[ve] played a major role in shaping the substantive character of the modern American legal system" by having "served as a major source—nay, *the* major source—of influential ideas about appropriate legal method" (Atiyah and Summers 1987, pp. 384, 405).

this bias. Accentuating ideological differences reasserts the (independent) influence that 'software' exerts on the legal practice by avoiding the dilution of the ideological dimension, yet without necessarily overlooking the complexity of the scheme of factors at play. Moreover, besides keeping comparisons more balanced, this tweak fosters another major contribution of comparative studies by encouraging deeper introspection into the observer's own system. Just as foreign institutional arrangements may cast doubt on the soundness or convenience of our own institutions, alternative ideological conceptions about the law which cannot be summarily dismissed for being the upshot of institutional eccentricities should at least spark a conversation about our own conceptions.

In the remainder of this essay, I will advance an argument that fits this template. My claim is that there is an interesting comparative point in the conceptions of the judicial office that are prevalent in the civil-law world and the American common-law culture.

3 The American Paradigm of Judging

Discussions about judges and the law in the United States show a distinctive peculiarity. For the most part, American scholars approach the legal phenomenon by focusing on courts of appellate review: they analyze appellate reported opinions, consider the appellate docket, and try to elucidate the way in which appellate judges decide cases. This appears to have been the case for well over one hundred years. As far back as 1930, Karl Llewellyn warned law students of what he thought was "the most important matter" they should be aware of in their encounter with legal education, namely, "the almost hopeless bias of all present and past discussion about law" implicit in the scholarly focus on "almost nothing else" but upper courts (Llewellyn 1930, p. 94). Decades later, Abe Chayes reported that "in the academic debate about the judicial function, the protagonist was the appellate judge . . . and the spotlight of teaching, writing, and analysis was almost exclusively on appellate decisions" (1976, p. 1285). More recent literature reviews show the same appellate-centered trend for a variety of scholarly approaches, ranging from theoretical accounts based on a certain image of the rationality of judicial decision-makers (Schlag 1991, pp. 1667–1668) to empirical studies on judicial behavior (Epstein 2016, pp. 2041–2050). Now, this does not mean that American scholars have forgone all epistemic ambitions over other realms of the legal practice. It does nonetheless hint at the fact that appellate decision-making has acquired the status of a paradigm in relation to the legal practice. This Section purports to explore how this distinctive perspective has shaped American scholars' ideological conceptions about judging and the law in general.

My purpose here is to report on the scholarly focus on appellate courts, not to suggest that it has been unfortunate. That such a perspective has been so prevalent in American thinking about law is not only a most interesting anthropological fact, but also one that can only be fully appreciated from a comparative standpoint. Observers well versed on different legal cultures have sporadically highlighted the feature. For instance, Frederick Schauer has noted that, aside from the importance that the judicial function has secured in legal cultures worldwide, "only in the United States could theories of law be so commonly conflated with theories of appellate adjudication…, law is all about hard cases, and conflicting theories of law turn out to be conflicting theories of how American appellate judges should decide the hard cases that come before them" (1988, p. 1717). Similarly, a scholar raised in another common-law jurisdiction such as HLA Hart once remarked that he felt an impulse to depict American legal thought as "marked by a concentration, almost to the point of obsession, on the judicial process, that is, with what courts do and should do, how judges reason and should reason in deciding particular cases" (1977, p. 969). Hart attributed the phenomenon to "the quite extraordinary role that the courts, above all the United States Supreme Court, play in American government" (1977, p. 970). The reactions by Hart and Schauer are indicative of how much of an outlier the American approach to law and judging is in the context of comparable legal cultures. Both authors seem astonished at the discrepancy. Moreover, there is a crucial underlying premise worth noting: the basis for their surprise is that both take as a given that the institutional platforms for the exercise of the judicial function in the United States and the other comparable cultures are basically the same.

The reasons for this appellate-centered focus are multiple, and some are undoubtedly related to institutional features. Common-law systems are to a large extent dependent on judge-made law through the pronouncements of higher courts, which have precedential authority even when interpreting statutes. It is certainly understandable that institutional features like these justify the "professional and scholarly concern on adjudication at the appellate level, for only there [does] the process reach beyond the immediate parties to achieve a wider import through the elaboration of generally applicable legal rules" (Chayes 1976, p. 1285). On the other hand, as Hart's referred astonishment implies, the appellate-centered perspective has not really emerged in common-law jurisdictions outside of North America. We may thus speculate that the true reasons are perhaps more idiosyncratic, and point to the paramount role that courts of review have historically played in the American legal system, for which they are highly regarded by the legal profession (Llewellyn 1960, pp. 3–4). But there are also factors more mundane. The simple fact that only appellate opinions were readily available in published volumes of reports made access to this material possible, which created a sort of cognitive bias toward the work of upper courts (Llewellyn 1930, p. 95). Judicial prestige and availability in print contributed to make of the appellate opinion a paramount historical document, the importance of which extends even beyond strictly legal studies (White 2010, pp. 47–62).

Arguably the most crucial step toward the enthronement of this perspective came via the institution of a new model for American legal education. Over the last decades of the nineteenth century, Harvard Law School's inaugural Dean, Christopher C. Langdell, introduced pedagogic novelties that redefined the canon of law school instruction in ways that persist fundamentally unaltered to this day (Kimball 2009). Langdell's take on *the aims* of legal education appears fairly conventional. In his view, for students to become "true lawyer[s]," they must develop the ability to apply the "principles or doctrines" that the law "consists of" to "the ever-tangled skein of human affairs" (Langdell 1871, p. vi). In other words, to Langdell, good law school education should aim at teaching students both what the actual rules command and how to think like lawyers. Now, when it comes to *the means* through which law school instruction is to accomplish these goals, Langdell's approach was truly groundbreaking. The driving force behind Langdell's program was his "conviction that law could only be taught or learned effectively by means of cases" (1871, p. v). Among the few innovations he implemented, the one that stands out the most is clearly the so-called Socratic method (or 'case' method), which radically transformed the protocol of classroom instruction. Yet the novelty I wish to highlight is one that accompanied this new teaching technique, that is, the significant changes in study materials that provided the basis for such renewed classroom dynamic. Langdell distrusted that students could gain professional competence by learning legal doctrines from the highly processed articulation that traditional treatises put forward. Instead, he thought that "the subject alike of study and instruction" should be the cases contained in the books of reports themselves, because "the shortest and best, if not the only way of mastering the doctrine effectually is by studying the cases in which it is embodied" (Langdell 1871, pp. v–vi). Now, Langdell also qualified this statement by pointing out that "the cases which are useful and necessary for this purpose [of systematic study] at the present day bear an exceedingly small proportion to all that have been reported" (1871, p. vi), which justified him in compiling the "*Selections* of Cases" (later known as 'casebooks') that would progressively displace traditional treatises as the core material for legal instruction.[5]

Langdell thus installed the appellate opinion as the main platform for analyzing and studying law. His reasons for opting for judicial pronouncements were twofold: not only did judicial opinions embody lawyerly logic in action, but also the appellate decisions were themselves the source of the substantive doctrines that students were expected to learn. As one would imagine, however, such a drastic change concerning study materials also had collateral effects that neither Langdell nor his immediate followers seem to have looked for or even anticipated. Exposition-wise, treatises and appellate judgments provide very different pictures of the law in action. Legal treatises tend to accentuate doctrinal harmony and stability by assembling the array of factual situations that the law already covers. By contrast, leading-case appellate opinions frequently expose the legal materials' defects, like recurrent gaps, contradictions, ambiguities, and lack of clarity, and show judges exercising a creative role in order to overcome these hurdles. No doubt, two conceptions of how the law works would look miles apart from one another if each took only one of these partial perspectives as paradigmatic. The Langdellian preference for judicial

[5]The impact of this innovation was significant. For example, while students of contracts would have typically studied from treatises like those by Story (1847) or Parsons (1853), after the Langdellian model spread casebooks became the primary material for instruction (although Langdell himself anticipated the occasional need for hornbooks in the form of "summaries").

cases seems to have ignited a process of change in the American legal mindset, consisting in a gradual shift from a paradigm chiefly based on the former perspective toward another where the latter one prevails. Some speculate that this law-specific shift came as part of a larger trend in American thought (White 1957). Be as it may, one of the most interesting aspects of this shift in American legal conceptions is that, because most legal cultures outside of the United States still maintain a fairly traditional mindset, its repercussions are especially, if not mostly, visible from a comparative standpoint.[6]

The appellate-centered focus comes so naturally to the American scholar that it is highlighted only occasionally and in general to criticize it for its limitations. Two evident concerns have been raised about it (although frequently in an undistinguishable manner). The first is that such a heavy focus on the appellate review simply neglects other important aspects of the legal practice. The law plays important roles in ways not directly connected to litigation and, moreover, even when courts do intervene, most of the times lawsuits do not advance beyond the trial level. There are thus plenty of reasons to find the partiality of the "picture [that is rendered by] this study of appellate courts alone" particularly problematic (Llewellyn 1930, p. 96). For instance, if we believe, alongside scholars interested in the 'law in action,' that the "[l]aw *is*, to the community, what law *does*," then such a straight disregard of the "mountain of the cases *un*appealed" makes it difficult to provide a measure of the law's "impact . . . on society—even within the realm of litigation" (Llewellyn 1930, p. 95). In a similar vein, the bias toward the work of appellate courts has been blamed for the fact that certain major developments in trial litigation and procedure have gone long unnoticed (Chayes 1976, pp. 1285–1288). In sum, the first difficulty of the appellate review bias is that it causes blind spots over areas of the legal landscape that scholars are supposed to have a direct interest in.

Yet there is also a second problem that is even more consequential. It is one thing to have a limited understanding of the law because the information available covers the phenomenon only partially, yet quite another that this partial knowledge leads to misrepresenting the practice because "the available bulks as if it were the whole" (Llewellyn 1930, p. 95). That is to say, the appellate-centered perspective may affect our comprehension of legal phenomena not only by keeping our attention away from important legal realms, but also by distorting our perception of those neglected realms via unwarranted extrapolation. The danger is for legal analysts to believe that they are knowledgeable about something only on the basis of the knowledge they do have about related phenomena, yet without establishing that the part of the thing they know about is representative of the whole. As early as 1930, Llewellyn himself identified this problem in his landmark book *The Bramble Bush*:

[6]In line with this shift, some have speculated that the American scholar's "affinity for case law" could perhaps explain why she "has displayed so little interest in European legal speculation" (Fuller 1934, p. 438).

> You find me trying to analyze the work of "courts" and "judges"—criticizing here, moved there to admiration. What judges? *Judges of appellate courts*. You find me dealing with "the law" and what it is and does. I say its center is the action of officials, *all* law officials—and no sooner say it than I slip off my own platform to land for lecture after lecture in discussion purely of these courts of high review: what *they* do. . . . We can, too, call attention, now and again, to the limitations of the picture thus set up [by legal scholars]. But we cannot keep the picture from distortion, as you go more and more deeply into a single part of it, neglecting all the others (Llewellyn 1930, pp. 94–96).

Llewellyn knew well that the sample of legal events he routinely had under consideration was unrepresentative of what courts do, how judges think, and how the law works, and yet he candidly acknowledged that this circumstance did not prevent legal scholars—even those aware of the difficulty like himself—from ascribing their conclusions to *all* courts, judges *in general*, and *the* law. What this suggests is that, by virtue of unwarranted extrapolations, the appellate-centered focus has frequently had implications as to the way in which American scholars conceive of judging and the law. This takes place via the practice of appellate decision-making acquiring the status of a paradigm for the social practice of law, even when most accept that "appellate cases are hardly representative of legal events" (Schauer 1988, p. 1720).

In what follows, I will explore two features that I believe exemplify well how the appellate-centered focus has led American scholars to conceive of the practice of judging in a distinctive way. One of these features concerns the perception of how much legal indeterminacy there is; the other presents a view of the judicial role as encompassing functions that would be more typically associated with a political office.

3.1 Legal Indeterminacy

Legal indeterminacy is a common, inescapable feature of legal systems at least at the level of positive rules. Authoritative legal materials determine outcomes, but they simply cannot cover all the possible cases that may come up (Hart 1992, pp. 124–130). Even those who reject this positivist stance accept the rough classification of cases into easy and hard, on the basis of how the available legal norms govern the situation at hand (Dworkin 1977, p. 81). My first point concerns the remarkable influence that the appellate-review bias has over the general perception of how ubiquitous legal indeterminacy actually is. Indeed, it seems reasonable to believe, as Ken Kress notes, that "[p]reoccupation with controversial appellate and Supreme Court cases engenders the illusion of pervasive indeterminacy. Focusing instead on everyday acts governed by law reveals the pervasiveness of determinate and correct legal outcomes" (Kress 1989, p. 296). Still, aside from this basic intuition, can an argument be made about the impact that the appellate-centered focus so prevalent in the American legal culture has had on the consideration of the issue of legal indeterminacy?

Comparative observers have pointed out that American lawyers and scholars seem to magnify the problem of legal indeterminacy (e.g., Maxeiner 2006). One cannot address the issue of legal indeterminacy in American legal thought without reference to the Legal Realist movement, whose members' advancement of strong views on this topic helped them make a name for themselves during the 1920s and 1930s. The Realists' arguments were surely controversial to a majority of traditionally minded legal scholars, who felt these new ideas directly challenged their scholarly methods (Schlegel 1995, p. 11; Moore 2000, p. 36). Yet, in due time these disruptive views seem to have become considerably influential, to the point where an important number of American scholars since the last decades of the 20th century identify themselves (quite imprecisely) as being "all Realists now" and, even more perceptibly, most American elite scholarship seems highly influenced by Realist tenets (Simpson 1981, pp. 677–678; Langbein 1998, p. 62). Indeed, judging by the impact that the Realist challenge had on American legal culture in comparison with other latitudes, it is understandable that American observers would think it to be "an American exclusive, [which] had no counterpart in England or in the European countries" (Gilmore 1961, p. 1047). Yet this is only partly true: critical views on judging similar to those held by American Legal Realists were certainly articulated in the main European civil-law jurisdictions, although not even remotely as influentially as in the United States (Dawson 1968, pp. 416–431, 480–502). This comparative contrast provides an interesting insight to understand the role of Realism in shaping the American ideological conception of judging (*compare* Atiyah and Summers 1987, p. vii).

There are at least two important discussions on legal indeterminacy. One is conceptual, and turns on whether legal norms are actually capable of regulating conduct and, if so, whether the law covers all possible cases or if it eventually runs out leaving gaps. Thereafter, a second point of divergence assumes certain mainstream answers to the conceptual questions and tackles the quantitative dimension of the problem: namely, how much determinacy vis-à-vis indeterminacy there is. In contrast to the philosophical orientation of the first questions, this second inquiry seems to be framed more directly as an empirical matter. As for the Legal Realist contributions to these discussions, members of the movement advanced arguments pertaining to both of these discussions. Nonetheless, they are most famous for their controversial stance in response to the second-order inquiry, that is, the well-known Realist claim that legal indeterminacy is a pervasive phenomenon. This Realist stance is better understood when compared with the divergent opinions of authors who hold first-order conceptual views similar to those of the Legal Realists about indeterminacy being inescapable—most notably, Benjamin Cardozo and (later in time) HLA Hart.[7] These jurists disagree with the Legal Realists as to *how much*

[7] Cardozo was not shy to proclaim that there are cases that "might be decided either way [because] reasons plausible and fairly persuasive might be found for one conclusion as for another"—"uncertainty" that he believed was "inevitable" (1921, pp. 165–66). It is here, where "judicial judgment moves untrammeled by fixed principles," that "the judge assumes the function of a lawgiver" (Cardozo 1921, pp. 128, 166). Indeed, in Cardozo's view, the fact that the legal materials

indeterminacy is to be found out there. Against Realism, Cardozo's view is that "[n] ine-tenths, perhaps more, of the cases that come before a court are predetermined—predetermined in the sense that they are predestined—their fate preëstablished by inevitable laws that follow them from birth to death" (Cardozo 1924, p. 60). In other words, although Cardozo accepts it to be undeniable that courts "have the right to legislate within gaps," he believes that "often there are no gaps" for them to legitimately exercise this power because, "[i]n countless litigations, the law is so clear that judges have no discretion" (1921, p. 129). Similarly, to Hart, "the life of the law consists to a very large extent in the guidance of both officials and private individuals by determinate rules..., even though uncertainties may break out as to the applicability of any rule ... to a concrete case ... at the margin of rules" (1992, p. 135). In contrast to moderate views like these, Llewellyn reports that one of the major achievements of Realism was, precisely, to debunk "the traditional pretense or belief (sometimes the one, sometimes the other) that there is no such area of uncertainty, or that it is much smaller than it is" (Llewellyn 1931, p. 1251).[8]

So Legal Realism's signature claim regarding the amount of legal indeterminacy is that it is pervasive. But how is the appellate-centered paradigm relevant to this discussion? The connection is easier to grasp once we understand how the debate unfolds. As noted, the quantitative question about indeterminacy is phrased in terms of an empirical inquiry, namely, as if the issue could be ultimately settled through scientifically suitable methods. Still, because such research would be too costly (if at all possible!), the arguments presented by all camps hardly ever move past anecdotal evidence or some incipient unsystematic empiricism, which may at best serve to make a prima facie case for each position. In other words, the different takes on the issue typically remain speculative in a sense analogous to Bertrand Russell's famous characterization of philosophical inquiry:

> Philosophy is that part of science which at present people choose to have opinions about, but which they have no knowledge about. Therefore, every advance in knowledge robs philosophy of some problems which formerly it had ... and will belong to science (Russell 1918, p. 281).

---

have left "the law unsettled ... cast[s] a duty upon the courts to declare it retrospectively in the exercise of a power frankly legislative in function" (1921, p. 128). Hart's argument on core and penumbra of legal rules is well known (Hart 1992, pp. 124–136).

[8]There are plenty of passages by Realist authors (and by their predecessors) on this issue. Anticipating the Realist Movement, Oliver W. Holmes believed that "[b]ehind the logical form [of judicial opinions] lies a judgment as to the relative worth and importance of competing legislative grounds ... You can give any conclusion a logical form" (1897, p. 466). In similar spirit, after wondering whether judges were "free of all control, thanks to the leeway offered by the ambiguities of [their] material," Karl Llewellyn claimed that, "by way of logic the strong judge can scale those walls ... his predecessors built" (i.e. controlling precedent) "when in his judgment that is needed" (1930, p. 77). Jerome Frank also pointed out that, every time a judge considers a dispute, she "can decide one way or the other and in either case can make [her] reasoning appear equally flawless" (1930, p. 66).

Positions on the amount of legal indeterminacy to be found out there are by and large *opinions* that we express in lieu of the knowledge we lack. Moreover, these opinions are rather clumsily ascribed to "the law" in general, missing the nuance that is standard of empirically verifiable claims (*compare* Schauer 2009, pp. 139–141; Schauer 2013, pp. 773–778). To my eyes, these facets reveal that the true nature of the views put forward is fundamentally ideological. It thus seems appropriate to wonder how it is that those who present such claims came to believe them and, subsequently, why a given audience would find views like these convincing. My thesis is that the appellate-centered focus is a crucial factor in considering both questions. For one, the Realists reached their assessments on indeterminacy on the basis of observations of appellate cases. What is more, one can speculate that the fact that appellate decision-making reached a sort of paradigmatic status—to which Realist scholarship surely contributed—may reasonably explain why Realist views ended up being so influential in the United States.

There are few doubts that the Realists' views on the law and its indeterminacy were inspired by, and based almost exclusively on, evidence drawn from *appellate* cases. This is clear from Llewellyn's authoritative review of Realist literature.[9] Indeed, Llewellyn notes how Realist authors "brought their batteries to bear in first instance on the work of appellate courts" (1931, pp. 1238, 1246). Consequently, this meant that most of the Realists' findings (up to then, at least) pertained to that realm—among these, the development of "more accurate reformulations of what appellate courts are doing and may be expected to do," including a revised assessment on the existence and scope of legal "uncertainty" (Llewellyn 1931, pp. 1251–1252). Now, there seem to be good reasons to believe that such an appellate-centered focus would expectedly cause a cognitive bias that misleads analysts regarding legal indeterminacy. This is the crux of Cardozo's criticism of this view. The then-Judge warned that, although legal indeterminacy is a marginal phenomenon, one could "easily seem to exaggerate it through excess of emphasis" (Cardozo 1924, p. 60), which would amount to "let[ting] these occasional and relatively rare instances blind our eyes to the innumerable instances where there is neither obscurity nor collision nor opportunity for diverse judgment" (Cardozo 1921, p. 128).[10] To Cardozo, this misleading emphasis "is likely to give a false impression, an overcolored picture, of uncertainty in the law and of free discretion in the judge" (1921, p. 164).

The most common explanation for why this may be the case is based on what we today know as the *selection effect* (Priest and Klein 1984). This alludes to the joint action of institutional and informal mechanisms connected to the judicial process, which create incentives and set in place hard constraints that in fact determine the *kinds* of disputes that in the end may make it to the courts. This idea highlights the

[9]Llewellyn does warn us that his review of Realism might be biased toward appellate courts because this was "his own main interest of the moment" (1931, p. 1235).

[10]A few lines below, Cardozo insisted: "We shall have a false view of the landscape if we look at the waste spaces only, and refuse to see the acres already sown and fruitful" (Cardozo 1921, p. 129).

fact that there are reasons to believe that the appellate docket provides a misleading picture of how the law works, especially regarding the clarity with which legal materials establish what the law requires. This is due to a combination of filters that work 'selecting' disputes for litigation and appeal. A *first filter* segregates the cases that are litigated from those that are not. The notion is quite intuitive: for the parties to decide to go through litigation and the expenses involved, each needs to believe that their own case has reasonable chances of prevailing. In other words, the issue in dispute has to be significantly open with regard to either the law or the facts—or both.[11] Thereafter, a *second filter* applies to the subset of litigated cases and separates them into two groups: those where the parties settle for the first court judgment on the merits and those that are appealed to an upper court. Compared to the first filter, this second one implements more complex selection criteria, in combining the cost/benefit considerations regarding the additional expenses related to the appeal and the procedural constraints that limit or preclude upper courts from reviewing questions of fact (which happens at some point of the court hierarchy in every legal system, either at the appellate level or higher up the ladder). The effect of this second filter seems to be that, in practice, only cases where the law is dubious enough will eventually continue to be litigated before an upper court.

The overlapping action of both filters leads us to think about cases in three different tiers: (i) non-litigated, (ii) litigated yet not appealed, and (iii) appealed. If the scheme works as described, a significant variation in legal indeterminacy is to be expected from one pool of cases to the next one. The underlying idea is that disputes where legal norms are largely determinative of the outcome (i.e., 'easy' cases) have fewer chances of being litigated and, when they so happen to be, the first judgment on the merits will rarely be appealed. As a result of this process of selection, the docket of upper courts will show a relatively disproportionate concentration of cases where the law is indeterminate (i.e., 'hard' cases). Therefore, it is reasonable to expect that the questions that judges—and, even more so, *appellate* judges—are presented with make up an unrepresentative sample of how the legal materials work more broadly in governing social life (Leiter 2007, pp. 12, 77). The idea is fairly intuitive. So much so that—curiously enough—even a few Legal Realists seem to have been aware of this dynamic of selection and its impact. Llewellyn himself—though in a manuscript only published recently—noticed that the problem of having to deal with rules that are "not in fact available in very guidesome form . . . happens

[11] Since both normative and factual issues converge on this first filter, it seems impossible to isolate the impact of legal indeterminacy as the cause for litigation. Hence, different observers typically postulate some component as being more relevant than the other. For instance, Benjamin Cardozo claims that the reason why disputes are litigated is due "most often not to the law, but to the facts" (Cardozo 1921, p. 129). By contrast, Max Radin believes that the most critical factor is legal uncertainty about the legal solution, which he identifies with the capacity to anticipate how the courts will rule: when the prediction "can be made with a fair degree of certainty and precision, . . . no [judicial] decision will be required," yet, when "prognosis is difficult and uncertain," judicial pronouncements "will consequently be called for" (Radin 1942, pp. 1270–1271). Llewellyn also believes that legal uncertainty may lead to litigation, albeit in a different way, and that only economically "large matters" make it to appellate courts (1930, pp. 59, 95).

exceedingly often in those cases which, having greater elements of doubt, get selected as peculiarly the province of those appellate courts whose writings are recorded" (Llewellyn 2011, p. 47). Similarly, Max Radin, who believed the law to be "sufficiently stable," warned that focusing on judicial decisions leads analysts to the impression that it is "less stable than it really is" because the controversies that are taken to the courts are for the most part those "marginal cases" where the law is in fact indeterminate (Radin 1942, pp. 1270–1271). Although each of these Realists focuses on only one on the 'filters' (Radin on the first, Llewellyn on the second), both of them appear to identify well the distorting effects of dispute selection.

Yet perhaps it is possible to interpret the evidence differently. For instance, Brian Leiter and Frederick Schauer have also underscored the appellate-centered focus implicit in Legal Realist scholarship, though for a slightly different purpose. Instead of focusing on explaining why Realist assertions about indeterminacy sound disproportionate to some, Leiter and Schauer advance a revisionist take on how to better understand those Realist claims in the first place. In these authors' view, the Realist contentions on law's pervasive lack of guidance were actually *meant* to underscore a feature only germane to appellate decision-making (Leiter 2005, p. 52; Leiter 2007, pp. 19–20, 41, 77–79; Schauer 2009, pp. 137–138; Schauer 2011, p. 16; Schauer 2013, pp. 758–759). Some of the notes highlighted earlier may seem supportive of this interpretation. For one, if the Realist findings on legal indeterminacy are to be exclusively ascribed to the realm of appellate review, then there is nothing odd about the Realists only considering evidence drawn from the pool of upper court decisions (thus dissolving the objection about this sample's unrepresentativeness). Moreover, this adjustment would also solve what would otherwise be an inconsistency in the views of the two Legal Realists quoted above, Llewellyn and Radin, who were aware of the inadequacy of the sample of appellate cases for assessing indeterminacy across the board. There is no doubt that recasting Realist claims in more restricted terms has the advantage of making them more commonsensical. Yet this comes at the high cost of making Legal Realism far less challenging than one would expect it to be according to the conventional story (Moore 2000, p. 36; Schauer 2013, pp. 764–766; *compare* Tamanaha 2010, pp. 1–5). For this and other reasons I will briefly state, I disagree with Leiter's and Schauer's claims that Realist authors actually intended to—and in fact did—restrict their assertions about the pervasiveness of legal indeterminacy to the subset of disputes that reach the appellate review. Evidence in support of this reading is simply too slim and somewhat contradictory.[12]

[12]In a couple of statements that get lost in the vast Realist literature, two authors do speak of indeterminacy in relation to "doubtful cases." Indeed, Walther Cook once expressed astonishment at the fact that it was "still possible for eminent members of the bar to assert that all a court does in deciding doubtful cases is to deduce conclusions from fixed premises, the law" (Cook 1927, p. 305). Similarly, Llewellyn reported that his fellow Realists had proven that the legal materials provide judges with resources to justify any of two opposing outcomes "in any case doubtful enough to make litigation respectable" (Llewellyn 1931, p. 1239). Still, Llewellyn was careful enough to report (in the same seminal piece) that Realist claims about indeterminacy and the role of legal rules go beyond appellate courts. Thus, he described Realists as characterized by their "[d]istrust of

Not only did the Legal Realists for the most part assert that indeterminacy was pervasive without caveats, but they also pointed out that their project reached way beyond the appellate review.[13] Furthermore, only by interpreting the Realists as arguing that indeterminacy is an overarching legal phenomenon can one both make sense of the criticisms denouncing Realism's overemphasis of the difficulty (Cardozo 1921, 1924; Hart 1977, 1992), and accommodate Llewellyn's candid fear about the bias that the appellate-centered focus introduces for drawing conclusions about the law in general (Llewellyn 1930, pp. 94–95).[14]

These quibbles aside, Leiter's and Schauer's arguments come straight to the point here because, like myself, they also stress the centrality of the appellate-review bias when it comes to assessing the scope of legal indeterminacy. At the bottom, their theses and mine account for the tensions that Realist claims present in terms of descriptive accuracy on the basis of the same idea—namely, that the claim about indeterminacy being pervasive may very well appear, at the same time, sound when confined to the appellate realm, yet farfetched when attributed to the law in general. This seems to be the case on the basis of a fairly uncontroversial assumption: namely, that the legal practice is vast and complex to the point where approaching it from alternative angles may produce remarkably different impressions. No doubt, there is one aspect that this circumstance does call into question, namely, the suitability of *global* claims about how the law supposedly works. Now, it is not my intention to criticize the Realist School for this mistake—which is, one must say, fairly common in legal thought. My point is rather to call attention to the underlying conceptions already present in a particular legal community for ideas like these to take hold like they have. Indeed, insofar as the Realists' unqualified assessments about indeterminacy are not reformulated with a more modest reach, they will make more or less sense to a given audience depending on the preconceptions of the legal practice that such a community holds. As I have argued, these ideological conceptions can come up as the result of a process through which a particular version or segment of the practice ends up acquiring a sort of paradigmatic status in relation to the whole. Accordingly, a legal culture that takes the appellate review as

---

traditional legal rules and concepts insofar as they purport to describe what either courts or people are actually doing, [and] of the theory that traditional prescriptive rule-formulations are the heavily operative factor in producing court decisions" (Llewellyn 1931, p. 1237). As for lower courts specifically, Llewellyn reported that, despite Realist research being incipient in the early 1930s, "[a] ll that is really clear to date is that until we know more here our "rules" ... give us misleading suggestions as to the whole body of cases unappealed" (1931, p. 1247).

[13] Llewellyn's review of Realism is insightful here as well, in noting that the epistemic ambitions of Realism "have grown out of the study of the action of appellate courts," and well "into the work of lower courts, of administrative bodies, of legislatures, of the life which lies before and behind law" (1931, p. 1250).

[14] Indeed, Llewellyn clearly did not believe that the difficulties of working with an unrepresentative sample could be solved as simply as through explicitly referencing a narrower universe of ascription for one's claims (namely, the appellate review). Quite the contrary, he thought that pointing out the difficulty, if anything, provided a reason for putting some effort into broadening the scope of analysis.

paradigmatic of how the legal practice goes (as seems to be the case in the United States) will be much more receptive to ideas about indeterminacy like those advanced by Legal Realism than other cultures whose dominant conceptions are construed around different paradigms (as it is the case in Europe or Latin America, for example).

3.2 *Judicial Statesmanship and Policymaking*

A crucial link in this argument is to underscore the fact that the legal practice in appellate courts is in several respects different from that in other legal realms. I have so far explored one of the reasons for this difference, namely, that it is far more frequent for appellate judges to be presented with factual situations for which the legal materials are indeterminate. To press the point further, I will now turn to another feature that sets the practice of higher courts apart from other judicial and non-judicial practices, which concerns the political role of judges in contemporary societies. (This second dimension should in theory count independently of whether legal indeterminacy is indeed an issue before upper courts; although in practice both circumstances add up to the complex reality of appellate judging). The claim is that the perspective of appellate judges is different—from, say, that of lower courts—in two important respects: regarding (i) the constraints that their decision-making is subject to, and (ii) the goals they must pursue in deciding cases. Let me explain these two briefly.

Judges are supposed to decide cases by applying the law. In fact, judicial opinions are almost exclusively written as if this was the only acceptable reason why the case must be decided in a certain way (Dworkin 1977, pp. 31–39), even in cases where it might be doubtful whether the law actually provides a solution (Hart 1992, pp. 135–136). Ascertaining what it is that the law requires is therefore one of the most central duties of judges—and one that can be quite burdensome when the legal materials are not particularly helpful, which is precisely what we mean when we speak of cases being 'hard.' Now, this requirement is enforced upon judges mainly through hierarchical judicial structures, which are set so that upper courts can control lower judges' decision-making as to whether they got the law right (and, to a lesser extent, mistakes regarding questions of fact). However, as courts stand higher up the ladder, instances of further review reduce considerably, until some tribunal is eventually entrusted with the "final word" on what the law is. Precisely due to this hierarchical arrangement, upper court judgments are less subject to control than those by inferior tribunals: the former simply face less chances of reversal or directly none at all. As Justice Robert Jackson famously pointed out about the Supreme Court, "[w]e are not final because we are infallible, but we are infallible only because we are final."[15] This translates into judges in upper courts having wider margins of maneuver than those of their lower-court colleagues: even when all judges technically have the same resources of craft available to them, those sitting higher up in the judicial ladder simply have far less concerns that their judgments will be reversed, and therefore can simply afford more interpretive leeway.[16] Although the notion of "who controls the controllers?" may sound cliché, it is somewhat fitting to portray the stark contrast between the systems of institutional checks that courts of review apply and the one to which these upper courts are subject (if any). Now, for this very reason, the point of view of appellate judges regarding law-finding must be different than that of lower judges, especially when cases are hard and judges must therefore put a considerable amount of effort into determining what it is that the law requires. This circumstance produces an interesting effect in connection with the next situational peculiarity of appellate courts.

The other difference concerns the aims of judicial decision-making. As a matter of fact, each tier of tribunals in the hierarchy of modern court systems performs a specific role, which does not strictly conform to the functions that the rules of procedure assign to these judicial echelons. Indeed, while the mission of lower judges is almost exclusively conceived in terms of dispute resolution, higher courts, and especially courts of last resort, are burdened with other responsibilities that go well beyond the judgment's immediate impact on the litigant parties. We may roughly split these additional tasks into two categories. First, one of the core missions of courts of review is to clarify, expand, or refine the law for its application in future cases.[17] Although this 'policymaking' (or, more controversially, 'lawmaking') function is characteristically associated with common-law systems, civil-law upper courts have been performing analogous tasks for a long time. Second, in certain circumstances high courts—and apex courts above all—are expected to pursue other goals that are valuable for the polity, like securing social peace, arbitrating political disputes, correcting distortions in the system of political representation, fostering judicial legitimacy and prestige, and even stabilizing the political regime in tumultuous times. Some have referred to the need to attend these latter considerations, even at the expense of legal requirements to the contrary, as a call for "judicial statesmanship" (Siegel 2008). It is important to understand that the

[15] Justice Jackson preceded the famous epigram with the following passage: "reversal by a higher court is not proof that justice is thereby better done. There is no doubt that, if there were a super-Supreme Court, a substantial portion of our reversals of state courts would also be reversed" (*Brown v. Allen*, 344 U.S. 443 (1953), p. 540 (Jackson, J. Concurring)).

[16] This seems to be one plausible interpretation for Llewellyn's famous distinction regarding legal constraints between weak and strong judges, both of whom contribute to the law in their own way (Llewellyn 1930, p. 77).

[17] As Justice Antonin Scalia (2010) explained: "any appellate court does more than decide the case in front of it. In fact, that's—to my mind—the least important thing that the court does. Any appellate court shapes the law. ... [As an appellate judge,] I am not about to give victory to a seemingly deserving party in this one case at the cost of causing injustice in hundreds of cases down the road. So the primary role of an appellate court, and especially of that appellate court which is at the apex, is to decide cases on grounds ... that will produce justice overall."

preceding two categories enumerate tasks that upper judges incorporate as further *duties* of office, insofar as courts may be criticized by the legal community and society in general whenever they fail to perform these satisfactorily.

The combination of all of these circumstances results in appellate judges approaching at least a portion of their cases in a singular way. Depending on the case and the kind of concerns at play or the pressures the court is facing, judges will be prone to balancing the results of their legal inquiries with other considerations, like the suitability of the holding as a sound rule for the future or whether the outcome will be politically palatable or achieve the desired goals. Whenever appellate judging is taken as paradigmatic of how the law works, this more complex perspective on judicial decision-making will bulk large in the dominant conception of the legal practice.

4 Conclusion

Allow me to conclude by going briefly over the argument. This essay begun with a critique of what I characterized as the prevalent form of argument in comparative studies about judging. The claim is that the way in which mainstream accounts portray the judicial practice as primarily determined by institutional factors is problematic in two senses. Not only does the emphasis on institutions downplay the influence that ideological conceptions have over the legal practice, but it also prevents observers from experiencing a proper comparative challenge to their own ideological commitments. This I believe underscores the need for comparative arguments that advance a different emphasis. The remainder of the essay advanced an argument tailored to meet this standard. On the one hand, it presents characteristic features of the American legal culture, such as widespread views about the pervasiveness of legal indeterminacy and the proper role of judges in the polity, as a product of ideological conceptions rather than institutional arrangements. On the other hand, in accounting for ideological conceptions as relatively detached from the institutional platform in the American legal culture, this study enables observers from other latitudes to experience a meaningful comparative contrast with their own conceptions. The idea is that the emphasis on ideology should encourage the observer not to dismiss alien conceptions as idiosyncratic or eccentric, but to consider their importance toward her own views by engaging in some introspection.

References

Atiyah PS, Summers R (1987) Form and substance in Anglo-American law: a comparative study of legal reasoning, legal theory, and legal institutions. Oxford University Press, New York
Cardozo BN (1921) The nature of the judicial process. Yale University Press, New Haven
Cardozo BN (1924) The growth of the law. Yale University Press, New Haven

Chayes A (1976) The role of the judge in public law litigation. Harv Law Rev 89:1281–1316
Cook WW (1927) Scientific method and the law. Am Bar Assoc J 13:303–309
Damaška MR (1986) The faces of justice and state authority: a comparative approach to the legal process. Yale University Press, New Haven
Dawson JP (1968) The oracles of the law. The University of Michigan Law School, Ann Arbor
Dworkin R (1977) Taking rights seriously. Harvard University Press, Cambridge
Epstein L (2016) Some thoughts on the study of judicial behavior. William Mary Law Rev 57: 2017–2073
Frank J (1930) Law and the modern mind. Brentano's, New York
Fuller LL (1934) American legal realism. Univ Pa Law Rev 82:429–462
Gilmore G (1961) Legal realism: its cause and cure. Yale Law J 70:1037–1048
Hart HLA (1977) American Jurisprudence through English Eyes: the Nightmare and the Noble Dream. Georgia Law Rev 11:969–989
Hart HLA (1992) The concept of law, 2nd edn. Clarendon Press, Oxford
Holmes OW (1881) Book notices. Am Law Rev 14:233–235
Holmes OW (1897) The path of the law. Harv Law Rev 10:457–478
Kennedy D (1997) A critique of adjudication: Fin de Siècle. Harvard University Press, Cambridge
Kimball BA (2009) The inception of modern professional education: C.C. Langdell, 1826-1906. UNC Press, Chapel Hill
Kress K (1989) Legal indeterminacy. Calif Law Rev 77:283–337
Langbein JH (1985) The German advantage in civil procedure. Chicago Law Rev 52:823–866
Langbein JH (1998) The later history of restitution. In: Cornish W et al (eds) Restitution: past, present, and future: Essays in Honour of Gareth Jones. Hart, Oxford, pp 57–62
Langdell CC (1871) A selection of cases in the law of contracts. Little, Brown and Company, Boston
Lasser M (2004) Judicial deliberations: a comparative analysis of judicial transparency and legitimacy. Oxford University Press, New York
Leiter B (2005) American legal realism. In: Golding M, Edmunson W (eds) The Blackwell guide to the philosophy of law and legal theory. Blackwell Publishing, Oxford, pp 50–66
Leiter B (2007) Naturalizing Jurisprudence: Essays in American legal realism and naturalism in legal philosophy. Oxford University Press, New York
Leiter B (2010) Legal formalism and legal realism: what is the issue? Legal Theory 16:111–133
Llewellyn KN (1930) The Bramble Bush. Oxford University Press, New York, 2008 (3rd edn., 11th printing, with a new introduction and notes by S Sheppard)
Llewellyn KN (1931) Some realism about realism: responding to dean pound. Harv Law Rev 44: 1222–1264
Llewellyn KN (1960) The common-law tradition: deciding appeals. Little, Brown and Company, Boston
Llewellyn KN (2011) The theory of rules. The University of Chicago Press, Chicago
Maxeiner JR (2006) Legal indeterminacy made in America: US legal methods and the rule of law. Valparaiso Law Rev 41:517–589
Moore M (2000) Educating oneself in public: critical Essays in Jurisprudence. Oxford University Press, New York
Oliphant H (1928) A return to stare decisis. Am Law Schools Rev 6:215–231
Parsons T (1853) The law of contracts. Little, Brown and Company, Boston
Pildes RH (1999) Forms of formalism. Univ Chicago Law Rev 66:607–621
Priest GL, Klein B (1984) The selection of disputes for litigation. J Legal Stud 13:1–55
Radin M (1942) In defense of an unsystematic science of law. Yale Law J 51:1269–1279
Russell B (1918) The philosophy of logical atomism. In: Marsh RC (ed) Betrand Russell logic and knowledge: Essays, 1901–1950. Routledge, London, 1988, pp 175–282
Scalia A (2010) Legally speaking: a conversation with Antonin Scalia, hosted by Calvin Massey. University of California at Hastings and Lawyer Magazine: UCTV. September 2010 (aired September 3, 2011). Available at https://www.uctv.tv/shows/20773

Schauer F (1988) Judging in a corner of the law. Southern Calif Law Rev 61:1717–1733
Schauer F (2009) Thinking like a lawyer: a new introduction to legal reasoning. Harvard University Press, Cambridge
Schauer F (2011) Editor's introduction. In: Llewellyn K (ed) The theory of rules. The University of Chicago Press, Chicago, pp 1–28
Schauer F (2013) Legal realism untamed. Tex Law Rev 91:749–780
Schlag P (1991) The problem of the subject. Tex Law Rev 69:1627–1743
Schlegel JH (1995) American legal realism and empirical social science. UNC Press, Chapel Hill
Siegel N (2008) The virtue of judicial statesmanship. Tex Law Rev 86:959–1032
Simpson AWB (1981) The rise and fall of the legal treatise. Univ Chicago Law Rev 48:632–679
Story WW (1847) [1844] A treatise on the law of contracts not under seal, 2nd edn. Little Brown, Boston
Tamanaha B (2010) Beyond the formalist-realist divide: the role of politics in judging. Princeton University Press, Princeton
White GE (2010) Patterns of American legal thought. Quid Pro Books, New Orleans
White M (1957) Social thought in America: the revolt against formalism, 2nd edn. Beacon Press, Boston

Two Worlds of Legal Scholarship and the Philosophy of Law

Alexander Somek

Abstract The cultures of legal scholarship and legal education are decidedly different in the US and in countries belonging to the civil law tradition, such as Germany and Austria. While North American legal academia has proudly transcended the horizon of mere doctrine and embraced a variety of interdisciplinary approaches, the civil law tradition appears to be still committed to the "science of law". It is argued that, in the context of the latter, the moment of transcendence is the preserve of the philosophy of law.

1 Introduction

The following remarks outline two different approaches to the study of law. For the purpose of this chapter, I refer to the continental European approach—more precisely, the mindset of German-speaking legal academia—as the "first" world. I am doing so for entirely historical reasons and therefore hasten to add that this explains why scholarship in the US, even though it is undoubtedly now "first" as regards its international relevance and impact, is cast as the "second" world. Occasionally and in passing, I will also speak of the world of training and education. It is the cosmos in which students are "trainees" and instructors "coaches". In this context, thinking is in demand only insofar as it is of assistance in showing off legal expertise.

2 Scientia Iuris

The first world is the world in which legal scholarship is still regarded as a "science" and in which it is taken to be the point of legal studies to introduce the initiates to the interpretive skills and a template of concepts necessary in order to determine and to

A. Somek (✉)
University of Vienna, Vienna, Austria
e-mail: alexander.somek@univie.ac.at

N. Bersier et al. (eds.), *Common Law – Civil Law*, Law and Philosophy Library 139,
https://doi.org/10.1007/978-3-030-87718-7_10

draw out what the law really is. There is, arguably, no widespread belief in the viability or intellectual respectability of this type of "science" in the second world.

But what does that mean?

It is often forgotten that the term *scientia iuris*—legal science—comprises both an objective and a subjective genitive. Legal science is not only the knowledge of the law as an object of study (objective genitive), it is also the form of knowledge that is adequate to its object and, to that extent, the knowledge in which the object, if it were a subject, would *recognize itself*. In other words, the law, if it could speak, would say to legal science that it welcomes to be known by it: "You apprehend me correctly, for you are spirit of my spirit." In the subject of knowledge, legal science, the object of this knowledge, the law, would consider itself to be adequately grasped. It is—subjective genitive—the law's very own way of knowing the law. Legal science inheres in the law itself. Borrowing from Weinrib, one can say that law is also a mode of understanding the law (*see* Weinrib 2012, pp. 15–16). The law is more than "a mere heap" of rules.[1] The law is also what lends unity to a system of rules. Legal science is the intellectual activity of drawing this out.

I profess belief in legal science in this "ontonomous"[2] sense, and know that I am, even though I am entirely right, taking a position that is widely considered to be eccentric.[3] In the Anglo-American world, the aforementioned Ernest Weinrib may well be the only one to join me. But even if one does not follow my own ambitious conceptualization, it is easy to see why the first world is the world of legal science, even though I take it that many inhabiting this world believe in legal science in a far less high-handed sense. If asked, they would possibly say that legal science proceeds methodically differently than a sociological, theological or moral-philosophical approach to the law. They would claim that it produces the knowledge that is relevant to the function of the legal system. It is the *proprium* of the jurists. Commonly, it is referred to, in German speaking circles, as "legal dogmatics" (*see*, more recently, Bumke 2017. *See* also Potacs 2019, pp. 26–27).

3 The Common Law

There is no "legal science" in the US. This is evident in the absence of "dogmatics" or of "legal formalism". If there is something that may well be dogmatics and that looks like it, then it is manifest in approaches to constitutional interpretation or, more importantly, in fragmentary "doctrines", which cannot really be distinguished from the law itself because they originate from court decisions. "Doctrines" are views of the law that, in precedents, coagulate into the law itself. But they remain

---

[1] I am drawing on language by Christine M. Korsgaard (2009a) here.

[2] "Ontonomy" is the study of how being develops conceptions of itself in order to understand itself (*see* Gabriel 2006, p. 164).

[3] My eccentricity is manifest in *Wissen des Rechts* (*see* Somek 2018).

fragmentary, tied to particular contexts or "clauses" of the constitution. They do not add up to a system (*see*, for example, Tiller and Cross 2006, pp. 517–533).[4]

But why is there no legal science? In my opinion, this is first of all due to the fact that the second world belongs to the wider circle of the common law. Overstating my point, a bit, for the sake of the argument, the common law is indifferent to large-scale systematization. Court decisions are neither true nor false. With the haughtiness inherent in *stare decisis*, they rise above any coherent scholarly edifice. They change the legal situation: "This is so because we have said so." One new decision suffices to maculate legal scholarship, even if it has merely faithfully and meticulously drawn out the implications of prior cases.

Consequently, the purport of legal knowledge is more modest in the common law tradition. The production of legal opinions is considered to be a "skill", a "craft" a "pragmatic" exercise, a form of "practical problem solving". What it really claims—what it is supposed to know—is largely left in an indeterminate state. What matters, instead, that it is an expedient tool if you have to appear in a court of law.

4 Transcendental Nonsense

The second world is the world where the attempt at consolidating the common law by means of building a conceptual system has received a particularly bad press (*see* Grey 1983, pp. 1–53). In this respect, the twentieth century marks the period during which the two major Atlantic legal traditions have grown apart. While the criticism of "dogmatics" by the free law movement (*see* Riebschläger 1968) and of the Marxist critique of law ran themselves into the sand owing to adverse historical circumstances on the continent (in particular, in Germany),[5] the realists' revolt against the American variant of legal science has turned out to be surprisingly successful in the long term (*see*, in lieu of many others, Singer 1988, pp. 467–544). The realists discredited any deduction from general principles or from basic concepts as "transcendental nonsense" (*see*, notably, Cohen 1935, pp. 809–849). As systems became discarded as cloud-cuckoo-lands the pretense of which merely served the purpose of obscuring the true bases of decision-making, these latent foundations were not considered to be amenable to reconstruction from a *jurisprudential* point of view. For the American realists, a moral judgment, a political ideology, or the personality of the decision-maker was tacitly doing the work. The basic conclusion that had to be drawn from their analysis was to focus on extralegal factors in order to understand how the law really works and how it ought to work.

This conclusion is still of relevance today, even in the modified form of the importance of so-called interdisciplinary legal scholarship. The extralegal factors are

[4]On the new doctrinalism, *see*, for example, Anne Fleming (2015), pp. 337–343.

[5]*See* the obituary in Rottleuthner (1982), pp. 124–153.

taken not only to explain the law, they are also supposed to inform sound legal policy. This is true, allegedly, of economic efficiency or of the social norms revealed in our conduct. I shall return to this below.

5 Skills Training as Subversion

The realists' revolt continues to have an effect to this day in the conviction that mere "doctrinal arguments"—the reasoning with cases or the interpretation of statutes—may not lead to a conclusive result: "You can argue either way" (*see* Frug 1988, pp. 869–927). There is nothing that legal science can do in order to give us the right answer. If there can be any such answer, the ultimate normative orientation must stem from other factors, such as economic efficiency, a moral principle, constitutional history or the deconstruction of the heterosexual matrix.

Outsiders who have been socialized in the first world and enter the second sometimes experience the relaxed attitude towards "doctrinal" arguments as liberating. One is relieved of the burden of having to come up with the seemingly compelling legal argument. The uncertainty about the conclusiveness of any such argument, which is often authoritatively suppressed in the first world, has found an outlet in the second world. One can argue either way. Truth does not have to be sought. Legal thinking is a sport. It is a trial of strength carried out in front of a third party who can only decide because he or she is loaded with moral or political prejudice. But that is merely part of being human (*see* Fish 1980, pp. 318–319).

American legal education contributes to the internalization of this rather skeptical perspective on legal knowledge. The overall intellectual perspective is thus supported by an institutional reality. "Thinking like a lawyer" is regarded as a bundle of skills and not as something that offers insights into anything. Nor does it have to be, for it would be absurd to confront the practice of juggling with the expectation that it provides access to truth. The production of legal expertise is strategic action that is to be mastered artfully. Therefore, legal method is taught neither by the luminaries of private law nor by the high priests of public law, but by separate "coaches", namely the Legal Research and Writing Instructors. Within the framework of the Legal Research and Writing Program, which is completed during the first year of study, certain technical conventions are rehearsed.[6] The aim is to convey something purely performative, such as the ability to write a well-structured and clearly formulated legal brief. "Learning how to think like a lawyer" means growing into adopting a pose and writing accessible texts. These are not at all minor achievements for those who have learned how to attain them.

What the descendants from the first world experience as liberating is often a source of bitter disappointment for novices. As a layperson, you first approach the

[6]For an overview of the study literature on this, *see* https://libguides.law.uiowa.edu/legalwriting (last visited 2/16/2021).

law with the expectation that it is determinate and at least moderately clear. Students may harbor no different idea. Soon, however, the initiates point out to them that the law cannot simply be established because the adversarial process has the effect of rendering it controversial. Students are making this experience already when they are pushed through the manic sequence of arguments and counterarguments in the course of moot court training. As part of this exercise, each team is expected to alternate between the plaintiff's and the defendant's side on the basis of the same set of precedents. Such socialization inadvertently conveys the message: Anything goes, and everything that sounds moderately persuasive can serve as a tool.

In this way, practical skills training exercises an intellectually subversive effect. The training component of legal education is not theoretically neutral. It creates indifference towards the legal arguments and, thus, breeds skepticism. Unfortunately, this impression eclipses the valid conclusion that is to be drawn from encounters with the common law tradition, namely, that the law emerges from a dialogical process that only comes to a temporary standstill in the form of decisions.[7] Every new case offers an opportunity to reopen the debate.

6 Hiding the Ball

The impression that the law cannot be ascertained is also reinforced by the teaching experience in the classroom. The "Socratic method" is the proudly presented symbol of American legal education.[8] Its prime directive is that every answer given by a student must be followed by a new question. In this way, the students are cornered and sometimes made to cry. The ethos of the Socratic method is based on the principle "no pain, no gain". Anyone who has been able to suppress tears in the classroom is well on the way to becoming a "tough lawyer".

A major theoretical effect of the Socratic method is, of course, to relieve completely the professor of the burden to reveal the right answer. The whole procedure is based on never giving any answer. Students are often led to believe that "the professor is hiding the ball" (*see* Schlag 1996). But they are mistaken. You can easily be a law professor without having any opinion of your own on any legal

[7] *See* Justice Breyer's remark in Dorsen (2005), p. 522: "[...] Law emerges from a complex interactive democratic process. We justices play a limited role in that process. But we are part of it. So are lawyers, law professors, students and ordinary citizens. The process amounts to a kind of conversation. That conversation is among judges, among professors, among members of the bar, among those who decide cases, among those who analyze and put together series of decisions, among those with practical experience at the bar. Law emerges from that messy but necessary conversational process. We judges participate in that conversation, when we decide cases and we can do so, too, when we speak more generally about the law and about the decision-making process itself."

[8] *See*, for example, the statement on the University of Chicago Law School website: http://www.law.uchicago.edu/prospectives/lifeofthemind/socraticmethod (last visited 2/16/2021).

issue. Perhaps it is even an advantage, because one's own belief does not stand in the way of further Socratic questioning.

The educational staging of ignorance, however, does not harm the cause. Legal arguments, written pleadings or the elegant appearance before a professional court are tools. They are supposed to lead to success. What is considered successful depends on what the individual wants.

7 Doctrine Plus Theory

But that's not the whole story. It is actually only the beginning. Since every form of mere "doctrine" is considered to have dubious intellectual credentials, it is not invested with the force to provide authoritative guidance. The quality of "doctrines" has to be assessed from an external point of view (*see* Posner 1987). The legal scholarship of the second world, which has a pronounced propensity towards small-scale world improvement, must address normative questions from an external point of view, because there is no reliable orientation to be gained from the internal point of view. "Doctrines" are merely social facts—patterns of thinking—that may be legitimately altered on the basis of theoretical insight. This insight, however, can only originate from another discipline.

It is those who in the US regard themselves as legal scholars in an eminent sense who are responsible for creating and conveying these insights. Anyone who wants to be someone in legal academia has to produce "interdisciplinary" work. The "other discipline" is the alias for the search for an external perspective providing the key unlocking the levers of external control, that is, of the normative impulses that are supposed to inform the adjustments of doctrines.

On a very basic level, such an external perspective and impulse is provided by the interests of clients, who would like to know where they stand, legally speaking. Their self-interest invests lawyering with a normative perspective that informs the prediction of court decisions and the use of doctrines to the advantage of clients.

Evidently, however, the mere self-interest of clients is incapable of informing morally defensible decision-making. When it comes to deciding cases, hence, the external controlling factor has to be impersonal. It may come in a variety of forms. "Originalism" is an attempt to provide a solid foundation for constitutional interpretation that anchors it in the historical study of the language of the common law.[9] From a distance, it may look like what we would call "historical interpretation". And yet, the matter is different because its relation to elementary "doctrines" of common law is not so clear and largely unsettled. Does an interpretation unearthing the original meaning have priority over the *stare decisis* principle? This is a question that is terribly difficult to answer. The mediation between the external and the

[9] An elegant defense and critical discussion of this approach can be found in Bennett and Solum (2011).

internal is often up for grabs. As is well known, law and economics developed for the purpose of such mediation the narrative of the common law's unconscious development along the lines of economic efficiency. The course of history is supposed to serve as a mediating factor. But invisible hand explanations are always doubtful and, hence, surrounded by a mystical ring (*see* Ullmann-Margalit 2017, p. 130). It can thus happen that the control of doctrine by the other discipline remains entirely external. This other discipline may have an impact, but this impact is not necessarily mediated from an internal perspective.

In any case, the best-known and most successful example of external control is Law and Economics (*see* Posner 2014; Shavell 2004). It has been trailed by related approaches, also taking their cue from the wealth-maximizing "homo economicus", such as Public Choice Theory,[10] Social Choice Theory,[11] Game Theory (*see* Baird et al. 1994) or, most recently, Behavioral Law and Economics (*see* Zamir and Teichman 2018). There is not much left of the "fancy theory" once invoked by Critical Legal Studies and parts of feminist legal theories, but when they were in bloom, one certainly would have found Foucauldian analyses of immigration law or possibly also deconstructive tax law. Nowadays, empirical social research is on the rise—under the title "empirical legal studies" (*see* Epstein and Martin 2014)—or empirical psychology, especially in connection with the investigation of unconscious racial prejudices in criminal procedural law and labor law (*see* Greenwald and Krieger 2006). It is not so clear, however, what the normative import of such empirical studies is.

Nevertheless, the selective infusion of doctrine with social science has undeniably had effects on some areas of law. This is true, in particular, of the influence of economic analysis on tort law, competition law or intellectual property law (*see* Hovenkamp 2008). These possibilities of grasping legal phenomena from the vantage point of another social science are regarded as intellectually respectable explorations of the law. But hardly ever is truth alone the issue. Academic jurists seize the interdisciplinary possibilities in the awareness that their work has to serve a good cause or to contribute to fighting an evil. The upshot of most scholarship is, thus, a view of what the law ought to be.

[10]Public Choice Theory essentially seeks to provide a "sober", economic analysis of political behavior (*see* Farber and Frickey 1991; Stearns and Zywicki 2009).

[11]Social Choice Theory is concerned with the difficulties and paradoxical outcomes of multi-person decision making. For a particularly successful example of the application of multi-person decision making models to individuals, *see* Katz (2012).

8 Interdisciplinarity

The juxtaposition of the external and the internal perspective, explains, at least in part, the enormous international success of American legal scholarship. Owing to its "interdisciplinary" orientation, Law and Economics, Law and Public Choice, Law and Social Choice, Behavioral Law and Economics and Critical Legal Studies (*see* Kelman 1988) are not tied to any particular legal tradition, even if it took an American intellectual milieu for them to emerge in the first place. Any project that approaches the law from the outside is not rooted in a particular legal system, but transcends national bounds. Not merely the glamour and prestige of Ivy League Law Schools and their popularization by American culture industries, but also the universality and diversity of "interdisciplinary approaches" explains the global significance of the second world of legal scholarship.

In comparison, the first world looks exactly the way it is, namely old-fashioned, tedious and pedantic. Even if years ago Reinhard Zimmermann (*see* Zimmermann 1995) was poking fun at some excesses of the American law review culture, the first world, even if sometimes influential in Asia or Latin America, struggles with obstacles of which the second world is free. Traditions of scholarship are inevitably more closely interwoven with national legal systems, sweep less broadly, and are articulated in vernaculars that outsiders rarely ever understand, let alone master.

But one must not rest content with this diagnosis. The second world has its own shortcomings. Legal scholarship is split into two halves, namely doctrine and interdisciplinary research. The basic dichotomy comes to light in the duplicity of even the smallest sample of legal analysis. The "doctrinal argument" is followed by a "policy analysis". Often, it is not clear how they are linked together.

From the point of view of the first world, this lack of integration is confusing. Arguably, it is indicative of two unsolved problems.

First, it raises the question whether the disassembly of legal science precipitated by legal realism has not thrown the baby out with the bathwater. The radical dismissal of doctrine stems from a time when "formalism" proudly proclaimed that the legal system is gapless and the deduction of legal conclusions from principles is morally neutral. These exaggerated expectations of jurisprudence, which are historically connected with conceptualism, can now be regarded as having been overcome, also in the continental tradition.[12] The demolition of the bizarre pretensions of legal science must not necessarily result in demoting a whole discipline to the status of habituated intellectual skills. In Germany, at any rate, legal scholarship has learned to admit of imperfection without surrendering to other disciplines (*see*, for example, the remarkable work by Görg Haverkate 1977).

Second, it may be possible to overcome the unconnected parallelism of the internal and external perspective by asking the legal question mentioned at the outset: Would the law agree to being known from an economic perspective?

[12]This has been the case at least since the emergence of the so-called "jurisprudence of interests" (*see* Somek 1992).

Which implies nothing less than the question: Are efficiency and wealth-maximization the ultimate principles of law? Whoever engages in the discussion of this question (and there are some in the US), begins to bridge the gap between the two worlds. The question, in fact, concerns the very essence of law. In his own work, Ronald Dworkin repeatedly and unwittingly made himself into an advocate of what from the perspective of the first world would be regarded as "legal science" (*see* Dworkin 1985, pp. 267–291).

Even if the internal dividedness of the second world cannot be the last word, we should remain fair and must not wrinkle our noses with old European snobbery. The two-track approach is still better than the absorption of the study of law into mere skills training. Degenerating into the latter is the danger inherent in the European approach if it merely prides itself in catering to the social demand for legal expertise. If legal scholarship does not engage in theoretical reflection of its merit, the merit will be *de facto* assessed by a well-paying corporate clientele and those wielding political power. Legal scholars may still proudly claim that what they do is of relevance to practice and therefore socially relevant; such relevance, however, merely reflects the self-interested motives of business-people or politicians. The merit of legal expertise is thus assessed in terms of money and power and not from the perspective of the intellectual respectability of the scholarship that informs it. It is for that reason that the two-track approach of American legal education, which offers skills plus interdisciplinarity, helps to sustain a crucial intellectual balance.

9 The Larger Picture

We should also not close our eyes to the intellectual rewards that American jurisprudence offers to those who are interested in the evolution of law and of the role that it plays in our society.

In the US, owing to the close connection between social science research and political-normative criticism, the reflective examination of more wide-ranging legal developments is understood as an important and valuable component of legal scholarship. The examples I have in mind are not studies of legal policy that are only addressed to specialists, but to the general public at large, since they are of concern to us all. The developments affect how all of us—or most of us—live. These are, in particular, those in which something like the "spirit of our times" comes to the fore, that is, the cognitive and normative orientations shaping our age. Part of American legal scholarship seeks to understand them and engages with them critically.

Examples of this type of scholarship abound. Cass Sunstein's and Richard Thaler's book on "Nudging" (*see* Thaler and Sunstein 2008) deals apologetically with incentives or informative signals that are supposed to help us to pursue voluntarily our self-interest or to demonstrate consideration for others. There are plenty of examples of this, ranging from the warning notice on the cigarette packet to the calorie information on the menu all the way down to the recommended "default" installation mode of the computer program. Sunstein has also written outstanding contributions to a psychologically prudent analysis of risk assessments and has warned against the hysteria that laypersons are susceptible to in this context (*see* Sunstein 2005). We live in a world of risk regulation. Sunstein's analyses challenge us to become circumspect in our own judgment.

Other examples of zeitgeist-sensitive work are Lawrence Lessig's groundbreaking studies on the behavior-regulating power of computer software (*see* Lessig 2006) or the innovation-stifling tendencies of copyright law (*see* Lessig 2004). Bruce Ackerman's gloomy picture of the downfall of the American Republic, which in his opinion is caused by the dominance of the president and the apparatus that serves him, falls into the same category (*see* Ackerman 2010). A special gem is a book by Leo Katz with the promising title *Why law is so Perverse* (*see* Katz 2012). Among other things, it examines the phenomenon of why the legal system sometimes forbids us to harm ourselves, or why it is notoriously incomplete. In an original way, Katz refers to the Social Choice Theory, which is tailored to interpersonal processes, in order to reconstruct the pitfalls of intrapersonal decision-making.

In works of this kind, the formative cognitive and normative orientations of the law are partially grasped and submitted to scrutiny. One encounters something that amounts to legal scholarship from the perspective of concerned and engaged citizens. The works pay attention to mentalities or certain ways of thinking that surround us and determine our life. The analyses and messages do not contain any expertise that would be requested by lawyers. They want to be more. They are close to life because they get to the bottom of how we live.

This proximity to life—and not merely the practice of law in a judicial or administrative context—indicates that zeitgeist-sensitive legal scholarship is part of something more comprehensive. I think I am not mistaken to call it "philosophy of law", for this is that part of legal scholarship that is interested in human life and not only in the generation of valuable legal expertise.

10 The Legal Relation

Christine Korsgaard begins her magisterial study *Self-Constitution* with the simple observations that we human beings are "condemned" to choice and action (*see* Korsgaard 2009b, p. 1). Even choosing not to act makes not acting into a type of action. The inevitability of choice and action is placed in a context that confronts us with the burden and opportunity of realizing a life plan (or of having to adjust to the unrealizability of such a plan). The inescapable nature of action reminds us permanently of the fact that we are able to *lead* our lives and can do more than just to let it happen to us.

Indeed, as individuals, we are present in this world only by virtue of consciously leading our life. We can write our own life story to a certain and quite indeterminate degree. Events that affect a human life plan arouse our special interest. These may be transitions such as wedding or biographical ruptures such as dismissals or falling away from religious faith.

It is therefore no coincidence that one of the most important legal philosophers of the twentieth century, John Rawls, places human life, understood as a project, at the center of his theory of justice (*see* Rawls 1971). In the end, he reconstructs the goods we need to have at our disposal in order to have a chance of seeing a life plan succeed.

In this vein, philosophy of law tries to understand why, in order to be able to realize life plans, we have to have legal relationships and what it is that we can demand from others within their context. This includes, for example, the expectation to find our legitimate desires, if we so wish, respected. We call these expectations "rights".

Without rights, life would have little value because it could not be lived autonomously. We want to be able to emancipate ourselves at any time from all relationships with others by pulling the social emergency break and presenting ourselves as a specimen of legal person in the abstract. The chillness and strangeness that arises among us when we appeal to our rights helps to rescue us from the loops and strictures of kindness that are characteristic of our informal or close dealings. For example, discriminatory practices are evil, not only because they lead to real disadvantages, but because they drive potential victims of discrimination into self-denial. People are frivolously lulling themselves into the hope of avoiding disadvantages when they hide their true faces. Discrimination law helps people to shed this illusion.

From the opposite perspective of duties, by contrast, the law demands that we make room for others and yield to their wants. The retreat that the law imposes on us goes very deeply and makes the profession of lawyers most difficult. The law expects its users to accept as premises ideas that they may find utterly stupid. In the legal order we do not encounter our own reason, but the reason of others, which could be our own if we were other people. Generally, therefore, the law represents practical reason in such a state of alteration.

11 Conclusion

So, what is considered to be the task of philosophy of law in the first world? My remarks have already indicated what this might be. Above all, it is up to us to keep the question of legal science alive. If we did not do so, we—teachers and students—could immediately sign off on the project of juridical skills training. At the same time, however, we must promote legal scholarship that is relevant to life, because everyone who is interested in his or her life must be interested, at least to a certain degree, in philosophy of law. Whoever wants to understand his life, inasmuch as it is touched by law, will necessarily end up in the quarter of legal philosophy.

However, we legal philosophers in the first world can take the following with us from the second world, where everything we take a live interest in is simply called "legal scholarship": In isolation from the other subjects of law, philosophy of law is at the peril of become sterile in the long run. It would not, to quote Hegel's famous word, put "its own time in thought", but, at best, its prehistory—and this is often be achieved in the interpretation of classical philosophical texts. The latter has happened in no small measure in the context of the philosophy of law that is written by philosophers. It lives institutionally predominantly in the seventeenth and eighteenth centuries. By contrast, our philosophy of law benefits from intensive contact with the other fields of law. Its vitality actually depends on it.

References

Ackerman B (2010) The decline and fall of the American Republic. Harvard University Press, Cambridge
Baird DG, Gertner RH, Picker R (1994) Game theory and the law. Harvard University Press, Cambridge
Bennett RW, Solum LB (2011) Constitutional originalism: a debate. Cornell University Press, Ithaca
Bumke C (2017) Rechtsdogmatik: Eine Disziplin und ihre Arbeitsweise. Mohr Siebeck, Tübingen
Cohen F (1935) Transcendental nonsense and the functional approach. Columbia Law Rev 35:809–849
Dorsen N (2005) The relevance of foreign legal materials in U.S. constitutional cases: a conversation between Justice Antonin Scalia and Justice Stephen Breyer. Int J Const Law 3:519–541
Dworkin R (1985) A matter of principle. Harvard University Press, Cambridge
Epstein L, Martin AD (2014) An introduction to empirical legal research. Oxford University Press, Oxford
Farber D, Frickey PP (1991) Law and public choice: a critical introduction. University of Chicago Press, Chicago
Fish S (1980) Is there a text in this class? The authority of interpretive communities. Harvard University Press, Cambridge
Fleming A (2015) The long shadow of doctrine. Univ Pa Law Rev Online 163:337–343
Frug J (1988) Argument as character. Stanford Law Rev 40:869–927
Gabriel M (2006) Der Mensch im Mythos: Untersuchungen über Ontotheologie, Anthropologie und Selbstbewusstseinsgeschichte in Schellings Philosophie der Mythologie. de Gruyter, Berlin
Greenwald AG, Krieger LH (2006) Implicit bias: scientific foundations. Calif Law Rev 94:945–967
Grey TC (1983) Langdell's orthodoxy. Univ Pittsburgh Law Rev 45:1–53
Haverkate G (1977) Gewissheitsverluste im juristischen Denken: Zur politischen Funktion der juristischen Methode. Duncker & Humblot, Berlin
Hovenkamp H (2008) The antitrust Enterprise: principle and execution. Harvard University Press, Cambridge
Katz L (2012) Why the law is so perverse. University of Chicago Press, Chicago
Kelman M (1988) A guide to critical legal studies. Harvard University Press, Cambridge
Korsgaard CM (2009a) The activity of reason. Proc Addr Am Philos Assoc 83:23–43
Korsgaard CM (2009b) Self-constitution: agency, identity, and integrity. Oxford University Press, Oxford
Lessig L (2004) Free culture: how big media uses technology and the law to lock down culture and control creativity. The Penguin Press, New York
Lessig L (2006) Code: and other laws of cyberspace: version 2.0, 2nd rev edn. Basic Books, New York

Margalit EU (2017) In: Margalit A, Sunstein C (eds) Normal rationality: decisions and social order. Oxford University Press, Oxford

Posner RA (1987) The decline of law as an autonomous discipline 1962–1987. Harv Law Rev 100: 761–780

Posner RA (2014) Economic analysis of law, 9th edn. Wolters Kluwer Law & Business, New York

Potacs M (2019) Rechtstheorie, 2nd edn. Facultas, Vienna

Rawls J (1971) A theory of justice. The Belknap Press of Harvard University Press, Cambridge

Riebschläger K (1968) Die Freirechtsbewegung: Zur Entwicklung einer soziologischen Rechtsschule. Duncker & Humblot, Berlin

Rottleuthner H (1982) Rechtsformen – Ein symphonischer Nachklang. In: Gessner V, Winter G (eds) Jahrbuch für Rechtstheorie und Rechtssoziologie, vol 8. Westdeutscher Verlag, Opladen, pp 124–153

Schlag P (1996) Hiding the ball. N Y Univ Law Rev 71:1681–1718

Shavell S (2004) Foundations of economic analysis of law. Harvard University Press, Cambridge

Singer JW (1988) Legal realism now. Calif Law Rev 76:467–544

Somek A (1992) Rechtssystem und Republik: Über die politische Funktion des systematischen Rechtsdenkens. Verlag Österreich, Wien/New York

Somek A (2018) Wissen des Rechts. Mohr Siebeck, Tübingen

Stearns M, Zywicki T (2009) Public choice concepts and applications in law. West Academic Publishing, St. Paul

Sunstein CR (2005) Laws of fear: beyond the precautionary principle. Cambridge University Press, Cambridge

Thaler RH, Sunstein CR (2008) Nudge: improving decisions about health, wealth and happiness. Yale University Press, New Haven

Tiller EH, Cross FB (2006) What is legal doctrine? Northwest Univ Law Rev 100:517–533

Weinrib EJ (2012) The idea of private law, 2nd edn. Oxford University Press, Oxford

Zamir E, Teichman D (2018) Behavioral law and economics. Oxford University Press, Oxford

Zimmermann R (1995) Law Reviews – Ein Streifzug durch eine fremde Welt. In: Zimmermann R (ed) Amerikanische Rechtskultur und europäisches Privatrecht. Mohr Siebeck, Tübingen, pp 87–131

Is China a Continental-Law Country?

Han Liu

Abstract The general knowledge about the Chinese legal system differs from its true nature. Therefore, the present gap between the law in action and law in the books from the outside needs to be bridged by a proper recognition of the underlying processes of the legal system in China. In order to do so, this chapter focuses on China's legal system not only from a doctrinal perspective but also by assessing its history, state doctrine as well as foreign influence. It offers the characterization of a hybrid nature of China's legal system, which is neither common nor continental. Thus, it concludes that Chinese law blends together the socialist tradition and Western elements, combining both continental and Anglo-American with ancient factors.

1 Introduction

What is the place of China in the world map of legal families? This is a question of interest to scholars and lawyers when discussing the divide and convergence of civil law and common law systems.

The Introduction to China's Legal Structure offered by the Law Library of Congress states that:

> The legal system of the People's Republic of China (PRC) is defined by the government as a 'socialist legal system.' Despite the official definition, however, China's legal system is based primarily on the model of Civil Law.

That, at least, represents the conventional account of the nature of Chinese law, held by most scholars and lawyers, foreign or Chinese: China belongs to the continental-law family. The enactment of China's Civil Code in 2020, which clearly resembles the German Civil Code, seems to reinforce that impression.

H. Liu (✉)
Tsinghua University, Beijing, China
e-mail: liuhan@tsinghua.edu.cn

N. Bersier et al. (eds.), *Common Law – Civil Law*, Law and Philosophy Library 139,
https://doi.org/10.1007/978-3-030-87718-7_11

However, careful observers would deem that conventional understanding inadequate. Indeed, part of contemporary Chinese law has been influenced by Anglo-American legal traditions, especially US law.

As Professor Upham points out,

> China has drawn on the US system in many substantive areas, from securities and corporate law to property law to criminal procedure (and even for a brief period in the early 2000s in constitutional law) (Upham 2017, p. 239).

Of course, here, we are speaking of mainland China. Hong Kong, as a special administrative region, is definitely a common law jurisdiction that has inherited its legal system from its English colonial past. But this point itself suggests the complicated nature of the Chinese legal system.

In another sense, it is also quite inappropriate to describe China as a "mixed jurisdiction" as scholars of comparative law use the term (Palmer 2001, p. 3). This term usually refers to relatively small countries or regions that have been colonized by European powers with different legal systems. By contrast, China was never entirely colonized by Western powers. Together with Japan, China is one of the few countries that tried to fundamentally reform its legal system on its own initiative during the modernization transformation, although this was triggered by the losses of wars against European empires. Moreover, what "mixed jurisdictions" have mixed are mostly civil law and common law. China, again, is different. Chinese legal system remains socialist, at least in name, but not only so. Reading the Chinese Constitution, for example, one can find that the cardinal spirit, basic structure, and most articles are socialist in nature. And perhaps more so with the 2018 Amendments, one of which has, for the first time, written Party leadership into the main text of the Chinese Constitution.

Thus, in comparative law, China occupies a special position. Officially, China claims itself to be a socialist legal system with Chinese characteristics. Legal circles largely think of China as a system of continental law. I, on the other hand, think of China as a mixed legal system that integrates the system of continental law, the system of English and American law, socialism and even ancient Chinese tradition. Numerous traditions seem in play at the same time. This curious mixture results from China's historical logic of modernizing its legal system.

2 Modern Chinese Legal Development and Its Historical Logic

The hybrid composition of Chinese law can be firstly understood by tracing its genealogy. Before meeting the West and western law, ancient China achieved its distinction as a "Sino Legal System" as many scholars call it: features such as the infusion of law with morality, criminal law as its main body, the importance of custom, and the strong influence of Confucian thought, all embodied such distinction. That tradition, which lasted for thousands of years until its encounter with the

Western powers in the mid-nineteenth century, influenced Japan, Korea, and other places around China: "comparative lawyers recognize a distinct tradition in East Asia, whose cultures emphasize social harmony and respect for social hierarchies. Some observers relate these traits to Confucian thought and suggest the existence of a Confucian legal tradition" (Merryman and Perez-Perdomo 2007, p. 4).

Anyone who knows a little about China's history recognizes that the 1840 Sino-British Opium War was the beginning of China's modern history. It was the British Empire who opened the door to China. Triggered by military loss and cession of territories like Hong Kong, China started its modernization campaign, including legal modernization. The driving forces for the late-Qing legal reform were both international and domestic. Internationally, the Qing Empire strived to abolish extraterritoriality enjoyed by European colonial empires in Chinese territories, especially in concession cities. Domestically, legal reform was regarded as a move towards modernization of political and social life—the move from status to contract.

Ever since that legal transformation process, China has largely learned from the civil law tradition, especially Japanese law and German law introduced through the intermediation of Japanese law. This was also true later, during the Republic of China (1912–1949) and after the Reform and Opening up starting from the late 1970s, except for a period of departure in the first 30 years of the People's Republic of China, when China largely learned from Soviet law in particular and the socialist legal system in general.

Then, the question is: why did the modern reform of Chinese law choose the continental law system represented by Germany, rather than the common law tradition represented by England? After all, it was England who open the door of the Qing Empire by trade and war, or trade war. And in the late 1890s and early 1900s, when the Qing Court further promoted large-scale legal reform and drafted legislations, one of the main intellectual, professional supporters was Wu Tingfang, the first Chinese who started a career as a barrister in England. Obviously, the reformers definitely knew about English law. Then why did they take the continental legal tradition, especially Germany and Japan, as the model to follow?

That's simply because of quite pragmatic considerations of the Qing Court and related elites.

First, the cost of learning from Japanese law was significantly lower than that of learning directly from European countries. China is closer to Japan both geographically and intellectually. Traveling to Japan was more convenient; Japanese language and culture had been greatly influenced by China in pre-modern history. Japan, therefore, was the first choice for Chinese students to study abroad. What's more, Japan has laid the institutional and intellectual foundation for the transplantation of a legal system from Europe to East Asia: at that time, it had completed the drafting of a Civil code and a Commercial code, mainly copying the German antetypes; it has also translated a vast amount of European literature and created a large modern vocabulary suitable for East Asian languages in the process of translation. For the Chinese intelligentsia, Japan represented the true modern and Westernized legal system in Asia at the time (Reynolds 1993, p. 182). China appears to be more like Japan than Europe, leading Chinese legal reformers to believe that copying Japanese laws would cause fewer compatibility problems than copying unfiltered European laws directly (Zhang 2018). Another factor was a political one. The Qing court wanted to learn from the Japanese constitutional system so that the Emperor and nobles could remain powerful after establishing constitutionalism: after all, in Japanese, rather than British, constitutional system, the Crown retains substantive powers.

Second, the German model appealed to the Qing dynasty, because it was an emerging continental power with a more centralized political system than Britain and had more in common with China. By contrast, the British Empire is known for its decentralized structure domestically and maritime empire internationally. After all, Japan, as China's model at the time, built its modern legal system largely on the German model. The decision to copy Japanese and German laws therefore suggested itself, especially with respect to the criminal and civil codes. An exception is commercial law: the Qing Empire finally adopted a mixture of Japanese and British laws, partly because of Britain's huge influence on China's foreign trade (Zhang 2018).

However, these practical factors cannot fully explain the reason why China, during the Republic of China era and post-Mao reform, still chose the civil law system, especially the German and Japanese tradition. There is a deeper reason behind that: the modernization of Chinese law is accompanied by the construction of a modern nation-state. The true explanation, thus, lies within the deeper logic of Chinese legal modernization: legal reform has been carried out along with the project of state-building and nation-building. The continental legal tradition, rather than the common law, fitted that vision and trend.

Actually, apart from the difference in concrete legal institutions, the civil law and the common law bear different ideational and ideological underpinnings. Professor Merryman points out that an important difference between the common law and the system of continental law is that while in the former the concept of extreme individualism prevails, in the latter the concept of statism prevails.

China held a statist conception of law similar to the continental tradition both in the ancient past and in its modern transformation:

> On the Continent the revolution seemed to require a rejection of the old legal order; in England it seemed to require acceptance and even glorification of it. (Merryman and Perez-Perdomo 2007, p. 22).

Apparently, the Chinese elites' will to be modern tries to reject, not glorify, its past.

During the late-Qing legal reform by the end of the nineteenth century and the beginning of the twentieth century, the legal reformists took statism as the guiding principle of the reform. For example, the famous constitutionalist and public figure Yang Du wrote a special article on the difference between statism and clannism in the legal reform, pointing out that:

> If clannism is immutable and statism inapplicable, it is better to abolish the new law and use the old law. If statism is supposed to be adopted, there can be no parallel path of clannism. Now the new criminal law, in fact, takes statism as its essence, namely the spirit of constitutional politics. (Hao 1996, p. 306)

Many contemporaries, whether legal reformists or revolutionary statesmen like Sun Yat-sen, the founding father of the Republic of China, had similar sentiments. For Western thinkers and statesmen in the eighteenth and nineteenth centuries, the point was to limit state power by constitutional arrangements to protect individual freedom and social autonomy. But in China, the point for most thinkers was quite the opposite. It was primarily to build a modern, centralized state in dire situations, free from foreign invasion and intervention. Reasons are obvious, given the historical context.

First, looking outward, China faced the serious threat from Western powers; it longed for sovereignty and autonomy against Western imperialism—invasions, "unequal treaties", extraterritoriality, etc. Patriotism, nationalism, and statism were zeitgeist. Second, looking inward, after the fall of the Qing Dynasty, multiple warlords fought among themselves, the country was torn apart, and the people suffered. It was expected that that such fragmented and nasty situation should be brought to an end as soon as possible; a united nation and a unified state had to be put in place. Third, looking into the future, as a developing country, in order to make China rich and powerful as soon as possible, the state had to adopt a series of top-down reforms, cultivate the market economy, take to the road of state capitalism, and promote the development of national economy (Hao 1996, p. 306). People would not wait for the spontaneous order to come into being by evolution. Continental statism holds that the state monopolizes legislative powers to make unified law. That appealed to the taste of China.

Along with statism, other features of the continental legal system met the needs of Chinese modernization of law. Not only because writing a code is much easier than producing a series of cases. Professor Merryman points out that the existence of codes is not a true mark of distinction of the civil law system (Merryman and Perez-Perdomo 2007, pp. 27–28). The real difference lies in their divergent understanding and conception of codification. Codes for continental countries are a formal expression of ideologies; they mark a new beginning in law and support a unified nation-state.

That understanding resonates with Chinese elites for generations, from the late Qing to today. China adopted the continental system mainly because it was the quickest way to modernize its legal system, using massive legislation backed up by a centralized political power—a revolutionary approach. The common law, by contrast, can only take shape over time—an evolutionary approach.

Back in the mid-nineteenth century, the loss of wars against Western powers, especially Britain, meant the loss of self-confidence of Chinese rulers and intellectuals about the traditional Chinese civilization. Chinese elites were keen to make their country modern, which means strong, rich, and being respected again. Sense of urgency preoccupied their minds and hearts. Mao once wrote the lines: "Ten thousand years are too long. Seize the day, seize the hour!" That captures not only the mentality of revolutionary Chinese leadership, but also that of each generation of Chinese elites since 1840, including legal elites, who bore the will to be modern swiftly.

Sense of urgency also haunted Chinese legal minds. Of course, Rome was not built in a day. But Chinese legal minds thought they can build a legal system within a few decades. This mentality of urgent reform itself, therefore, is in conflict with that of the common law which sticks to the archaic tradition and takes a long-term view towards law. Law, for the English lawyers, is a cause of centuries. By contrast, the continental legal system can be formed and erected in a relatively short period of time. With strongmen like Napoleon and Bismarck who wished to lay down a code, and legal scholars able to write it, a state can have a code within years. Through the centralizing organizational power and the work of scholars, a relatively complete system can be formed in a noticeably short time.

Another advantage of learning from continental law is that it facilitates the transplanting of laws. All the state needs are a strong central government and enlightened elites. Developed civil-law countries have already written codes. Developing countries can easily translate and transplant them. Therefore, since modern times, many countries have chosen the civil law system to build their legal systems. Not necessarily because it's good, but because it is feasible given time and resource constraints.

That historical logic applied in the post-Mao legal reform too. Since the authorities initiated the Opening Up, they deviated from the Soviet model and looked to the West.

This happened primarily for economic reasons: as China tries to become more developed, it must develop a private and market economy. The market economy must be equipped with legal functions, such as property law and contract law. Because of the need for a vast amount of supporting legislation in a short time, China naturally continued the previous acceptance of German law and Japanese law. By contrast, the excessive power of judges in the British and American laws conflicted with the People's Congress system in China, so it was not feasible to imitate the British and American laws.

3 The Architecture of the Contemporary Chinese Legal System

3.1 Private Law: Continentalization with Common-Law Characteristics

China's move towards a continental system is embodied chiefly in the area of private law. The Chinese Civil Code represents that fruition. Honoring the French and German Civil Codes, the Chinese Civil Code followed the continental tradition and the Roman law tradition, tinged with some articles on civil rights in the digital age—privacy and personal information rights. There is no doubt that China's Civil Code belongs to the civil law tradition. Only in some small areas, it borrows some elements from the common law. For example, the institution of administrator of the estate was written into the Chinese Civil Code, which was largely absent in previous Chinese law. It, of course, derives from the common law.[1]

But commercial law is different. Historically speaking, from the late Qing Dynasty, it had been highly influenced by the English tradition. Contemporarily, the influence of American law holds sway. Professor Tang Yingmao shows that China has transplanted some institutions from the United States, so "China has subjected her securities market to extremely tight control" (Tang 2017, p. 203), with the "strong intervention" of government (Tang 2017, p. 205). "A share offering to public investors is subject to the CSRC's approval. This is consistent with other key markets such as that of the United States." (Tang 2017, p. 206) In terms of the disclosure of information in a securities market, the foundation of modern securities law, "the Chinese model has generally followed the US model in this regard." (Tang 2017, p. 209) Similar developments took place in intellectual property, anti-trust, and so on.

3.2 *Criminal Law and Procedure: Socialist, Continentalization, and Common Law Elements*

The trend of continentalization takes place in criminal law, like in civil law, but not that easily and quickly. Contemporary Chinese criminal law, both code and case law, structurally has been modeled on the Soviet model. Still, many jurists are trying to reform Chinese criminal law by importing German and Japanese elements. Leading criminal law experts at top law schools like Peking, Tsinghua, and Remin are predominantly of German or Japanese background. The debate and struggle between traditional Soviet doctrines and German-Japanese doctrinalism still unfolds among scholars and practitioners. De-Sovietization is *en vogue* in classrooms of elite law schools, but not in courtrooms, police stations, and the prosecution. It remains to be seen where the reform will lead.

On the other hand, however, the Chinese reform of criminal procedure followed the American model. The reform is to change the Soviet inquisitorial system to an adversarial system. It may be quite unfathomable for outsiders to understand how the Chinese audience was amazed by the O.J. Simpson trial in 1994 and how it elicited an onging effect on judicial reform in China. The 1996 revised Criminal Procedure Law marked a critical shift away from the inquisitorial system and to the adversarial system. The principle of reasonable doubt has entered Chinese criminal procedure law in 2012, as did the exclusionary rule. Of course, the Chinese criminal justice system is still evolving, yet it begins to exhibit a hybrid nature (Yi et al. 2011, p. 172).

---

[1] Civil Code of the People's Republic of China (promulgated by the NPC., May. 28, 2020, effective Jan. 1, 2021), CLI.1.342411(EN) (Lawinfochina), at Art.1145–1149.

Another noticeable development in judicial reform is the introduction of some form of case law in Chinese adjudication, called the "guiding cases". Since 2010, China's Supreme People's Court has extracted a series of judicial decisions into binding decisions that courts at all levels can refer to while dealing with similar cases. These guiding cases, ranging from security and land use to murder and corruption, have become a potentially important new tool for judges to handle a sea of cases. As Professor Deng observes, "the current guiding case system and common law system have the tendency to become more and more similar systems in reality" (Deng 2015, p. 1). No doubt, the guiding cases system is to regulate lower court's judicial behavior, similar to the function of precedent in the common system, albeit guiding cases are non-binding. But given the authority of the Supreme People's Court, lower-level courts are expected to comply (Zhang and Ginsburg 2019, p. 302). With that, China has largely formed a *de facto* system of precedent.

3.3 Public Law: Socialist Grounding and Influence of American Law

China remains a socialist system in terms of constitutional law. In the world of constitutional law, given the existence of China, the socialist system, contrary to the understanding of many students of comparative law, never totally becomes extinct. Reading the Chinese Constitution, socialism still dominates the whole text. In reality, the Chinese Communist Party remains the ruling party. And in the past decades, the Party's control over the whole state system and government machinery became even stronger. The Party's leadership has been written into Article One of the Chinese Constitution by the 2018 amendments.

But again, the Chinese constitution itself includes other elements. The Constitution of 1982, currently in force, introduced some Western ideas. For example, Cheng Siyuan, then the Deputy Secretary-General of the Chinese People's Political Consultative Conference, refered to the stability of the U.S. Constitution to suggest limits on amending power. He indicated that the United States experienced only one constitution throughout its history of more than two centuries (Xu 2003, p. 406). Cheng suggested that the amending power should be restrained to maintain constitutional stability. Echoing Cheng's suggestion, many drafters put forward one-fifth of the national people's representatives as a threshold to propose constitutional amendments, which was eventually written into the 1982 Constitution.[2]

In the vertical constitutional structure, American influence also affected the Chinese Constitution. The Constitution borrowed from American federalism and

[2] Xianfa [Constitution] art. 64 (1982) (China): "Amendments to the Constitution are to be proposed by the Standing Committee of the National People's Congress or by more than one-fifth of the deputies to the National People's Congress and adopted by a majority vote of more than two-thirds of all the deputies to the Congress."

changed China's central-local relations, seeking to decentralize state power (Shen 1997, pp. 23–24). Thus, many observes attribute the reason why China made an economic miracle to its de facto economic federalism. Indeed, back in 1956, Mao Zedong referenced America's decentralized system about China's problem of over-centralization of legislative power (Shen 1997, p. 23). In the early 1980s, while, Deng Xiaoping expressed that excessive centralization of power was still a huge problem. The 1982 Constitution finally granted legislative powers to local governments (Shen 1997, p. 23).

American influence on Chinese constitutional law reached its climax in the early 2000s. In the case of *Qi Yuling v. Chen Xiaoqi* in 2001,[3] the Supreme People's Court declared, in response to a local court, that the Constitution can be cited as legal authority in adjudicating civil-law cases. This declaration changed the long-standing tradition that the judiciary cannot invoke the Constitution in adjudication.[4] Following this landmark opinion, Huang Songyou, then the chief judge of the SPC's First Civil Tribunal, published an article in the People's Court Daily, the official newspaper of the Chinese Supreme Court, putting forward the institution of constitutional judicial review modelled upon the American practice:

> In 1803, when the United States Supreme Court decided the case of Marbury v. Madison, Chief Justice Marshall declared in the opinion: "a law made by the legislature repugnant to the constitution is invalid." The case was the forerunner of judicialization of the constitution. . . .Now, judicialization of the constitution has become the universal model every country's judicial practice adopts; almost every country has established the institution and procedure of constitutional litigation. . . .Because we have not set up a specialized constitutional court, our model of judicialization of the constitution can follow the American, ordinary-court model. All the controversies concerning constitutional questions shall be tried by our ordinary court according to the ordinary procedure. Courts trying such kind of cases shall take the Constitution as the foundation for their judgment. The realization of the judicialization of the constitution will definitely exert a positive, important influence on building the rule of law in our country. (Huang 2001)

[3]Zuigao Renmin Fayuan Guanyu yi Qinfan Xingmingquan de Shouduan Qinfan Xianfa Baohu de Gongmin Shou Jiaoyu de Jiben Quanli Shifou ying Chengdan Minshi Zeren de Pifu (最高人民法院关于以侵犯姓名权的手段侵犯宪法保护的公民受教育的基本权利是否应承担民事责任的批复) [An Opinion with Regard to Whether Violating People's Constitutional Right of Education by Means of Violating the Right of Name Calls for Civil Law Responsibility] (promulgated by Sup. People's Ct., June 28, 2001, effective Aug. 13, 2001) (Chinalawinfo) (hereinafter "*Qi Yuling*").

[4]Generally, the Supreme People's Court established this principle by two replies to the inferior courts. The first is *Zuigao Renmin Fayuan Guanyu zai Xingshi Panjue zhong Buyi Yuanyin Xianfa Zuo Lunzui Kexing de Yiju de Fuhan* (最高人民法院关于在刑事判决中不宜援引宪法作论罪科刑的依据的复函) [*The Supreme People's Court's Reply to the Innappropriate Reference to Constitution in Criminal Cases*] (promulgated by Sup. People's Ct., July 30, 1955) (Chinalawinfo). In the reply, the Supreme People's Court stated that it is inappropriate to cite the Constitution in criminal cases. The second is *Zuigao Renmin Fayuan Guanyu Renmin Fayuan Zhizuo Falü Wenshu Ruhe Yinyong Falü Guifanxing Wenjian de Pifu* (最高人民法院关于人民法院制作法律文书如何引用法律规范性文件的批复) [*The Supreme People's Court's Reply about How to Cite Legal Reference When Writing Legal Documents*] (promulgated by Sup. People's Ct., Oct. 28, 1986) (Chinalawinfo). In the reply, the Supreme People's Court sets clear criteria as to which sources can be cited in legal opinions.

However, due to political backlashes, that judicial interpretation faded several years later in 2008. China's path toward the American style of judicial review was blocked. But still, one can get a sense of how American constitutional law influences China.

Continental constitutional thinking only exerted its influence in China in quite recent years. Since the 2010s, German constitutional law, for example, has increasingly impacted Chinese constitutional scholarship. Two German constitutional law casebooks were published, both edited by Professor Zhang Xiang, the Secretary-General of the Chinese Constitutional Law Association (Zhang 2012, 2016). The number of Chinese constitutional scholars trained in Germany has increased greatly in recent years. In another vein, the growing impact of German constitutional scholarship coincided with a hidden logic of *Qi Yuling*, that is, applying the Constitution in ordinary civil adjudication. Apart from judicial review, *Qi Yuling* in fact offered another way of judicializing the Constitution the privatization of the Constitution, i.e. to grant individuals private rights of action under the Constitution in civil lawsuits (Cai 2004).

As for administrative law, the hybrid nature of Chinese law is more eminent. As Professor He, a leading expert of Chinese administrative law, observes:

> In general, the contemporary Chinese administrative law community is like an international hypermarket of multinational administrative law, where a variety of different concepts, principles and systems are exhibited and purchased. Administrative law is an amalgamation of continental law tradition and Anglo-American law elements. ... This kind of influence begins to seep into administrative legislation. The law on administrative punishments and the administrative permit law, the two are unique legislation, can also be regarded as the results of the impact of different legal traditions: administrative punishment and administrative licensing this separate legislation seem to inherit and develop the tradition of continental law countries classification of administrative behavior, and one of the solutions (especially the program relies on) obviously affected by the common law tradition. In the administrative Procedure Law drafted by the Administrative Legislation Research Group, we also see the intersection of different traditions of continental law and Anglo-American law. (He 2007, p. 49.)

What can be added to He's account is the American influence on Chinese administrative litigation. The idea that citizens can sue the government in an ordinary court, rather than a specialized administrative court, definitely stems from across the pacific. Indeed, legal experts with a background in American law and institutions like the Ford Foundation and the Asia Foundation stood behind the drafting of some pillar legislations in administrative law, including administrative litigation law, state compensation law, administrative penalty law, administrative procedure law (Liu 2020, pp. 145–146).

3.4 Ancient Chinese Tradition

Recently, the ancient Chinese tradition looms large in Chinese law. Authorities emphasize that Chinese law should own its past. The modern Chinese revolutions, republican and socialist, may be considered revolts against the past. The past was viewed by Chinese elites, especially legal experts with foreign training, as a negative burden that should be thrown into the dustbin of history. But, with the rise of China, China's past is now thought of as a source of legal construction. That has generated much practical influence in concrete legal changes.

Take the recent constitutional change which establishes for the first time in the PRC the institution of a supervisory commission for example. The 2018 Amendments to the Chinese Constitution establishes a new state organ in charge of anti-corruption—the National Supervisory Commission. With that constitutional change, the National People's Congress (NPC) passed the National Supervisory Law in the same year to concretize rules about both party and state organ supervision. This new state organ, however, is rooted in ancient Chinese legal tradition: originating in the Qin and Han dynasties and lasting for more than two thousand years, an independent institution investigated and reported the conduct of government officials to ensure government ethics and justice.

Take the mediation system as another example. Since 2008, the new leadership of the higher courts in China altered the direction of Chinese judicial reform from a Western, professionalized, formalized goal to a more indigenous, populist, informal one, which was dubbed as "China's turn against law" (Minzner 2011). The Chinese judicial system revitalizes the practice of mediation, especially before formal trials. In some types of cases, mediation is compulsory before trial. Of course, mediation carries its ancient heritage—the Confucian idea of having fewer litigations and stressing the value of harmony.

4 Conclusion

Law is ideological in nature. It exhibits a nation's aspiration, plan, and character. Contemporary Chinese law is a mélange of the socialist tradition and Western elements, including both continental and Anglo-American ones, tinged with ancient factors. That is so because different exigencies exist almost simultaneously: to boost the market economy, to centralize state power, to modernize the structure of government, to enhance human rights protection, to reinforce Party leadership, etc. The Chinese legal system, because of its developing nature, is largely a patchwork in terms of its substantive content.

And China's reception and adoption of foreign legal system follow a dialectic of occidentalization and orientalization. In the past forty years, China tried to boost its economy while at the same time keeping its socialist political regime. It adopted a pragmatist approach towards receiving foreign law. Learning from the West but at the same maintaining political autonomy, curbing its political impacts, runs through the modern legal history of China and is also reflected in the construction of the contemporary legal system.

The last, but not the least, question remaining for this chapter is: given that the Chinese legal system has merged various heterogeneous elements, why do Chinese legal scholars still claim it to be within the family of continental law? The answer given in this chapter is that Chinese law wants to find its place in contemporary families of legal systems. While socialist law remarkably withers in general, and the ancient Chinese legal system seems largely in conflict with the project of legal modernization, the identity of continental law can help Chinese law be comparable to other legal systems like the US or Germany. The cover of continental law allows Chinese law to be intelligible and recognizable to outside observers.

References

Cai D (2004) Applying Chinese constitution like private laws (中国宪法实施的私法化之路). China Soc Sci (中国社会科学) 2:56–67

Deng J (2015) The guiding case system in Mainland China. Front Law China 10:1–26

Hao T (1996) On modern China's choice of continental legal system(《论近代中国对大陆法系的选择》). Stud Legal Mod (《法制现代化研究》): 302–314

He H (2007) The foreign sources of Chinese administrative law (中国行政法学的外国法渊源). J Comp Law(《比较法研究》)6:42–59

Huang S (2001) Judicialization of the constitution and its significance (宪法司法化及其意义). People's Court Daily(《人民法院报》) August 13

Huang Songyou (黄松有), Xianfa Sifahua jiqi Yiyi—Cong Zuigao Renmin Fayuan Jintian de Yige "Pifu" Tanqi (宪法司法化及其意义—从最高人民法院今天的一个《批复》谈起) [The Significance of Judicializing the Constitution—On a Supreme People's Court's Reply Today], Renmin Fayuan Bao (人民法院报) [People's CT. Daily], Aug. 13, 2001., http://politics.csscipaper.com/lawclass/constitution/ 23907.html

Liu H (2020) Regime-centered and court-centered understandings: the reception of American constitutional law in contemporary China. Am J Comp Law 68:95–150

Merryman JH, Perez-Perdomo R (2007) The civil law tradition: an introduction to the legal systems of Europe and Latin America. Stanford University Press, Redwood California

Minzner C (2011) China's turn against law. Am J Comp Law 59:935–984

Palmer V (2001) Introduction to the mixed jurisdictions. In: Palmer V (ed) Mixed jurisdictions worldwide: the third legal family, pp 3–18

Reynolds D (1993) China, 1898–1912: the Xinzheng revolution and Japan. Cambridge University Press, Cambridge

Shen Z (1997) Examples of borrowing foreign law in contemporary China: Part I(当代中国借鉴外国法律的实例(上)). China Legal Sci (《中国法学》) 6:22–28

Tang Y (2017) The Chinese model for securities law. In: Chen W (ed) The Beijing consensus? How China has changed western ideas of law and economic development. Cambridge University Press, Cambridge, pp 203–222

Upham F (2017) Lessons from Chinese growth: rethinking the role of property rights in development. In: Chen W (ed) The Beijing Consensus? How China has changed western ideas of law and economic development. Cambridge University Press, Cambridge, pp 119–143

Xu C (2003) (Constitutional history of the People's Republic of China) [中华人民共和国宪法史] (2003). Fujian People's Press, Fuzhou

Yi Y et al (2011) The course of rule of law: summary of 2011 China-US rule-of-law dialogue (《法治的里程——2011中美法治对话综述》). Tsinghua Law J (《清华法学》)6:160–176

Zhang T (2018) The development of comparative law in modern china. In: Reimann M, Zimmermann R (eds) The Oxford handbook of comparative law, 2nd edn, pp 228–252
Zhang T, Ginsburg T (2019) China's turn toward law. Virginia J Int Law 59:306–389
Zhang X ed. & trans. (2012) 1 Selected German constitutional cases: fundamental rights (德国宪法案例选释第一辑:基本权利总论) . Law Press (法律出版社) Beijing
Zhang X ed. & trans. (2016) 2 Selected German constitutional cases: freedom of speech (德国宪法案例选释第二辑:言论自由). Law Press (法律出版社) Beijing

Dworkin and the Aspirations of International Law

Lars Vinx

Abstract In his last publication, 'A New Philosophy for International Law,' Ronald Dworkin set out to establish the continuing relevance of an old jurisprudential puzzle, the question whether international law can be said to exist. But Dworkin failed to vindicate the continuing relevance of that question or to explain why legal scholars were once interested in it. Like his positivist opponents, Dworkin took the existence of international law for granted and argued merely that an interpretive conception of international legal order was to be preferred to the application of Hart's theory of the rule of recognition to the international case. It will be argued here that Kelsen's theory of international law is better placed to provide the missing explanation of why the existence puzzle continues to be relevant.

1 Introduction

The jurisprudence of international law was once animated by the question whether international law can be said to exist, whether it has the quality, to speak in the language of Hobbes and Austin, of law properly so-called (*compare* Hobbes 1996, p. 111 and Austin 1995, pp. 123, 171). While interest in this puzzle seems to have receded in the last few decades,[1] many of the greatest legal theorists of the twentieth century, whether they wrote in a civil or a common law context, put significant efforts into resolving it. Of late, the issue has begun to receive renewed attention (*see* Pavel and Lefkowitz 2018; Lefkowitz 2020).

This chapter will argue that the question of the existence of international law continues to be jurisprudentially relevant. It will do so by comparing Ronald Dworkin's thoughts on the puzzle of the existence of international law with Hans

[1]Recent philosophical debate has centred on the moral legitimacy of international law. *See* for instance Buchanan (2007).

L. Vinx (✉)
University of Cambridge, Cambridge, UK
e-mail: lv330@cam.ac.uk

N. Bersier et al. (eds.), *Common Law – Civil Law*, Law and Philosophy Library 139,
https://doi.org/10.1007/978-3-030-87718-7_12

Kelsen's. On the first few pages of his last publication, Dworkin promises to rehabilitate the existence puzzle (Dworkin 2013, pp. 2–3). But upon closer inspection, his argument fails to resurrect the puzzle in its original form. Dworkin seems to agree that there is no real question as to the existence of international law and ends up defending the claim that an interpretive conception of international law is needed, in lieu of Hartian positivism, to offer a morally attractive account of the content of current international law. It will be argued here, by appeal to Kelsen's theory of international law, that this perspective fails to appreciate the source of the original existence puzzle and that it consequently misunderstands the reasons for its continuing relevance.[2]

2 Kelsen and the Existence Puzzle

The puzzle of the existence of international law arose from the prevalence of sovereigntist accounts of legality in the nineteenth and early twentieth century. A sovereigntist account of the nature of law takes it that all proper laws are sovereign commands. The sovereign, in turn, is understood to draw their authority not from any form of legal authorization by to enjoy it as a result of the uncontested possession of supreme political power. Sovereigntism will commit its proponent not merely to the conclusion that international law is not proper law, but to the more radical view that international law cannot ever develop into proper law. If proper law is validated by exercises of sovereign authority, and if it is of the essence of sovereignty for the bearers of sovereign authority to be free from legal obligation, then it will follow that there can be no proper international law, no international law that is objectively binding for sovereign, politically independent states. International anarchy, tempered by an attachment to customary rules of international decorum, or the dreaded despotism of a world state will be the only two available models of global order.

Hans Kelsen read this line of reasoning as a *reductio ad absurdum* of the sovereigntist account of the nature of law (*see* Kelsen 1920). If a theory of the nature of law entails that it is impossible for there to be international law, that theory, Kelsen claimed, must be flawed. If we are to acknowledge that the existence of international law is possible, we must reject sovereigntism. Laws are not to be validated by appeal to the factual authority of a sovereign, but rather by reference to a fundamental rule of legal system, the basic norm, the validity of which must be presupposed in all juristic thought. A basic norm, given suitable circumstances, might confer objective bindingness on laws that have been produced by agreements

[2] Kelsen's theory of international law has not received a great deal of attention in English-language systematic jurisprudential debate on the nature of international law (*see* Dyzenhaus 2020). Kelsen-scholarship has produced some excellent discussions (*see* von Bernstorff 2010; Kammerhofer 2011). A bibliographical overview of Kelsen's works on international law is available in Bersier (1998). For a recent general interpretation of the Pure Theory *see* Kletzer (2018).

among states or that have come to be established as customs in the intercourse of nations. Whether there is international law depends on whether the assumption that there is an international legal order turns out to be a fruitful juristic hypothesis. Though Kelsen and the members of his school had difficulty in agreeing on a formulation of the basic norm of international law (see von Bernstorff 2010, pp. 160–165), they successfully established the view, later adopted by Hart, that there is no *a priori* reason to think that there could be no international law.

Kelsen's legal theory does not rule out that there might be circumstances in which the hypothesis that there is international law would not be fruitful. One might conceive, after all, of a condition such that all the world is united in one state, with all human beings subject to one municipal legal system. One might equally conceive of a condition such that different polities exist, but do not interact with each other in any way, perhaps as a result of unbridgeable geographical isolation. But in a world characterized by the existence of relatively centralized units of political power (also known as states) that have control of delimited but contiguous territories, that regularly interact with one another, and that develop common norms of intercourse or enter into explicit agreements, the hypothesis that international law exists, Kelsen argued, will turn out to be fruitful.[3]

Though Kelsen rejected the notion that a legal system must be grounded on a sovereign authority that stands above the positive law, he did not fully abandon the state-centred focus of civil-law jurisprudence. Kelsen famously argued that, from the point of view of legal science, the state is identical to the law and that jurisprudence is therefore nothing more than the legal theory of the state (*see* Kelsen 1928, pp. 114–204; *compare* Vinx 2007, pp. 78–100). The Pure Theory of Law, in line with these claims, exhibits a marked tendency to transfer traditional characteristics of the sovereign state to the legal system.

Kelsen argues, for instance, that a legal system, unless it is a mere part of a larger system, must be normatively independent. Its authority must be self-contained, drawn from the system's own basic norm (Kelsen 1920, pp. 4–9, 85–101). What is more, Kelsen claims that any legal system possesses a property of completeness. Once we assume that there is international law, there will be no international conflicts that are not amenable to a legal assessment (*see* Kelsen 1952, pp. 304–307). Kelsen rejects the view that sovereign states possess a natural freedom akin to the Hobbesian right of nature, a freedom which states, according to some sovereigntists, have never fully abandoned but only partially restricted, in voluntarily entering into treaties that impose certain limited obligations.[4] He holds, in contrast to that view, that it is of the essence of any legal order to claim a monopoly on the legitimate use of coercive force (*see* Kelsen 1944, p. 3 and Kelsen 1952, pp. 13–15). States that are subject to international law, accordingly, are entitled to use force only in response to a violation, on the part of other states, of their legal

---

[3]For more detailed discussion *see* Vinx (2016).

[4]For a particularly radical version of this view, which was widely cited in German-language debate in the early twentieth-century, *see* Kaufmann (1911).

rights. It does not matter that public international law, as of now, is still rather thin in content. If two states have a legal dispute, then the complainant must either be right to argue that a violation of their rights has taken place, and appropriate sanctions are then to be imposed on the delinquent state, or the complainant's claims must be spurious, in which case they may take no further, unilateral resort to force, in virtue of the principle that whatever is not prohibited by law is to be regarded as permitted.

International law's property of completeness goes along with a degree of subordination of municipal to international law. If international law purports to order all uses of force on a global scale, then it must purport to delimit a state's authority to use force and thus to explain under what conditions a state's use of force is not an international but a domestic concern. It does that, according to Kelsen, by assigning authority to control the use of violence in a certain territory to those who have achieved stable *de facto* control of it. From a jurisprudential perspective that acknowledges the existence of international law, then, states turn out not merely to be bound by international law. Their own authority is taken to be constituted by an international legal order (*see* Kelsen 1920, part 2).[5]

Kelsen's theory of international law is exposed to the charge of wishful thinking. If an international legal order that exhibits the property of completeness and that authorizes national legal orders can be brought into existence through a mere juristic hypothesis, then something must have gone wrong, or so it seems. After all, we still appear to live in a world of states that lay claim to sovereignty. Kelsen himself fuelled this suspicion by embracing a construction of the relationship of national and international law that was designed to accommodate his theory of international law with the facts of politics. Kelsen was concerned to argue, for instance, that his view that international law validates national law does not entail that national norms in conflict with international norms lack validity. The existence of such a conflicting norm merely authorizes the application of an international sanction (*see* Kelsen 1992, pp. 117–119). The Kelsenian existence and supremacy of international law, other words, seem to turn out to be less legally and politically consequential than we might have thought. If the claim that there is international law is true only if it is understood to have very few interesting legal or political implications, why bother with the question whether international law is law properly so-called?

[5]A short summary of the position in Kelsen (1992), pp. 107–125. Hart argued that Kelsen's understanding of the relation of national and international law is irredeemably flawed. *See* Hart (1983). Hart's assessment has come to be widely accepted in Anglo-American debate, but it strikes me as uncomprehending and confused. For further discussion Vinx (2016).

3 Hart on International Law

When H.L.A. Hart addressed the old chestnut of the existence of international law, in the final chapter of *The Concept of Law* (*see* Hart 1994, pp. 213–237), he did not come to answer the question, like Kelsen, but to bury it. It was one of Hart's aims to show that the issue was much less central to legal theory than earlier debate had assumed, to establish that it did not raise any deep questions about the nature of law. Hart agreed with Kelsen, of course, in rejecting a sovereigntist account of the nature of law. He agreed as well, accordingly, that the sovereigntist argument against the very possibility of international law was to be dismissed. But Hart was willing to concede that scepticism about the actual existence of international law had not been altogether unwarranted.

International law, Hart averred, is analogous to paradigmatic instances of legal order in some respects, but disanalogous in others. It is not a misuse of the term 'law', accordingly, to talk of international law, but one should remain aware, or so Hart cautioned, writing in the late 1950s, that international law still falls short of being a fully developed legal order in some important respects. Hart claimed that international norms have not yet come to be united into a legal system by a rule of recognition, grounded in an international practice of recognition. International law, in contrast to municipal law, Hart argued, does not yet exemplify the union of primary and secondary rules that forms the capstone of a fully developed legal order (*see* Hart 1994, pp. 236–237).

While it does make important concessions to a sceptical view of international law, Hart's account of international law allows that the practices and rules of international law might develop into a genuine legal system. The question whether international law is proper law is transformed from one that concerns our understanding of the very nature of legal order into an empirical issue that concerns the factual state of development of international legality. Has international legal practice developed its own practice of recognition and thus transformed itself into a legal system of its own?

Hart's approach has helped to defuse the existence puzzle in a second, less direct way. His theory of legal system is unburdened from the legacy of state theory that structures Kelsen's understanding of legal order. It is therefore open to a pluralist understanding of legality which allows for the co-existence of several independent and interacting legal orders (*see* Barber 2010, chapters 9–10). There may be international law, and it may, from its own point of view, claim generate obligations that are binding on states. But for a Hartian, it need have no pretensions to supremacy or completeness. Whether such claims should be attributed to international law must depend on the contingent content of its rule of recognition, assuming it has one.

4 Dworkin on Hart on International Law

Hart's reframing of the issue has been widely accepted and the old puzzle, as a result, has moved to the margins of jurisprudential debate. It is commonly assumed, nowadays, that contemporary international law is proper law. But this fact is taken to be explicable on Hartian grounds, by appeal to the claim that international law is now more developed than it was in Hart's time, and to raise (or answer) no deep jurisprudential questions (*see* Besson 2010).

Dworkin's 'new philosophy of international law' challenges that consensus and attacks legal theorists who work within the Hartian paradigm for paying no attention to the existence puzzle. The facts that are relevant for assessing whether international law is proper law, from a Hartian point of view, or so Dworkin argues, have not changed dramatically enough, between the 1950s and the present, to justify an assessment of the status of contemporary international law that differs from the negative verdict Hart gave in *The Concept of Law*.[6] Dworkin himself does not in fact think that the existence of international law is seriously in question. What he argues is that legal theorists who take their cues from Hart lack a compelling account of why contemporary international law can be said to be proper law.

Those who aim to establish the existence of international law on Hartian grounds argue, according to Dworkin, that 'a sovereign state is subject to international law but [...] only so far as it has consented to be bound by that law, and they take that principle of consent to furnish an international rule of recognition', expressed in rough outline in art. 38 of the *Vienna Convention on the Law of Treaties* (Dworkin 2013, p. 5). In this approach, the principle of consent plays two slightly different roles, as Dworkin acknowledges. It binds states to rules they expressly agreed to be bound by and it subjects them to international customs and legal principles that are generally recognized, by the community of 'civilized nations', as legally binding. The 'law for nations [...] is grounded in what nations – or at least the vast of those that others count as "civilized"—have consented to treat as law' (Dworkin 2013, p. 6).

Positivists are drawn to this consent-based account, Dworkin argues, because they think it holds out the promise of a reconciliation of the sovereignty of states with the bindingness of international law. If all international legal obligations are based on consent, if even so-called peremptory norms of international law are binding only because they represent an agreement in moral opinion among 'civilized nations', then it follows, in the view that Dworkin attributes to the positivist, that international legal obligations are compatible with state sovereignty, since no state will ever be subjected to an international obligation against its will (Dworkin 2013, pp. 6, 10).

As Dworkin is quick to point out, this supposed reconciliation of sovereignty with international law involves an obvious *non-sequitur*. If the agreement of some states, of the majority of states that count as 'civilized', can validate rules that bind other

---

[6]"But nothing has actually changed. The old grounds for challenge remain; they are only ignored." (*See* Dworkin 2013, p. 2).

states—states that are civilized but non-consenting or states that do not qualify as civilized—there will be some states which are subject to obligations that do not result from their own will. The aim of reconciliation, if it is to be successful, clearly calls for a stricter understanding of the principle of consent, one that requires each state's individual consent to any obligation to which it may be held. But international law will be unable to serve any useful purpose, Dworkin fears, it will fail to reduce 'the threat some states offer to others,' unless it escapes 'the straitjacket of state-by-state consent' (Dworkin 2013, p. 7).

The consent-based account of international law would fail, Dworkin goes on to argue, even if we set that problem aside and chose to adopt the stricter reading of the principle of consent, for several further reasons. The first is that the consent-based account leaves it open how rules agreed upon are to be interpreted (Dworkin 2013, pp. 7–8). States are committed, in virtue of membership in the UN, to abstain from violations of the territorial integrity of other states, unless these take place in the course of defence against another state's aggression or are authorized by the UN Security Council. But how, Dworkin asks, are we to interpret the term 'territorial integrity'? Does the protection of territorial integrity make it impermissible, for instance, to perform an airdrop of humanitarian supplies without the permission of the state in which a humanitarian crisis is unfolding? To say that states consented to a particular view on this matter when entering the UN is unconvincing, and problems of interpretation cannot be offloaded to a court endowed with the power to bindingly decide on all contested questions of interpretation of international norms. Such a court does not presently exist, and there is little appetite among states, Dworkin observes, to create it.

A second problem concerns the issue of how to understand the notion of *opinio juris*. The consent theorist claims that states are bound by those international customs which they have decided to accept as legally binding. But the notion of acceptance which the consent theorist wants to account for takes it that states *recognize* certain international customs as legally binding, in expressing an *opinio juris*, not that they make those customs legally binding through expressing the opinion that they are. To claim that accepted customs are legally binding because they are accepted is therefore incoherent. If state acceptance is a mere recognition of a customary norm's legal standing, there must be some criterion other than factual acceptance that explains why a customary norm is deserving of acceptance. Consent-theory, however, must fail to supply that more basic standard (Dworkin 2013, p. 9).

There is a question, moreover, Dworkin points out, as to why it should be deemed legitimate to hold states to treaty-based obligations, in the present, that a state entered into a long time ago, perhaps under a different political regime, and which may fail to adequately reflect current circumstances. 'It seems unfair that people should suffer serious disadvantage only because politicians chosen by entirely different people under entirely different constitutions signed a document many generations ago' (Dworkin 2013, p. 10). Dworkin goes on to observe that some domestic constitutions, like the American, turn treaty-based obligations into part of 'the Supreme Law of the Land.' If such incorporation were necessary for international law to be binding, however, it would make the bindingness of international law contingent on domestic law: '...what domestic law creates it can destroy: a state would not be bound by international law if it were free, through its domestic processes, to unbind itself' (Dworkin 2013, p. 10).

It is a little hard to see what these two points are supposed to have to do with each other. But perhaps Dworkin's claim is that since international legal obligations are assumed to be objectively binding on states, irrespective of whether they are incorporated into domestic law, the normative question of whether a state should continue to be held to an obligation that it entered a long time ago is especially pressing. If we were to adopt a theory that grounds international obligations in state consent and that holds that treaty-based obligations will bind conclusively and indefinitely, the pattern of international obligations would come to lack the ability to adapt to changing circumstances, in line with perceived moral requirements.

Dworkin apparently takes this problem to be related to the question of what makes treaties binding. It is obvious that consent theory must rely on the principle that states are bound by treaties they entered into: *pacta sunt servanda*. This principle, of course, cannot itself be grounded in consent. It is what explains the bindingness of consent. But the principle itself, Dworkin suggests, stands in need of further explanation. We need to know why (and to what extent) treaty-based obligations are to be regarded as binding. The attempt to apply a Hartian analysis of legal system to international law, Dworkin claims, does not help with answering this moral question (Dworkin 2013, p. 10).

5 From Fit to Justification

Dworkin argues, as we have seen, that Hartians fail to take the existence puzzle seriously enough. But what exactly is the critical conclusion that Dworkin wants to draw from that claim? He should not want to argue, it would appear, that a Hartian approach is in principle incapable, like the sovereigntist theory of old, to acknowledge the possibility of the existence of international law. There seems to be no doubt that an international practice of recognition that accounts for all apparent international obligations could, in principle, come into existence.

To be sure, Dworkin repeatedly suggests, as we have seen, that a positivist account of international law must take the form of a theory that aims to ground all international obligations in state-consent. That view, however, is clearly mistaken. There simply is no reason to think that an international practice of recognition that recognizes peremptory norms of international law and that lays down the criteria under which norms are to be accorded that status could not arise. The development of such a practice might go along with or follow upon the creation of an international tribunal empowered to give authoritative interpretations of all international obligations and it could, for all we know, specify the conditions under which treaty-based obligations are to be regarded as defeasible or to be adapted to changed circumstances.

Of course, an international practice of recognition of this kind does not presently exist, but this fact leaves open several further possibilities as to how a positivist account of the foundations of current international law might play out. It might be argued that there is, so far, no international practice of recognition at all, as Hart claimed, not even one that grounds the existence of international law entirely in state consent. While Dworkin does at times suggests that this is the view a Hartian would be forced to adopt—most pointedly in the claim that the facts have not changed since Hart wrote *The Concept of Law*—most of his discussion seems concerned to press a slightly different claim. Dworkin's central line of attack appears to concede that a Hartian might plausibly hypothesize that there now is an international practice of recognition, but that this hypothesis fails to explain the existence of international law in a way that fits current international legal practice.

The Hartian hypothesis, Dworkin suggests, would force us to adopt an implausibly austere conception of the content of international law, one that implies that some of the norms that are commonly regarded to belong to international law, or that many scholars would very much like to be able to designate as legal norms, are not proper laws. We would have to concede that there are currently no peremptory international norms, that all existing international obligations are based on state consent, and perhaps that the circumstances under which they will be regarded as defeasible are not clearly defined in the law.[7] A Hartian account of international law, as a result, will be too threadbare to succeed on the dimension of fit. State practice and legal scholarship increasingly reflect the conviction that there are peremptory norms of international law that are validated by their intrinsic qualities, and that international law is, to some degree, subject to the moral pressure of the ambition towards legitimacy. The prevalent understanding of international law, such as it is, Dworkin argues, takes existing international law to have a prominent non-consensual element, and a good theory needs to account for that.

What Dworkin argues, then, is that the Hartian account mishandles what Dworkin supposes is the non-consensual element of existing international law. For Dworkin, this perceived failure to give a satisfactory account of an important dimension of international law, of course, is not a mere descriptive deficiency: '. . .the question of *why* these documents [The UN Charter and the Vienna Convention] constitute some kind of legal system is crucial because how these rules and principles should be interpreted hinges on it' (Dworkin 2013, p. 3) The positivist approach is as unattractive on the dimension of justification as it is deficient on the dimension of fit. To make full sense of the aspirations embedded in contemporary international legal

[7] As Kramer (2018), p. 51 points out, Hart (1994), p. 225 appears to suggest that such a view is incoherent because it overlooks that states will be unable to impose obligations on themselves unless there are acceptance-independent power-conferring norms. If that was Hart's view, he was mistaken, as Kramer argues, 'because voluntarists deny not the possibility of acceptance-independent norms but instead the possibility of acceptance-independent obligations.' There is no reason why a practice of recognition could not give rise to an international legal order in which all obligations are derived from state-consent.

practice, one must turn to an interpretive account of international law (*see* Dworkin 1986, chapters 1–3).

6 Dworkin's 'New Philosophy of International Law'

The attempt to apply Dworkinian interpretivism to international law faces an obvious hurdle, as Dworkin acknowledges. Dworkin's interpretive version of natural law theory is concerned not to eliminate the difference between the law as it is and the law as it ought to be. The law is not simply derived from the system, whichever it may be, of true moral principles. Rather, it is derived from a morally optimizing interpretation of past practice. Law consists of 'rights and obligations [. . .] properly enforceable on demand through institutions like courts' (Dworkin 2013, p. 12). But when judges ask themselves what rights and obligations parties are entitled to see them enforce, they do not answer the question on the basis of an abstract political morality alone. Rather, they draw their answer from 'the political constitution, legislation pursuant to that constitution, and past judicial decisions' (Dworkin 2013, p. 12). It is those materials which are to be given an interpretation that shows them in their best light. For legal interpretation to take this constraint of fit seriously is itself a moral requirement, in Dworkin's view, to which he refers as a demand for integrity. The laws' claims are more binding than those of abstract justice since the law protects the legitimate expectations of its subjects, by treating them in line with a coherent system of principles expressed in practice (*see* Dworkin 1986, chapters 6–7).

An interpretive account of international law would have to walk the same fine line. It would have to offer a morally optimized interpretation of actual international legal practice that respects a constraint of fit and thus secures the integrity of international law. The importance of the demand for integrity is arguably more pressing in the international context than in the domestic. If interpretation in the international sphere were not grounded in past practice, its results would obviously be open to the charge that they do nothing more than to elevate the interpreter's moral opinions to the status of legitimately enforceable law. The distinction between the law as it is and the law as it ought to be, from the point of view of abstract justice, would collapse. International law would become what the most powerful interpreters think it ought to be.

What allows us to maintain the distinction between legal interpretation and abstract moral reasoning in the domestic context, Dworkin explains, is the fact that our interpretive efforts can take their start from an accepted institutional background by reference to which we will be able to distinguish between adjudication and legislation. To identify legal rights and obligations we take the position of a judge, if perhaps only virtually, and ask ourselves what considerations a judge would have to make, in order to honour the ideal of integrity, when they decide whether some claim ought to be regarded as enforceable on demand. A comparable institutional framework, however, is unavailable in the international sphere:

> We can draw that distinction easily for national legal systems, because we find institutional structures there that provide an appropriate vocabulary. These structures broadly distinguish between courts, which have the responsibility and power to enforce rights and obligations on demand, and other sorts of political institutions, like legislatures, that do not. So we can helpfully frame our basic political question in institutional terms: We can ask what rights courts have the responsibility and right to enforce. But no such structure, in any but the most rudimentary form, is yet in place in the international domain, and none can be expected soon (Dworkin 2013, pp. 13–14).

Though the international lawyer lacks the full institutional background that, in the domestic context, underpins the project of developing an interpretive theory of law, we can, Dworkin argues, make up for that lack through a feat of juristic imagination. In order to answer interpretive questions concerning international law, to ascertain what international rights are enforceable on demand, we may simply assume, for purposes of argument, that there is an international court that has compulsive jurisdiction on all questions of international law and whose judgments are enforceable against any state:

> If we can imagine such a court, even as fantasy, then we can frame a tractable question of political morality. What tests or arguments should that hypothetical court adopt to determine the rights and obligations of states (and other international actors and organizations) that it would be *appropriate* for it to enforce coercively? This is a moral question, but a special one, because judicial institutions with compulsory jurisdiction and sanctions at their disposal are subject to special moral standards of legitimacy and fairness. They have no right to declare and enforce general standards of comity, decency or wisdom. We can identify a general theory of what it would be appropriate for such an institution to enforce as the foundation of international law (Dworkin 2013, p. 14).

The sketch of the foundations of international law that Dworkin develops by appeal to the question of how an imaginary international court would have to decide which international rights are enforceable on demand proceeds in two steps.

In the first step Dworkin argues that states are subject to a moral duty to govern legitimately, that is, to ensure that the use of coercive force by their own institutions is as morally justifiable to citizens as circumstances allow it to be (Dworkin 2013, pp. 16–19). Since international order is a part of the framework that each state imposes on its own citizens, together with other states, this duty entails a more particular duty on states to accept and to support forms of international order that enhance the legitimacy of the rule they exercise over their subjects. States must be willing to 'mitigate the failures and risks of the sovereign-state system' (Dworkin 2013, p. 19), which include the danger that a state may sink into tyranny and deprive its citizens of the opportunity to participate in the exercise of political power as well as engage in systematic violation of human rights, the danger that a state may be unable to protect its own citizens against the aggression of other states, and the danger that states may fail to coordinate their policies in ways necessary to realize and protect important global public goods.

The duty to mitigate the legitimacy-undermining potential consequences of an unbridled system of state-sovereignty is somewhat akin to the well-known Rawlsian natural duty to create and support just institutions (*see* Rawls 1999, pp. 293–301). As in the case of Rawls's natural duty, the duty-bearers face the problem that there are a number of different ways in which the duty might conceivably be discharged. The duty to mitigate therefore needs to be specified, in the second step, by a principle of salience (Dworkin 2013, pp. 19–22). The latter requires that states be willing to fall in with nascent or established norms of international cooperation that improve the political legitimacy of the states that form part of the international system. The UN Charter and the institutions for which it provides, for instance, are a salient pattern. States are, therefore, subject to the law of the United Nations, not because they have consented to accede to it, but because compliance with the pattern is now the required way in which a state must discharge its duty of mitigation.

Dworkin's general claim is that the combination of the duty to mitigate with the principle of salience answers to what he regards as the weaknesses of the positivist account of current international legality. Dworkin's sketch sustains the claim that there are norms of *jus cogens* and shows, in outline, how to argue for them. It thus makes room for non-consensual elements of international law, but it does so in a way, Dworkin hopes, that will respect the integrity of international law. Established patterns of cooperation, whether customary or treaty-based, rightly lay claim to the special attention of international lawyers. The salience of these patterns helps to provide the needed specificity to the duty to mitigate.

7 Interpretivism and Illegality

Dworkin's sketch of the general foundations of international law raises an obvious question. Could the duty to mitigate the shortcomings of a sovereigntist international order justify unlawful departures, on the part of states or coalitions of states, from established patterns of coordination, if to do so promises to establish new custom that better legitimates the exercise of political power on the part of members of international society? Dworkin appears to think that the answer to the question should be negative. Referring to Thomas Franck's view that the NATO intervention in Kosovo was morally mandatory though it was illegal (*see* Franck 1999), Dworkin remarks:

> That is a dangerous description, particularly from an eminent international lawyer. International law is fragile, still nascent and in critical condition. The proposition that a sense of moral duty can justify violations of international law threatens to strangle the child (Dworkin 2013, p. 23).

The claim that the intervention was illegal, Dworkin argues, is a product of a consent-oriented positivist approach to international law which the interpretive approach is meant to replace. While there can never be moral justification to set aside the law that derives from a compelling interpretive account, interpretivism need not concede that the Kosovo crisis confronted the world with a tragic conflict of law and morality. Interpretation can shoulder the task of reform that a positivist would have to consign to the strategic lawbreaking on the part of states powerful enough to establish new custom.

Dworkin's development of this claim delivers rather less than might be expected. Dworkin suggests that article 2 (4) of the UN Charter might plausibly be interpreted not as preventing all forcible intervention not authorized by the UN Security Council but as merely outlawing 'the use of military force aimed at territorial change or political dominion' (Dworkin 2013, p. 23). However, he immediately concedes that such a view will not do, at least not without further qualification, as it would, in effect, empower hegemonic states, under a humanitarian pretext, to interfere in the affairs of the weak at their own discretion—a danger that came to pass in the 2003 invasion of Iraq. What is needed, Dworkin thinks, is a framework that constrains the unilateral use of force but does not subject humanitarian intervention to the stringent constraint of approval by all members of the UN Security Council. He therefore proposes that the UN General Assembly pass a resolution to declare that interventions are permissible, even without the consent of all members of the Security Council, if such intervention is approved by the majority of members of the Council, and if the ICJ declares it to be necessary, upon the request of the General Assembly, to prevent crimes against humanity. Dworkin candidly admits that the proposed resolution would amount to 'fresh legislation [. . .] rather than an interpretation of the Charter as it stands' (Dworkin 2013, p. 26). What the interpretive approach contributes, then, is merely the argument that for the General Assembly so to legislate would not conflict with article 2 (4) of the Charter.

Dworkin reasons along similar lines to address the need for international law to coordinate state behaviour to tackle climate change (Dworkin 2013, pp. 27–29). The general assembly could not legislate, Dworkin concedes, to impose binding emissions quotas in states, and Dworkin's imaginary international court would not be entitled to enforce such legislation. However, if almost all states were to decide to enter into a convention to empower the General Assembly so to legislate—with a quadruple majority representing a majority of states in the assembly, a majority of the world's population, a majority of the members of the Security Council and a majority of the permanent members of the Council—the General Assembly could, according to Dworkin, lawfully acquire a power to impose binding emissions quotas on all states. What interpretivism contributes, once more, is the argument that the procedure in question could lawfully be created without universal state consent. States have a duty to mitigate the danger of climate change, the proposed scheme would possess salience, and its procedural safeguards would adequately protect individual states against abusive uses of the power to impose quotas. States not party to the proposed convention would therefore be bound to their quota.

8 Does Interpretivism Make a Difference?

Let me explain why I claimed above that Dworkin's interpretive account of the foundations of international law delivers less than it appears to promise. International interpretivism stops short of arguing that interpretation alone will suffice to establish the existence of the pattern of obligations which is needed, in Dworkin's view, to adequately protect human rights and to coordinate state behaviour in ways conducive to the realization of international common goods. What interpretivism does, by itself, is merely to support the claim that existing international law makes it possible for states lawfully to create a process for the legislative enactment of international norms that would not require universal state consent even while its outcomes would bind all states.

Though Dworkin, at times, seems to want to tar the contemporary positivist with the brush of the sovereigntist denier of international law, the dispute with the Hartian positivist, as we have seen, is neither about whether there could be proper international law nor about whether such law currently exists. It is noteworthy as well that Dworkin is more interested in institutional reform than in directly vindicating the legal standing of certain substantive moral principles. The dispute with the Hartian positivist, as Dworkin describes it, boils down to the question whether existing international law would permit the establishment of mechanisms of decision-taking which are capable to generate outcomes binding on all states, even those who have not consented to be subject to those mechanisms. There is no reason to think that a Hartian positivist would have to disagree with the view that the changes to international law envisaged by Dworkin would be morally and politically desirable. And as I pointed out above, a Hartian approach does not rule out the possibility that a practice of recognition that does give rise to something like the framework proposed by Dworkin might in time develop. An attempt to read a Hartian rule of recognition into existing international practice might, to be sure, make current international law out to be more firmly wedded to the requirement of state-consent than Dworkin thinks is appropriate. And that might entail, from a Hartian point of view, that the changes advocated by Dworkin could only be brought about with the consent of all who are to be bound, or else through some process of political change that, however desirable its outcome, is not itself lawful.

It is not clear, however, how much turns on this difference from a practical point of view. Dworkin's interpretive sketch of the foundations of international law, after all, is unlikely to bring forth the actual change in the absence of its acceptance by governments, legal scholars, and the citizens of the several states that form part of international society. If such acceptance prevailed a political transformation towards a global practice of recognition that realizes something like Dworkin's proposal, whether authorized by existing international law or not, would in any case be rather likely. The simple truth of the matter, of course, is that a concurrence in opinion among states of the requisite sort does not presently exist, irrespective of whether it is portrayed as a view about what the law is or as a view about what it ought to be. Interpretivism does nothing to solve that problem.

9 Sovereignty and Objective Validity

As we have seen, Dworkin plays up the significance of the difference between his interpretivism and a Hartian approach by suggesting that legal positivism must be committed to a consent-based understanding of international law. Positivism, in Dworkin's understanding, claims that law is grounded in past legal decisions alone, it excludes moral principles that might figure in an interpretive account from the sources of law. If that understanding of the sources of law is applied to international law, it will follow, Dworkin seems to think, that all international obligations must be based on the explicit consent of the duty-bearing state, simply because there is no international legislative authority and no judicial authority with compulsory jurisdiction.

I have already suggested that the connection between positivism and consent is more contingent than Dworkin seems to realize. There could be an international practice of recognition that sustains an international law with a non-consensual dimension. But Dworkin's account of the motivations of positivism in international law is open to a more fundamental criticism. As Dworkin sees it, positivism's adherence to the view that international obligations must be derived from consent results from the aim to reconcile the existence of international law with the doctrine of state sovereignty. Since positivism, allegedly, sustains consent theory, positivism itself will seem attractive, Dworkin thinks, since it helps to bring about that reconciliation (Dworkin 2013, p. 10). But the desire for reconciliation between the claim that there is international law that is binding on states and the claim that states are sovereign is misconceived, in Dworkin's view. The 'Westphalian' doctrine of state sovereignty is what ails international order, and it must be overcome if international law is not to be strangled in its cradle. What we need, and what Dworkinian interpretivism is supposed to deliver, is an account of the foundations of international law that does away with the doctrine of sovereignty.

This line of reasoning seems to concede that a consent-based account of international law would, in principle, be capable to reconcile the existence of objectively binding international law with state sovereignty. Dworkin's real argument against such an account, as we have seen, is not that it fails to account for the existence of international law but rather that a consent-based account of the foundations of international law would offer a morally less attractive rendering of the content of international law than the doctrine laid out in Dworkin's interpretive sketch. According to Kelsen, the initial concession—that a demand for state consent will bring about reconciliation—should not be made in the first place. There is no way to harmonize the existence of objectively binding international law with the doctrine of sovereignty, not even for the positivist or for the positivist theorist of consent, at least if the doctrine is understood in the way that motivated denials of international law (see Kelsen 1920, pp. 102–241).

To illustrate the point, consider one of Kelsen's contemporaries. Heinrich Triepel's consent-based account of international law might serve as an example of an unsuccessful attempt at reconciliation (*see* Triepel 1899).[8] Triepel was staunchly committed to the view that a sovereign state cannot have any obligations other than those which it chooses to impose on itself by entering into treaties with other sovereign states. And yet, Triepel was equally staunchly committed to the view that there is international law and that it is objectively binding upon states. Once a state has imposed an international obligation upon itself, it cannot be released from that obligation unless the other contracting parties decide to waive it. States, Triepel argues, must not be permitted to invoke a *clausula rebus sic stantibus* to wiggle out of their treaty-derived obligations. To allow them to do so, at their own judgment, would, in effect, undercut the objective bindingness of international law.

If we take the sovereigntist legal theory that motivated nineteenth-century scepticism about the existence of international law seriously, Triepel's position looks like an incoherent halfway house. The sovereigntist claims that the sovereign's will is not only the sole source of law but stands above it.[9] Once that claim is taken at face value, it becomes hard to see how a sovereign could ever be subject to objectively binding legal obligations, whether these are self-imposed or imposed by some other authority. A sovereign government that has entered into a treaty might judge, at some later point, that to stick by its terms is no longer in the nation's interest. If sovereignty, in the domestic context, includes a power to waive constitutional restraints, to decide on the exception, as authors who were also deniers of international law tended to believe (*see*, for instance, Jellinek 1914, pp. 332–375), must it not entail, in the international context, that a sovereign can unmake any of its international obligations?

One might try to avoid that conclusion by arguing that there is a background norm of international law that requires that sovereigns abide by their treaty-derived obligations, whether they now wish to be held to those norms or not. Such a norm might take a more complicated content than the simple principle that treaties must be kept. One might, for instance, conceive of a background norm that lays down conditions under which a treaty-based obligation may be repudiated. The crucial point is that the background norm cannot itself have been created by an exercise of sovereign authority, whether individual or collective. What is more, it must lay claim to objective validity if international law is to be proper law. If there is to be international law, no state's declared view as to what its legal rights and obligations are can ever claim to be conclusive. Even if, for instance, the background norm in international law that makes treaties binding were to contain exceptions, a state's claim that it is permitted to withdraw from some treaty-derived obligation would still

[8]Triepel's reconciliation was rejected both by Kelsen (1920), pp. 120–151 and by sovereigntists like Jellinek (1914), p. 377, n. 1.

[9]For expressions of this view in German debate to which Kelsen responds *see* Kaufmann (1911) and Jellinek (1914), pp. 375–379. Jellinek (1914), p. 377 puts the point as follows: 'Where the observance of the law of peoples comes into conflict with the existence of the state the rules of the law, by contrast, recede [. . .] the law of peoples exists for states, not the states for the law of peoples.' For a more recent theory of international law that shares some of the flavour *see* Goldsmith and Posner (2007).

have to be either be objectively true or false, depending on whether the relevant exceptional circumstances obtain or not. A state's mere claim that is vital interests are affected cannot make it true that it is permitted to withdraw from the obligation.[10]

Let me try to clarify the point by rephrasing it. The idea of the objective bindingness of law is incompatible with the existence of a sphere of a-legality. In Kelsen's conception of legality, as we have already seen, a legal system necessarily makes a claim to completeness. Where there is law, any possible act of any subject of the law will either be deemed legal or illegal, that is, it will either be an act that is legally permitted, and coercive interference with which is prohibited, or it will be an act that violates a duty-imposing legal norm and therefore warrants the imposition of a sanction. There are no acts which are beyond legal assessment or exempt from legal evaluation.[11] This principle, Kelsen argued, applies to those who act in the name of the state as much as to anyone else. If it makes sense to speak of sovereignty, as normative independence, then only as a property of legal order itself, not as a power wielded by organs of government.[12]

An area of a-legality, by contrast, will arise wherever the applicability of the distinction between legality and illegality to an agent's acts is held to depend on further, meta-legal conditions, the satisfaction of which is to be adjudicated by the sovereign. The *clausula rebus sic stantibus*, for example, might be read in a way that gives rise to a sphere of a-legality. The clause might be taken to imply, say, that a state's actions are evaluable as legal or illegal only if a situation of normality obtains, and that the judgment as to whether that is the case is left to a sovereign. The binding force of any obligation that a state may have incurred through consent, in that view, is contingent on the duty-bearer's judgment that there has been no material change in the underlying circumstances, which is just another way to say, of course, that it is not conclusively or objectively binding.[13] This understanding of treaty-based obligations fits into a wider picture of international society that portrays states as living in a condition akin the state of nature. Specific consent-derived obligations, in such a view, are not expressive of a genuine legal order that claims completeness and a monopoly on the legitimate use of coercive force. They are partial and revocable restraints on an a-legal natural freedom which states continue to possess.

What Dworkin overlooks is that it is a picture of this kind that motivated the sovereigntist denial of the existence of international law. To claim that the state is truly sovereign is to claim that it cannot be conclusively bound, that it is not, in the last instance, subject to legal order. It is immaterial whether a state's obligations are held to arise only from consent or also from peremptory duty-imposing norms. If

[10]This point is pressed in Kelsen (1920), pp. 204–240. For extended discussion of Kelsen's idea of the objectivity of law *see* Vinx (2007).

[11]Lauterpacht (1933) is an extended attempt to apply this idea to international law.

[12]For further discussion *see* Vinx (2007), pp. 78–100.

[13]This is the key claim in Kaufmann (1911), perhaps the most widely cited German work on the theory of international law in the first half of the twentieth-century. Carl Schmitt's famous claim that the sovereign is he who decides on the exception, in Schmitt (2005), p. 5, is likewise built on the idea that the essence of sovereignty consists in the sovereign's ability to enter a sphere a-legality.

obligations based on consent are held to be objectively binding, they are as incompatible with sovereignty as obligations that stem from *jus cogens*. If international law is to be proper law, if it is to be objectively binding, there is no way to reconcile sovereignty with the existence of international law—just as there is no way, for similar reasons, to reconcile the classical doctrine of sovereignty with the existence of proper constitutional law.[14]

To avoid this conclusion one could, of course, redefine the notion of sovereignty and declare a sovereign state to be one that can be conclusively bound to international law but only with its own consent. Or one might argue that states ought to enjoy protection against external interference to the extent that to do so serves morally valuable purposes (*see* Endicott 2010).[15] But such openly normative or moralized understandings of sovereignty do not match the understanding that motivated the existence puzzle. The proposed redefinitions would make it inexplicable why anyone should ever have thought that the doctrine of sovereignty stands in tension with international law. Short of such exercises in redefinition, the only way to concede that there is international law is to admit that a state, at least from a legal point of view, cannot be truly sovereign. We must either deny that the state is sovereign or deny that there is international law. *Tertium non datur*.

10 Dworkin, Kelsen, and the Aspirations of International Law

There are of course attempts to avoid this stark alternative. A constitutional pluralist might argue that international obligations are conclusively binding even against the will of states, but only from the point of view of the international legal system, which latter is only one of several interacting but independent legal systems, each with their own ultimate standards of validity. International law's claim to be objectively binding need not be accepted from the point of view of a national legal order for the two systems to interact. There is, admittedly, a possibility of conflict. But the danger of conflict can be reduced to a tolerable level, or so we are promised, if the two systems engage in dialogue and refrain from pressing a claim to supremacy (*see*, for instance, Krisch 2010).

Dworkin would surely have held that such a response amounts to a political fudge, and one that threatens to sell the claims of international law short. If

[14]Sovereigntists typically apply the idea that a sovereign may enter a sphere of a-legality both to constitutional and to international law. Carl Schmitt is the most famous case in point (*see* Vinx 2013).

[15]To put the point above in another way: Sovereignty is not to be confused with what international lawyers call sovereign equality. The latter is a legal status secured to states by international law that goes along with certain legal obligations. The question whether the legal protections which this status offers to states are morally justifiable may be interesting and important, but it has nothing to do with the existence puzzle.

international law is to fulfil an ordering function for international society, states must be brought to recognize that its norms are objectively binding. A legally uncontrolled sphere of a-legality must not be allowed to reappear in the interstices of the several interacting systems of a pluralist legal order. The claims of international law must be enforced, if need be, against recalcitrant states. Dworkin is quite clearly committed to the view that international law is complete, in something like the Kelsenian sense, and that the obligations which it imposes are conclusive.

However, Dworkin does not explicitly own up to that commitment. The assumptions of completeness and objective validity remain undefended in his theory of international law. As Dworkin himself points out, they do have unproblematic application in the domestic context—where a state exists, is typically seen to be legitimate, successfully claims a monopoly of force, and manages to enforce its law within a certain territory. It is an essential feature of the state, as we understand it, that it refuses to give the subjects of its law any access to a sphere of a-legality. The state imposes it legality/illegality-dichotomy on all acts of all its subjects. Once this authority is taken to be unproblematic, it will follow that the state's courts are the proper place to settle thorny questions concerning the interpretation and application of the law. The claim, moreover, that they ought to do so in line with a principled interpretive conception of the legal material that shows the law in a morally justified light will, in that case, have obvious moral attractions.

But whether this line of reasoning translates into the international sphere is doubtful. What really drives the consent-oriented understanding of international law is not a simple jurisprudential mistake—the unwillingness on the part of scholars to exchange dreary Hartian positivism for morally inspiring and exciting Dworkinian interpretivism—but the fact that the assumptions of completeness and objectivity have no unproblematic applicability to international society. And we clearly cannot paper over this problem with a mere feat of the juristic imagination. To claim that we can determine the content of international law by asking what that content would appear to be from the interpretive point of view of a hypothetical judge on an international court with compulsory and universal jurisdiction begs the decisive question. The move assumes that to be objectively binding and complete is what the practice we refer to as international law is meant to be. But that, of course, will be denied by latter-day sovereigntists when it suits their purposes. Dworkin's claim that nothing has changed since Hart wrote *The Concept of Law* might have to be given a more radical interpretation than Dworkin himself was willing to embrace. If proper law must be objectively binding, the original puzzle of the existence of international law is still very much with us.

Kelsen arguably saw this point much more clearly than Dworkin. If the very notion of the objective validity of law is incompatible with the understanding of sovereignty that gives rise to the existence puzzle, if sovereignty is nothing more than the normative independence of a rule-based legal order, then we are left, Kelsen argued, with either the view that international law is valid only to the extent that it has been incorporated into the domestic legal system whose point of view the jurisprude has chosen to occupy, or else with the view that national law derives its validity from a basic norm of international law. To claim that there is objectively binding international law, Kelsen argued, one must embrace the latter approach.[16]

The Pure Theory of Law does not deny that international law, much like constitutional law, frequently gives rise to problems of application (*see* Kammerhofer 2011). If international legal obligations are to be objectively binding, binding on states against their will, then what a state's obligations are cannot depend on the duty-bearing state's say-so. But the attempt to rely on international norms to arbitrate specific disputes will often give rise to reasonable disagreement and force norm-appliers to exercise discretion, given that international law is relatively thin in content and still to be regarded as complete. Under these circumstances, the law's claim to objectivity can be made real, Kelsen suggests, only where it is *authoritatively* applied by *impartial* adjudicative institutions (*see* Kelsen 1944, pp. 3–67). The claim to objectivity translates into the demand that states must enjoy effective legal remedies against the aggression on the part of other, stronger states. It is this aspiration—which Kelsen described as 'an eminently ethical idea and one of the few genuinely valuable and undisputed components of modern cultural consciousness' (Kelsen 1920, p. 204)—that motivated his tireless advocacy for an international court with universal and compulsory jurisdiction, not as a heuristic fiction that helps us to think what doctrines we might find morally acceptable in the international sphere, but as a real institution.[17]

It might be argued that if this was Kelsen's view, he ought not to have claimed that objectively binding international law already exists. He should have concluded, in the interest of intellectual honesty, that it does not, at least until institutions that can give meaning to the claim to objectivity have been put in place. In my view, one can read Kelsen's account of the existence of international law in a more charitable way. States frequently do make appeal to the international legality of their actions for justificatory purposes and, at least when doing so, they pretend that they accept they are bound to objective international obligations. The assumption that the legality of a state's actions bears on their legitimacy, moreover, is deeply embedded in the global political culture. Kelsen reminds us what it would take to turn appeals to international law on the part of members of international society into something more than self-serving hypocrisy.

What is needed to give bite to the claim that proper international law exists, from a Kelsenian perspective, is not so much the working out of a morally attractive doctrine of the substantive content international law, but the acknowledgement of a political commitment to creating the institutions that can make good on international law's promise to objectivity. To overburden the project of international legalization with attributions of specific doctrinal content which may turn out to be contentious is

---

[16]Hart argued that Kelsen's understanding of the relation of national and international law is irredeemably flawed (*see* Hart 1983). Hart's assessment has come to be widely accepted in Anglo-American debate, but it strikes me as uncomprehending and confused. For further discussion Vinx (2016).

[17]Kelsen offers a similar argument for constitutional adjudication. Constitutional laws will remain *leges imperfectae* unless they are judicially enforced (*see* Kelsen 2015).

likely to be counterproductive. It may turn out to be a more feasible avenue towards international legal reform simply to take states at their word and to hold them to their apparent acknowledgment of the proper legality of international law.

The contrast between Kelsen's and Dworkin's views on the foundations of international law signals more than a tactical difference as to how to further the goal of the creation of a proper system of international law. Kelsen and Dworkin set out from different understandings of the aspirations of international legality. For the common lawyer, the law, as far as its content is concerned, is already what it ought to be.[18] The task of institutionalization is to build the mechanisms that will enforce the rights already identified by way of a morally optimizing interpretation undertaken from the point of view of a hypothetical judge. For the continental public lawyer, by contrast, the task is to create institutions that can bindingly decide on what rights are to be attributed to subjects of the law in the first place. The interest in making sure that international law will turn into law proper, from this perspective, is one in the realization of the intrinsic benefits of the establishment of legal order, not one in the protection of specific fundamental rights. Kelsen takes these benefits to consist, in large part, in the opportunity to settle international conflicts peacefully, and to do so in a way that does not automatically give the upper hand to larger and more powerful states (*see* Kelsen 1920, pp. 204, 314–320).

The observations offered in this chapter do not purport to assess which of these two visions of the development of international law is more realistic and attractive at the end of the day. What has been argued here is that the continental perspective might have something to contribute to a renewed debate on the nature of international law. Dworkin's conception of the foundations of international law assumes that the project of the further development of international law can still appeal to a substantive liberal consensus; a consensus which, though it may not be unanimous, is nevertheless truly global. What Dworkin's 'new philosophy of international law' does, in effect, is little more than to offer the outline of a legal argument for how to get around a Russian or Chinese veto in the UN Security Council. But one might doubt that we have reason to be confident that the march of liberal democracy towards global triumph, however desirable, is bound to resume any time soon. The challenge of creating a genuine international legal order, in times to come, will likely have to overcome more serious political and moral disagreement than Dworkin lets on, and that suggests that Kelsen's less ideologically committed reflections on the puzzle of the existence of international law might be worth another look.

---

[18] I adopt the phrase from Allan (2020).

References

Allan TRS (2020) Why the law is what it ought to be. Jurisprudence 11:574–596

Austin J (1995) In: Rumble WE (ed) The province of jurisprudence determined. Cambridge University Press, Cambridge

Barber NW (2010) The constitutional state. Oxford University Press, Oxford

Bersier N (1998) Hans Kelsen (1881–1973) biographical note and bibliography. Eur J Int Law 9: 391–400

Besson S (2010) Theorizing the sources of international law. In: Besson S, Tasioulas J (eds) The philosophy of international law. Oxford University Press, Oxford, pp 163–186

Buchanan A (2007) Justice, legitimacy, and self-determination. Moral foundations for international law. Oxford University Press, New York

Dworkin R (1986) Law's empire. Fontana Press, London

Dworkin R (2013) A new philosophy for international law. Philos Public Aff 41:2–30

Dyzenhaus D (2020), Kelsen's Contribution to Contemporary Philosophy of International Law. Available at SSRN: https://doi.org/10.2139/ssrn.3571343

Endicott T (2010) The logic of freedom and power. In: Besson S, Tasioulas J (eds) The philosophy of international law. Oxford University Press, Oxford, pp 245–260

Franck T (1999) Lessons of Kosovo. Am J Int Law 93:857–860

Goldsmith JL, Posner EA (2007) The limits of international law. Oxford University Press, New York

Hart HLA (1983) Kelsen's doctrine of the unity of law. In: Hart HLA (ed) Essays in jurisprudence and philosophy. Oxford University Press, Oxford, pp 309–324

Hart HLA (1994) The concept of law, 2nd edn. Oxford University Press, Oxford

Hobbes T (1996) In: Tuck R (ed) Leviathan, rev stud edn. Cambridge University Press, Cambridge

Jellinek G (1914) In: Jellinek W (ed) Allgemeine Staatslehre, 3rd edn. O Häring, Berlin

Kammerhofer J (2011) Uncertainty in international law. A Kelsenian perspective. Routledge, Abingdon

Kaufmann E (1911) Das Wesen des Völkerrechts und die clausula rebus sic stantibus. JCB Mohr, Tübingen

Kelsen H (1920) Das Problem der Souveränität und die Theorie des Völkerrechts. JCB Mohr, Tübingen

Kelsen H (1928) Der soziologische und der juristische Staatsbegriff: Kritische Untersuchung des Verhältnisses von Staat und Recht, 2nd edn. JCB Mohr, Tübingen

Kelsen H (1944) Peace through law. University of North Carolina Press, Chapel Hill

Kelsen H (1952) Principles of international law. Rinehart & Company, New York

Kelsen H (1992) Introduction to the problems of legal theory (trans: Litschewski-Paulson B, Paulson S) (eds) Clarendon Press, Oxford

Kelsen H (2015) The nature and development of constitutional adjudication. In: (trans: Vinx L) (ed) The Guardian of the constitution: Hans Kelsen and Carl Schmitt on the limits of constitutional law. Cambridge University Press, Cambridge, pp 22–78

Kletzer C (2018) The idea of a pure theory of law. Hart, Oxford

Kramer M (2018) HLA Hart. Polity Press, Cambridge

Krisch N (2010) The case for pluralism in postnational law. In: de Burca G, Weiler JHH (eds) The worlds of European constitutionalism. Cambridge University Press, Cambridge, pp 203–261

Lauterpacht H (1933) The function of law in the international community. Clarendon Press, Oxford

Lefkowitz D (2020) Philosophy and international law: a critical introduction. Cambridge University Press, Cambridge

Pavel CE, Lefkowitz D (2018) Skeptical challenges to international law. Philos Compass 13:1–14

Rawls J (1999) A theory of justice, rev edn. Harvard University Press, Cambridge

Schmitt C (2005) Political theology: four chapters on the concept of sovereignty (trans: Schwab G). Chicago University Press, Chicago

Triepel H (1899) Völkerrecht und Landesrecht. CL Hirschfeld, Leipzig

Vinx L (2007) Hans Kelsen's pure theory of law: legality and legitimacy. Oxford University Press, Oxford

Vinx L (2013) Carl Schmitt and the analogy between constitutional and international law: are constitutional and international law inherently political? Glob Const 2:91–124

Vinx L (2016) The Kelsen-Hart debate: Hart's critique of Kelsen's legal monism reconsidered. In: Telman J (ed) Hans Kelsen in America - selective affinities and the mysteries of academic influence. Springer, Dordrecht, pp 59–83

von Bernstorff J (2010) The public international law theory of Hans Kelsen: believing in universal law. Cambridge University Press, Cambridge

www.ingramcontent.com/pod-product-compliance
Ingram Content Group UK Ltd.
Pitfield, Milton Keynes, MK11 3LW, UK
UKHW020817290926
15470UKWH00003B/1221
* 9 7 8 3 0 3 0 8 7 7 1 7 0 *